Sanaz Fotouhi was born in Iran and grew up and was educated in Japan, America, Hong Kong and Australia. She holds a PhD in English Literature from the University of New South Wales. She currently lives in Australia.

THE LITERATURE OF THE IRANIAN DIASPORA

Meaning and Identity since the Islamic Revolution

Sanaz Fotouhi

I.B.TAURIS
LONDON • NEW YORK • OXFORD • NEW DELHI • SYDNEY

I.B. TAURIS
Bloomsbury Publishing Plc
50 Bedford Square, London, WC1B 3DP, UK
1385 Broadway, New York, NY 10018, USA
29 Earlsfort Terrace, Dublin 2, Ireland

BLOOMSBURY, I.B. TAURIS and the I.B. Tauris logo
are trademarks of Bloomsbury Publishing Plc

First published in Great Britain 2015
This paperback edition published in 2022

A catalogue record for this book is available from the British Library.

A catalog record for this book is available from the Library of Congress.

ISBN: HB: 978-1-78076-728-4
PB: 978-07-5564-924-2
ePDF: 978-0-8577-2430-4
eBook: 978-0-8577-3766-3

Series: Written Culture and Identity

Typeset in Garamond Three by OKS Prepress Services, Chennai, India

To find out more about our authors and books visit
www.bloomsbury.com and sign up for our newsletters.

Dedicated to all the Iranian Writers in Diaspora:
Past, Present and Future

CONTENTS

LIST OF ILLUSTRATIONS

ACKNOWLEDGEMENTS

The idea for this book has been in the making for the last ten years. While the idea and vision were conceived during my days as an undergraduate student at the University of Hong Kong, the final product, after being carried to Australia, Iran and Afghanistan, was finally born in Hong Kong, where I am submitting this manuscript.

In this process, I have been fortunate enough to be assisted, sometimes in mysterious ways, by forces and people who conspired to eventually make this happen. I owe a huge thank you to all those who assisted me.

First of all, I cannot deny the forces of the universe, those beyond my understanding, which guided me and gave me hope when I was ready to give up.

Then, I need to thank my family for putting up with me in the process of the PhD that turned out eventually to be this book. Especially, my partner in life, Amin Palangi, who put up with all the ups and downs, and supported me in the various stages of this project. And my parents, especially my dad, whose spiritual guidance has been the compass that keeps me on the right path.

In the making of this book, I owe a thank you to Professor Bill Ashcroft, who saw the potential when I was ready to give up, and Dr Michelle Langford who assisted me, so hugely, in seeing the ideas through and articulating them. Without them this book would never have manifested to be what it is today.

In the process of the transformation of this book, I owe a thank you to Dr Laetitia Nanquette for reading the early drafts of the manuscript, and an even bigger thank you to my good friend soon-to-be Dr Mahsa Salamati for her meticulous and incredibly valuable feedback on the various drafts of this book. In the final stages of this process, I owe a thank you to Nick James for copyediting the book to perfection.

I have to also thank my friends in Hong Kong, who always provide me a refuge when I need time to come back to my Asian home. Especially, this time, to Felix Ng for offering up his house as my writing sanctuary where in silence and peace I managed to finish the editing. I also need to thank Marina Ma and Dr Roland Vogt – who were at the height of taking care of new-born twins – as well as Jonathon Lee, for giving me more space to continue the finishing touches of this manuscript. I also owe a thank you to Jojo Yue for her emotional support in the final stages of this process.

Finally, thank you to the wonderful writers, without whom this book would not exist!

INTRODUCTION

ESSENCE OF DESIRE FOR A BETTER WORLD

> I don't feel *turmoil* anymore. [...] And I don't mind being a chameleon; my father used to call me that as a compliment. [...] My childhood was like *ahsh*, like soup with beans and noodles and spices and yogurt and lemon juice – contrasting tastes and smells and hopes and ideas. It may be true what you say about peacefulness of belonging to one culture completely, but you forget that I've never *completely* been one thing or another. I was brought up in this country; I am a lot of things.[1]

Growing up outside Iran like Layla, the Iranian–American young girl in Susanne Pari's *The Fortune Catcher* (1997) who goes back to Iran and faces the reality of the duality of her identity, I never really felt I fully belonged to any one culture. I desperately longed for home, the never-changing paradisiacal images of which had formed a great part of my sense of identity and belonging; but I also wanted to belong and feel at peace in the country in which I lived. I discovered Pari's novel by accident in a dingy basement bookstore in Hong Kong, where I was studying at the time. It was the cover, with a soft gazing half-veiled face of a woman – still a surprisingly fresh image in the late 1990s - that attracted me to the book. When I picked up the book it was the above quote that really spoke to me.

As one of the first novels in English by an Iranian woman living outside Iran, it brought back nostalgic sights and sounds of home. But it offered much more than that. Here was a book that not only reflected my own condition, but also pointed hopefully towards the possibility of a future without the turmoil of non-belonging. Reading it, I felt that, through Layla, I had an opportunity to negotiate my own sense of identity.

Although I had always been attracted to and sought solace in diasporic literatures, it was refreshing to see an Iranian expression of this experience that resonated so acutely with my own. I no longer felt that I was the only one with those feelings. But it was not just personal sentimentality that attracted me to Pari's novel. The book spoke to me on another level. In *The Fortune Catcher* I recognised a similarity of subject, themes and issues with other diasporic writings that I had studied over the years. The sense of nostalgia, placelessness, identity crisis, and hope for a better future in the host country could have been conjured up by almost any diasporic writer from anywhere in the world. The book also foregrounded the voices and experiences of marginal characters through strategies similar to those often encountered in post-colonial Indian, Caribbean, African and Asian writing in English. It was this thematic and subjective resemblance of Iranian writing to other diasporic and post-colonial writing that planted the seed for what eventually became this book.

After reading *The Fortune Catcher*, I became intrigued to know if there were others like Pari. This curiosity led to the eventual discovery of an emerging world of Iranian writing in English. As I read other fiction and memoirs by diasporic Iranian writers, the similarity between their work and that of other diasporic and post-colonial writing became even more apparent. But as the number of Iranian writers grew, particularly after 9/11, I realised that what differentiated these books from other diasporic and post-colonial writing in English was that they were collectively dealing with issues that were specifically Iranian. It was in this discovery that I gained the desire to follow the trajectory of this body of work.

This book, then, traces the history of the emergence of Anglophone diasporic Iranian literature and highlights its importance as a new category of writing in world literatures in English, examining its significance for the people who write it and are reflected by it. Over the last few decades, there has been a gradual expansion in the creation and study of world literatures in English. One can trace this trend in the production and consumption of work from the Indian subcontinent, as well as from Africa, South East Asia and the Middle East. The success of writers from these areas has not only brought them to the attention of popular audiences and academics alike, but it has also contributed greatly to an increased understanding of their respective cultures on a global level. But, in this conversation, the voices of Iranian writers in English have been missing. This is not surprising. Compared to some of those from regions named above, the global Iranian diaspora is a relatively young community with some of its members still struggling to establish themselves within their new setting. Additionally, Iran's real exposure to the West and Western cultures, and vice versa, has been relatively short compared to some of the other colonised countries and regions. So while writers from colonised countries were writing from a point of relative but mutual historical and cultural familiarity, even if sometimes that familiarity lay in the language (which gave them the ability to embed themselves into the literary scene and culture from the outset), the lack of intimate familiarity with Western cultures, including its languages and literatures, was a major cause for the rather slow emergence of Iranian diasporic literature in English, particularly literature of merit.

However, over the last few decades, during which the study of diasporic and world literatures in English has been progressing, the Iranian diaspora have also been gradually creating a body of work that is now ready to make a significant contribution. With more than 30 years of history, the Iranian diaspora have not only established themselves, but have also gained considerable cultural, linguistic and literary merit, sufficient to be considered part of the serious debate on world literatures in English. Like any body of work by a diasporic community, this literature contributes to the way the Iranian diaspora are situated. It has become a vehicle through which they are represented and represent themselves.

This book is one of the first studies of the body of Anglophone diasporic Iranian literature and its contribution to world literatures in English. Its aims are to introduce and situate diasporic Iranian literature in English, and to examine its significance for the diasporic Iranian communities in the maintenance, reconstruction and negotiation of their identities.

What does this book do?

Given the increasing number of novels and memoirs published in English by the Iranian diaspora, which at the time of the publication of this book stands at well over 200, this book serves as a guide, introducing a range of existing and emerging Iranian writing for both scholars and general audiences. If we look at the history of the study of diasporic Iranian literature in English, it is relatively short. It has only been recently that this body of work has seriously come to the collective attention of readers and scholars.

This, however, is not to say that before this Iranians were not writing abroad in languages other than Persian or English. From the late nineteenth and early twentieth centuries Iranians of a certain educated and aristocratic class, though small in number, had begun to travel and migrate, marking Iran's increasing contact with foreign countries. Indeed, the origins of diasporic Iranian writing in foreign languages can be traced back to the scattered writings of this group of early migrants and travellers. For instance, the first French novel by an Iranian woman should be credited to Amineh Pakravan (1890–1958) for her *Le Prince sans histoire* (1921), which was awarded the Prix Rivaro in 1951 and praised by French literary critics. This was followed by her posthumously published *Destinées Persanes* (1960).[2] Similarly, Freydoun Hoveida (1925–2003) should be mentioned for the significant contribution of his French novel *Les quranraines* (1961) followed by a string of other successful novels, *L'aerogare* (1965), *Dans une terre étrange* (1968) and *Le losange* (1969).

In English the pioneers can be traced back to the late 1950s, to Najme Najafi for her books *Persia is My Heart* (1953) and *Reveille for a Persian Village* (1958), followed by Freydun Esfandiari (also known as FM.2030) (1930–2000) for his novels *The Day of Sacrifice* (1959), *Beggar* (1965) and *Identity Card* (1966). They were followed by a group of writers who emerged at the brink of the revolution, including Donne Raffat, who published *Caspian Circle* (1978), and Nahid Rachlin, who wrote her first novel *Foreigner* in 1979.

Despite the relatively long history of scattered diasporic Iranian writing in languages other than Persian and English, however, it was not until after the revolution, which resulted in the mass migration of a significant number of people from a cross-section of Iranian society, that a distinct body of work began to emerge from the diaspora. It took nearly two and half decades for this literature to develop into a sustained body of work and to be acknowledged by literary critics and scholars as an emerging genre.

In the early 2000s, when I first became interested in this topic, there was virtually no scholarship on this work. Pioneering scholarship gradually emerged only after 9/11 with the sudden increase in books and interest in narratives from the Middle East. However, this interest on the part of publishers, audiences and scholars was primarily focused on, and framed in relation to, the Arab/Muslim woman's position after America's declaration of 'War on Terror'. It has only been since then that Iranian writers have become serious subjects of interest for both Iranian and non-Iranian scholars and audiences. While numerous essays were published about Iranian writing in diaspora, particularly between 2001 and 2007,[3] it has only been since Gillian Whitlock dedicated an entire chapter of her book *Soft Weapons*[4] (2007) to Iranian women's memoirs that diasporic Iranian writing in English was discussed as a serious and emerging discourse. Since then, a series of other scholarly endeavours have expanded the field. In 2007, for instance, Jasmin Darznik submitted a PhD thesis on the topic.[5] In 2008 the *Multi-Ethnic Literature of the United States* (MELUS) published a special issue on Iranian–American Literature,[6] and Persis Karim, one of the pioneers of this field, along with a group of diasporic Iranian writers, established the Association of Iranian American Writers (AIAW), building a 'network of writers who have roots in Iran and America and who seek to build a literary community'.[7] AIAW gave many emerging and established Iranian writers the chance to showcase their work, organise conferences, communicate and exchange ideas through forums and blogs. Partially due to AIAW, interest in various aspects of diasporic Iranian writing increased and different aspects of this body of work are regularly addressed in papers, conference panels, reviews, special journal issues and articles. For instance, in 2009 AIAW organised an event to celebrate '30 Years of Iranian–American Literature' at which distinguished Iranian writers in English debated their situation as writers in America. Unfortunately AIAW as a formal body ceased to exist in April 2013, but its legacy continues through an informal Facebook group that brings information to writers and readers alike.

Other groups, too, have played a significant role in the introduction of this literature. The International Society for Iranian Studies (ISIS), for instance, which had previously included panels on Iranian diasporic writing in Persian, added panels on diasporic Iranian writing in English in their 2008, 2010 and 2012 conferences. Since then Iranian literature in English has become an important part of this bi-annual gathering. In 2011, Persis Karim and Babak Elahi edited a special section in *Comparative Studies of South Asia, Africa and the Middle East*[8] that focused on Iranian diasporic literature. More recently, Daniel Grassian published the first book-length study of diasporic Iranian literature in English in 2013.[9]

However, despite this increasing scholarship, there appears to be an under-representation and analysis of a cross-section of texts. Until recently, much of the work on diasporic Iranian writing in English focused on a number of significant and well-known titles. Consequently work by lesser-known or more obscure writers, who are nonetheless making a significant contribution to the field, has been largely ignored. This undermines the ever-growing breadth of the genre for both readers and scholars, and leaves out significant writers whose works are published by smaller publishers.

One of the aims of this book is to introduce and examine a cross-section of books by drawing on a large and varied range of English memoirs and fictions by diasporic Iranian writers, and to address specific topics that surround them, in order to reflect the diversity and complexity of the literary landscape. For this reason, issues and subjects are approached through a variety of perspectives in multiple texts and through various scholarly lenses. As a result, some sections include detailed content analysis of one or several books while other parts only refer to titles that deal with specific issues. This method enables us to reflect on the diversity, complexity and multiplicity of the body of work at hand. This is why I have not limited my approach to a specific number of texts. It is also why, given the significant number of memoirs and fictions, as well as an increase in poetry, that the book has been organised around recurring themes.

In addition, I have included an appendix, listing as many memoirs and works of fiction by diasporic Iranian writers in English as I could find, currently published, available in bookshops or on the internet at the time of publication of this book. As a first of its kind this will serve as a reference for general readers and scholars interested in locating these texts.

As a significant aim of this book is to situate this body of work within the existing global conversation and body of theories on diasporic writing in English, it traces the history of its emergence against the social and political, national and international events and histories that have shaped its landscape. Diasporic Iranian literature in English occupies an ambivalent discursive space, constructed at the junctions of Iranian history and literatures and Western literatures and philosophies, and reflects the complexities and multiplicities of Iranian migratory experiences. Often written against the grain of history, like the many characters that occupy it, it is a hybrid form that defies precise classification. Reflecting this complexity, the book is conceived at the intersection of the history of this literature alongside the history of Iranian migratory experience, and within the framework of multiple overlapping discursive and theoretical spaces that it occupies.

Given the close relationship of this literature with social, political and historical events, the book divides the emergence of diasporic Iranian literature in English into three waves that coincide with significant social, political and historical events in the last three and half decades. It traces the origins of the first wave back to the 1979 revolution and ensuing American hostage crisis in Iran. It associates the beginning of a second wave with the events of 9/11 and its aftermath, and it identifies a third wave, which has begun to emerge after the controversial 2009 Iranian presidential elections.

Although the body of work examined here originates outside Iran, its contextual origins have to be traced back, understood and analysed in relation to Iranian history and the recent history of Iranian diaspora. This book, then, traces and analyses the emergence of this literature in relation to specific historical and social contexts out of which it has emerged.

In the last century, Iran was subject to two revolutions: the constitutional revolution of 1906 and the Islamic Revolution of 1979. Between these two revolutions, Iran was heavily influenced by British, American and Russian presences. It was, historians believe, this contact that influenced Reza Shah's drive for modernization in the 1930s. Inspired by Turkey's Mustafa Kamal Atatürk, Reza Shah pushed Iran into the modern age. He saw modernisation as reflected in a secular society. Consequently, he attempted to replace religious systems with modern and secular ones. But the most memorable and controversial consequence of modernisation came in 1936, when he began an anti-veil offensive. In a controversial decision, Reza Shah ordered men to wear suits and Western-style hats, and women to unveil. To enforce this, he sent soldiers to pull the veil from women's heads. This affected Iranian women's development and ironically inhibited their ability to achieve equal rights. Many women who had lived their entire lives under the veil were shocked by the idea of unveiling and refused to leave their homes altogether, let alone work or go to school alongside men. Ironically, while the modernisation scheme was designed to allow women for the first time in Iranian history to enter into society, into the workforce, and to get an education, the forced unveiling kept many conservative women indoors.

Caught between tradition and modernity, many Iranian women never had or gained the opportunity or ability to express themselves. Although modernisation affected the façade of the country, it did not change core values. While some families levied more freedom to women, the majority still operated according to strict gender and public/private dichotomies that had ruled Iranian society for centuries. Within this dichotomy, women's voices were still silenced and the stories of their lives kept within the domestic realm. Following the Islamic Revolution and the consequential forced re-veiling of women in the early 1980s, women's situation became even worse and their voices were further silenced.

This book situates and analyses the emergence of diasporic Iranian literature, particularly women's literature, as a historical response arising from silences that have historically dominated Iranian women's lives. For instance, it traces the importance of historical engagement for diasporic Iranian women writers and argues how, by drawing on history, they are reconstructing their sense of historically silenced identities and subjectivities. Similarly, it situates and examines the sudden increase in the number of Iranian women's memoirs after 9/11 as a response to the historical silences and other forms of historical imposition both in Iran and abroad. On a similar theme, it traces the historical representation of Iranian women as mothers and daughters, and examines how diasporic Iranian writers are engaging with this history to recreate and reconstruct the Iranian mother and daughter beyond historically imposed imagery.

However, women's voices have not been the only silences throughout Iranian history, and certainly not the only kind of silence to which diasporic Iranian writers are responding. After its encounter with modernisation, Iran was on its way to becoming one of the Middle East's most economically developed countries. But it had climbed the economic ladder at the price of discontent among the majority of its population. While the changes introduced affected all aspects of Iranian life, including, as Ali Mirsepassi points out, 'economic relations, social institutions and cultural patterns of the country',[10] what was neglected was the complex process needed to accommodate social change, particularly for the transformation of a predominantly religious society into a secular one. For many, things like unveiling were an unfathomable sacrilege against the very sanctity of Islamic beliefs that had formed the basis of much of Iranian identity for centuries. Any attempt to discredit traditional ways was not only frowned upon by popular clerics and the majority of people, but also seen as a real threat to the core values underpinning Iranian identity and society. Consequently, Reza Shah's secularisation affected everyone. While it favoured only a small number, who became the ruling class, it alienated the government from the people.

In this system there was very little room for expression of discontent. Those who opposed were dealt with harshly by the feared secret police, SAVAK. The written word in all its forms – local and imported books, newspapers, pamphlets – was subject to heavy censorship. The government was especially sensitive to subjects and words that hinted at discontent or revolt. As Azar Mahloujian tells us 'the authorities were sensitive to such words as "red" and "red rose," which symbolized the bloodshed during revolution, or "black night" and "high walls," which symbolized prison and repression'.[11] Thus, the possession of books such as Maxim Gorki's *Mother*, for instance, which tells the story of a mother's unconditional support of her socialist son in Russia, meant paying a hefty price. As Mahloujian goes on to argue 'the publication or possession of forbidden books [was] dangerous for all concerned – writers, readers, booksellers and publishers – so those who [were] not political activists [would] seldom risk reading them', because dealing with these books could 'lead to [at least] a three-year jail sentence'.[12] Everyone was aware of the lethal consequences of possession of and engagement with forbidden material. The government made this message clear by occasionally prosecuting high-profile revolutionary writers. Consequently, in this system, the voices of any alternative political parties, as well as those who contested for change, were silenced, and censored from the mainstream pages of history.

This book examines the emergence of diasporic Iranian literature against the history of political censorship that has affected Iranian expression. But, while censorship existed prior to the revolution, it reached its apex after the establishment of the Islamic government. Soon after gaining power, the Islamic regime opted for 'the reestablishment of traditional institutions and the removal of all modernist reforms'.[13] This included reforming the education and legal systems, and restoring religious systems. The traditionalists 'felt confident that by Islamising education they [could sow] the seeds of a process which would mature into conflict between children and their un-Islamic parents'.[14] In 1980, however, there was a reversal of what had happened decades earlier as the government passed a law requiring women in the work place to cover their hair. A year later the law of veiling was extended to all women, Muslim and non-Muslim, in all public places. The violation of this law was punishable by a maximum jail sentence of one year.[15] Inevitably in this religious system, the public expression of women's voices, bodies and sexualities was highly censored.

As a result, Iranians, faced with 'secularist modernization on the one hand and religious orthodoxy and traditionalism on the other',[16] became even more bewildered and confused. While the implementation of secular laws and reforms had affected the lives of traditional Muslims within Iran, the re-implementation of Islamic laws and reforms affected 'the lives of all Iranians'.[17] Yet, the tables had turned. Now it was the upper and upper-middle classes, those who had been the supporters of the Shah, who 'found themselves alienated from the regime',[18] as rules and censorships were imposed on almost all aspects of their everyday lives. There were defined rules 'on women's dress in the street; a continued ban on music and dancing in public; there was propagandistic output of radio, television and the press', and there was 'a constant fear of reprisals if they expressed their disenchantment too loudly'.[19] Also affected were minorities such as Jews, Zoroastrians, Armenians and Baha'is, who lost almost all their rights. While they were discriminated against in and by the government, they also faced open discrimination from many who boycotted their businesses and insulted their beliefs.

Soon after the revolution, writers and publishers too faced stricter censorship laws. There was intensified censorship on anything that hinted at political and social discontent. Added to politically censored subjects were those that were deemed to be against the Islamic values of the state. As Mahloujian observes,

> the new government banned books written by or about the Shah, as well as books dedicated to him or the royal family. Eventually, this censorship extended to books on Marxism, Darwinian evolution, and anything else seen as contradictory to religious doctrine.[20]

Similarly, anything that dealt with dancing, drinking and sexual relationships, or women's bodies, was strictly censored. Many books by Western writers that advocated a Western lifestyle were also pulled off bookshelves and university reading lists. Lecturers, like the now-prolific Azar Nafisi, the author of *Reading* Lolita *in Tehran* (2004), who taught foreign literatures and languages, were pressured to change their curricula or leave their posts. Even Iranian classical poetry that dealt with love, eroticism and wine, despite its symbolism, was heavily censored, making uncensored classic and loved books of poetry by Hafez and Rumi rare to find commodities, even on the black market.

Because the Islamic revolution and its aftermath caused such a great deal of confusion among the population, and discriminated against many, and because of its relative historical proximity, this period is one with which many diasporic Iranians writers are engaging. In fact, narratives that deal with the Islamic revolution and its aftermath, occupy the biggest thematic category by Iranian writers in English. These narratives often deal with the trauma of the revolution and the process of exile. This book pays particular attention to the different narratives in response to the historical censorships and discriminations that emerged as the result of the revolution.

However, it is not only the silences and discriminations inside Iran to which diasporic Iranian writers are responding. Following the revolution, millions of Iranians were forced to leave Iran and re-settle across the globe. Like any other diasporic community, the Iranian community too faced the difficulties of re-settlement, exile and identity crisis. However, while leaving Iran might have offered escape from persecution, many who left, especially those who migrated to the United States, faced a double exile. Aside from having to cope with the difficulties of migration, they also faced the burden of contradictory images of Iran and Iranians, pre and post-revolution, which have informed popular Western understandings of Iran and its people. These representations, which often construct stereotypical images, have historically hampered the Iranian diaspora's integration into new communities. As Lila Azam Zanganeh puts it, Iran has been present in Western literature since antiquity: '[W]hether as a haven of exotic sensuality or a stronghold of fanatic religiosity, Iran has, since ancient times, inflamed the popular imagination.'[21] The image of pre-revolutionary Iran that had flourished in the Western mind was one that frequently had its origin in dated explorer travelogues and tourist accounts, as well as exotic fictional narratives. Put another way, the representation of Iran throughout Western history fits Edward Said's definition of the Orient in *Orientalism*, as a land that 'had been since antiquity a place of romance, exotic beings, haunting memories and landscape, [and] remarkable experiences'.[22] Indeed, descriptions of Iran (or Persia, as it was known up to 1935) were often characterised by effusive elaborations of it as 'a pleasant dream', with 'intriguing alleys and secretive walls, open spaces and courtyards, and avenues that slit down the middle with watercourses and lines of trees'.[23] It was the land in which 'within the same space contains a greater variety of contrasts of scenery'[24] with its people described as 'the most cheerful people in the world [. . .] [who] delight in familiar conversation; [. . .] [and] contrive every means to add to the pleasure of their social hours'.[25] However, despite lengthy and often florid descriptions of Persia and the Persians in many books, they still reflect a sense of Western superiority. This is particularly evident in descriptions of the condition of Iranian women. In most such accounts, women, who occupied a separate territory, out of the Western male narrator's gaze, remained an enigma. Western writers, who were both 'fascinated and repelled by the veil' and by the situation of women, created the assumption and convention that 'veiled women were necessarily more oppressed, more passive, more ignorant than unveiled women', which led to 'exaggerated statements about the imprisoned existence of women in "the Orient"'.[26] Since the historically exotic and Orientalist representation of Iran has been one of the other major underlying themes that diasporic Iranian writers are responding to today, this book examines the various responses to stereotypical representations in diasporic Iranian literature in English.

However, the image of Persia as an exotic and wonderful land of adventure, and of its gracious people, began to dissipate in the wake of the 1979 revolution. While the onset of forced re-veiling reinforced some of the already-existing negative images of Iran, it was the ensuing American hostage crisis that led to the emergence of a strong anti-Iran attitude in the West. The hostage crisis, which began on 4 November 1979 when 63 Americans were taken hostage at the American embassy in Tehran and held for 444 days, unfolded as nightly television and radio drama for the American public. This incited many negative perceptions of Iran and Iranians, who were portrayed as 'non-rational', 'hungry for martyrdom', and 'unwilling to compromise'.[27] Long forgotten were exotic utopian adventures into Persia and its harems. Instead, Iran became the demonic, inaccessible, anti-American dystopia with escalating numbers of human rights violations. While the non-stop coverage of the hostage crisis played an especially important role in the construction of this anti-Iranian attitude, this representation resonated far into the future, continuing to affect the way in which Iran and Iranians are seen and represented in the West even today.

Consequently, many Iranians who migrated to the West, particularly to the United States, were faced with a new sense of identity crisis, one that stemmed from open discrimination. This put additional pressure on the perils of migration, and the persecution that they had faced in their homeland. The negative imagery that surrounded them rendered them invisible and silent. For many diasporic Iranian writers, writing has become a means to regain their sense of identity and make themselves visible against the backdrop of this negative history.

This book examines diasporic Iranian narratives in relation to theories of narrativity and subjectivity. It shows how through the process of narrating their own stories writers are overcoming their 'otherness' and reconstructing their own sense of diasporic Iranian identities in the West. Although both Iranian men and women have suffered a great deal as the result of discrimination, I believe Iranian men and masculinities have been far more greatly affected. While images of the hostage crisis represented Iranian men as angry, bearded, hostage-taking fanatics, these were accentuated by the more recent post-9/11 debates and by Arab and Iranian women's narratives that were used to point to the seemingly patriarchal and oppressive nature of Muslim/Middle Eastern men. This is why one of the recurring elements in diasporic Iranian literature stems from this negative stereotypical representation of Iranian men and masculinities.

Despite the social, cultural and historical specificities of their situation, diasporic Iranian communities share great similarities with other global diasporic communities. Like other migrants, the Iranian diaspora too have left 'their homeland for any number of years, maybe even for the rest of their lives', and often 'construct a new identity abroad through the use of imagination, nostalgia, and memories'.[28] Their literature, too, like other diasporic literature, is often a reflection of this desire to maintain an historical connection with their homeland. Given this similarity of expression, this book situates diasporic Iranian literature through existing theories of diasporic literary expression. In particular, it examines the recurring elements of historical engagement as a way to maintain a sense of identity, reflecting what Stuart Hall calls 'historicisation' of a sense of cultural identity.

In describing this literature, however, I couple the word diasporic with utopian and will use the word utopian throughout this book to describe this writing because I believe the combination of the two best describe the disposition of diasporic Iranian literature in English. Here 'utopian' is not in reference to something being of, or referring to, Utopia, an idealised paradisiacal island, state or place. Rather, I draw on Ernst Bloch's contemporary definition of utopian theory in which utopia is 'no longer a place but a hope itself, the essence of desire for a better world'.[29] As he puts it, 'everybody lives in the future'.[30] Everyone, he argues, has 'dreamed of the better life that might be possible'.[31] But it is not only dreams and daydreams that constitute this utopianism. For Bloch, even 'thinking means venturing beyond'[32] what already exists into the future and is, in effect, utopian.

I find this definition of utopianism reflective of migratory experiences and present in their literature, where writers are drawing on their experiences to construct and reflect hopeful future possibilities. But, I find this definition even more appealing because the utopian process of looking forward is not simply a Not-Yet, better, hopeful future, in a 'mere vacuum of an In-Front-of-Us'.[33] Rather, it is highly reflective of the past in projecting the future. This utopianism, while looking into the future, is also based and rooted in the past because the past always has a powerful influence on how we view our future.

Much of the work by diasporic Iranian writers in English, while reflective of the past, is indeed also continually projecting forward, constructing and negotiating the future. In fact many writers are aware that, as much as maintaining a connection with an uninterrupted past can alleviate pangs of exile, it can also hamper a community's ability to look into the future, move forward and integrate into their host community. There is a realisation that 'such return is always in danger of becoming a disabling nostalgia',[34] and many Iranian writers consciously reflect on the past, even changing some of its elements, in such a way as to project a desired future.

Given that diasporic Iranian literature generally seems to operate at the intersection of this utopian reflection of the past and projection into the desired future, there is great similarity between this work and post-colonial literatures, or what Bill Ashcroft calls post-colonial utopianism. Like post-colonial writers, diasporic Iranian writers draw on elements of the past to transform them, rewrite them, to reconstruct themselves, their past and future, against colonial/domineering forces. This is why throughout this book I draw on theories of post-colonial literature to address certain points.

In choosing to read these works through the conceptual framework of post-colonialism, however, I am not claiming that Iranian writers share the same historical and political motivations for writing as writers from former colonies. This would be historically inaccurate, of course, since Iran, as a nation, has never been officially colonised by any outside forces. The post-colonial theory with which this book engages has its bases in Elleke Boehmer's definition, according to which 'colonialism was not different from other kinds of authority, religious or political, in claiming a monopoly on definitions in order to control a [. . .] reality'.[35] My engagement here is close to Homi Bhahba's definition of the term 'post' in post-colonialism, where the term 'post' does not indicate 'sequentiality [. . .] or polarity'.[36] Rather, it indicates 'moving beyond' to resist the attempt at holistic forms of social expression.

It is from the vantage point of the junction of Boehmer's definition of colonialism and Bhabha's interpretation of 'post' that this book views the unifying and totalitarian pre- and post-revolutionary regimes of Iran, as quasi-colonial and oppressive forces that have rendered many Iranians marginal both in Iran and abroad, and examines the specific techniques that writers use to draw on the past and to reflect and project a desired future. On the one hand, it examines how, by drawing on and adapting elements and techniques of post-colonial literatures, Iranian writers are reconstructing the past, opening up new spaces of expression, and negotiating a sense of future identity for themselves. On the other hand, given their unique position, it situates and examines their significant contribution to post-colonial literatures at large. Taking this body of work as a whole, this book approaches diasporic Iranian literature in English as a manifestation and reflection of the desire to maintain, reconstruct and negotiate diasporic Iranian identities.

Issues of language

This book deals with fiction and memoirs, and some poetry, written in English by members of the diasporic Iranian community across the globe. It was a conscious decision to only examine work produced originally in English, as opposed to in translation, because of the fascinating interaction and intersections that are created by the marriage between Iranian culture, literature and experiences, and the English language. This book, therefore, focuses on an analysis of this intersecting space. It shows how the interconnection of Iranian writers and their culture with various discourses of the English language has opened up new and transformative spaces of expression through which diasporic Iranians maintain, reconstruct and negotiate their personal and communal subjectivities and identities.

It is the consequent construction of some fascinating discursive spaces that this book is most interested in. If we look at the body of work produced in English by the diasporic Iranian community over the last few decades, the choice to write in English operates on different levels. For the writers it is a means of expression and communication with the people of their host country. As such it can be seen as a way of establishing dialogue and introducing their own culture and ideologies into their new environment. On another level, the choice to write in English offers exciting new opportunities.

English provides many who previously did not have the ability to express themselves in their home or host cultures with new linguistic possibilities of expression. For some, English has given them the ability to tell their stories, to speak, and to have a voice where they previously did not have any. This means that through this new language, and by becoming a speaking subject, they can reconstruct their own sense of damaged identity and redefine already established stereotypes through their narrations.

This is where their use of language begins to be more than a mere means for expression. In this context, language can be seen as a tool that can be adapted and used to resist, challenge and negotiate certain representations. In post-colonial criticism, the use of and challenge to the dominant language of the coloniser is often one of the greatest strategies for transformation, critique and negotiation of recognition. Language can be seen as an imposition by domineering forces, 'a conscious strategy of cultural hegemony'.[37] The exclusive use of language does not promote recognition between Self and Other, but instead advocates hierarchy and misrecognition. This is why the employment of the dominant language is such an important strategy for post-colonial writers.

For diasporic Iranian writers too, the decision to use English plays a significant part in the process of reconstruction, maintenance and negotiation of their subjectivities through literature. English has often been the language used to discriminate against them in the West, and it has been English that has given them voice and allowed them to recreate their sense of subjectivity. Therefore, as much as this book is concerned with the contents of diasporic Iranian writing and how it can lead to transformation, it also analyses the formal linguistic changes and challenges that are taking place in this process. For instance, it considers how diasporic Iranian writers' engagement with the English language is changing, transforming and appropriating some aspects of the language and literature to make it more reflective of their own experience. It, for example, looks at the ways in which these narratives insert and draw on elements of Persian literature in their expressions in English, which as much as changing and adding new dimensions to English literature are also transforming certain aspects and elements of Persian literature.

In addition, the decision to focus solely on work produced in English stems from a relative lack of study of this group of writers. According to Nasrin Rahimieh[38] diasporic Iranian writers can be divided into three groups. There are those who write only in Persian, aimed exclusively at Persian-speaking audiences. These include well-known and already established authors such as Ali Jamalzadeh, Bozorg Alavi, Esmail Fassih, Goli Taraghi and Shahrnush Parsipour, whose works have also been translated. Then, there are those who write in English (or languages other than Persian)[39] and have launched their careers in a foreign language, such as Nahid Rachlin, Gina Nahai and all those dealt with in this book. Finally, there are those who launched their writing career in Persian after migration and have established themselves abroad as Persian writers, such as Shahla Shafigh. However, while the first and last categories are usually older, first-generation migrant writers, the second group are often second-generation or those who migrated in their youth and have spent most of their lives outside Iran.

Although Persian writers in the other groups have produced far more work over the last few decades, a number of factors determine why this study has focused solely on those who launched their writing careers in English. First, the majority of established writers who continue to write in Persian after migration already have an avid readership, network of critics, reviewers and studies that analyse various aspects of their work both in Iran and abroad. These writers are often successful even after migration, continuing to win prizes in absentia in Iran and are very present in various Iranian Studies societies across the globe. Often their works in translation have gained them considerable attention from readers, reviewers and academics in and beyond Iran. Among them one of Iran's first female novelists, Goli Taraghi, who migrated to Paris after the Iran/Iraq war broke out in 1980, has continued publication, and was awarded the Bita Prize for Iranian literature by the Iranian Studies Centre at Stanford University in 2009. Shahriar Mandanipour, an acclaimed Iranian writer whose books were banned in Iran between 1992 and 1997, settled in the United States when he went there for a festival in 2006 and did not return, obtaining instead a fellowship at Brown University. His success was soon reflected in the translation of his book *Censoring an Iranian Love Story* (2009), which gained him a review by James Wood in *The New Yorker* (2009), revealing the book as a reflection of harsh censorship laws in the Iranian publishing industry that affect researchers, writers and academics. Mandanipour went on to be nominated for the prestigious Neustadt Prize in 2010 along with writers like Margaret Atwood and Haruki Murakami. Similarly, Sharhnoush Parsipour, best known internationally for her translated works and the recent film adaptation of her novella *Women without Men* (2004), was awarded an honorary doctorate of letters in 2010 by Brown University alongside seven other delegates including Nelson Mandela and Morgan Freeman.

While the above writers have had great success within and beyond a Persian readership, those who have established themselves as diasporic Persian writers have also gained considerable attention from readers, critics and scholars, and have been the subject of many studies both in Iran and abroad.[40] Over recent decades numerous centres and associations, such as the Iranian Writers Association (in Exile) and Iranian Pen Centre in Exile, have created support networks for these budding writers. Similarly, websites such as the BBC Persian have dedicated sections to Persian writers in exile, debating, featuring and introducing their works for a Persian readership.

However, as mentioned earlier, as a consequence of the relative youth of the group who have launched their writing careers in English, it has only been in the last decade or so that this body of work has come to the attention of readers and scholars. Indeed, this book is among the first few book-length studies of this group of writers.

Although this book approaches diasporic Iranian literature in English from a scholarly perspective, it is also the manifestation of my own personal experiences as a young diasporic Iranian woman. This is why, as I write this book, I want it to be accessible to readers who share similar experiences to my own. It is for this reason that, while each chapter addresses a different aspect of diasporic Iranian writing in English, each will also begin with a personal anecdote. While this approach fulfils my creative desires and injects a personal perspective into this study, it is also a way to showcase the fact that the issues I deal with are real issues with which many Iranians living abroad have had to deal with at some point during their migratory lives.

CHAPTER 1

HISTORY – 'REMEMBERING AND NARRATING THE PAST'

Iranian communities in diaspora seem to have an inherent obsession with history. Although at times hidden beneath the surface, if one looks closely, this can be seen reflected in deeper aspects of their lives. I first noticed this interest in history in a gathering of Iranians in Canberra where, as a new addition to my husband's well-known family in the community, I was welcomed by a party. Although I had lived most of my life abroad, I had, somehow, managed to avoid large Iranian gatherings. But that night, as I sat there politely observing the people who now formed my community, I had the sudden realisation that many had a consistency, almost uniformity, about them. They were mostly ageing men and women who had made the quiet suburbs of Canberra home some 30 years ago. Many had not returned to Iran since then, and carried themselves as if they were still middle class Tehrani citizens of the 1970s. Everyone was dressed up, almost to excess. Most women wore colourful dress suits, resembling what might have been fashionable when they left Iran. Their blonde hair perfectly blow-dried; their jewellery self-consciously displayed, a distant remainder of their once rich lives in Iran. The men wore suits with ties and spoke of the Shah's regime as if it was still an existing government. Later that night, as I listened to nostalgic poetry accompanied by the soothing sound of traditional Iranian instruments, I felt that these men and women were still very much living in a distant past.

As I settled into Canberra, I noticed that this connection to a historical past played a far more integral role than I had assumed at first encounter. It was a subtle undercurrent, a running theme in many aspects of their lives. Many of them attended regular gatherings at each other's houses. Being invited was like being transported from the eucalyptus tree-lined streets of Canberra back to Iran. One could smell the rich aroma of cardamom tea and saffron rice, even before ringing the doorbell to enter houses decorated with Iranian handicraft and pictures of ancient Iran. The bookshelves of these far-flung houses in the suburbs were often lined with classical Persian poetry and philosophy books. Their television, if turned on, would be tuned to one of various Iranian channels beamed by satellite from Iran and the United States. Gatherings at these houses consisted of poetry and book readings. Sometimes, people reminisced about their grandparents, their homes in Iran, and what that they had left behind. Sipping tea out of slim-waisted golden-rimmed glasses, one could easily forget that one was not in Iran, if not for the sudden entrance of one of their Australian-born adult children. These young adults, who often came at their parents' insistence, spoke Persian with an accent, but listened intently as they tried to make sense of a poem, or learn something about the history of their cultural past. Sometimes, after a while, they would leave to attend other parties with their Australian friends. It was these gatherings that for me highlighted the importance of and connection with history. While for the older generation, these events were the epitome of their identity, for their children it was a way to understand their past so that they could negotiate their identities in Australia.

In coming across different diasporic communities through the internet, and seeing the kinds of activities they engaged with, I soon realised that this was not exclusive to Canberra. It appeared that all over the world, Iranians have had a tendency to formulate gatherings around activities that had an undercurrent of engagement with some element of their Iranian past: in the way they set up their houses, in poetry and book readings, in celebrations of age-old Persian events, or religious gatherings.

As I realised the presence of this historical engagement, I recognised a thematic similarity between these gatherings and the books authored by members of the diaspora. Like in these real-life gatherings, though at times indirectly, most books by diasporic Iranian writers, whether memoir, fiction or even poetry, have an undercurrent of an historical theme. Reading these books was like entering into those Iranian houses and gatherings in Canberra. However, the nature of the engagement with history in diasporic Iranian literature appears to be as varied as people's engagement with it in real life, and it should be viewed as a response to each individual's level of commitment and understanding of its importance and significance. While, for example, for a large number of writers the use of an historical theme is a deliberate attempt to highlight and address inherent issues, for many more, reference to the past is as natural a running theme through their narrative as it is in their everyday lives, in the parties and gatherings. In looking at their work, however, no matter what form engagement with history takes, history is not just a theme that is picked up by some and ignored by others. Rather it is central and pervasive, present in most of their writings in various forms. While in some it emerges in and through a memoir, a personal recollection of a specific event, time period or locale, in others it comes as reference, or sometimes challenge, to historically cherished elements of Iranian culture, such as its literature. In some cases, engagement with elements of the past is a deliberate strategic response to the grand narratives of history, as a way to highlight and foreground marginalised and silenced voices of the past. In other cases, understanding and recounting history is a means for negotiation of diasporic presents and futures.

In this sense, Iranian diasporic communities are very similar to other diasporic communities. Like other migrants, the Iranian diaspora have left 'their homeland for any number of years, maybe even for the rest of their lives', and often 'construct a new identity abroad through the use of imagination, nostalgia, and memories'.[1] In their literature too, Iranian migrants often express similar sentiments to migrants from other countries. One of the most important tenets of this shared diasporic experience, and a recurring theme in this literature, is the maintenance of a continued sense of cultural identity. Leaving their home, the Iranian diaspora were faced with social isolation and homesickness that affected and disrupted their continued sense of identity, subjectivity and historical identification. This is a natural experience for any migratory group. Migration disrupts the sense of historical belonging, because, to put it in Bhabha's words, it leaves the immigrant in a state of 'unhomeliness'. Unhomeliness leaves the subject in displacement, with 'borders between home and world [...] confused'.[2] To overcome this sense of incredulous terror, the displaced often try to retain their sense of identity and belonging, by 'maintain[ing] a longing for their homeland and [a] desire to either return or preserve their nostalgia as a form of identification'.[3]

However, such a relationship becomes more complicated in colonised, patriarchal and totalitarian societies in which, generally, what is historically specific is not representative or inclusive of the identities of those it claims to represent. Thus, in the works of those who want to resist the hegemony of official history, particularly the colonised and marginalised, engagement with history is not necessarily about maintaining a continued sense of identity. Rather, it becomes an issue of what Ashcroft calls 'appropriation and interpolation' of master narratives of history. In these works, engagement with history is about tapping into the very discursive formations and practices of history to challenge it in order to transform it, to reconstruct and negotiate new histories that are representative of multiple experiences and futures.

Taking the complex relationship between history and maintenance, reconstruction and negotiation of identity into account, there are two prominent ways in which diasporic Iranian writers are engaging with history. On the one hand their literature could be read through Stuart Hall's concept of 'historicisation'. Emphasising historical connections, particularly for a diasporic community, may be an attempt to maintain a collective historicised sense of identity and belonging. On the other hand, this engagement can be seen through a post-colonial lens through which, by tapping into, appropriating and interpolating the grand narrative of history both in Iran and abroad, writers are deliberately challenging and transforming its elements, to reconstruct and negotiate histories reflective of their own identities, experiences and desired futures.

Historicisation and maintenance of identity

As Stuart Hall believes, history, among many other factors, and particularly in the form of collective and shared experiences, is a central tenet of how we form our identities. Cultural identities, he proposes, are formed through 'historicisation', which is identification 'constructed on the back of a recognition of some common origin or shared characteristics with another person or group, or with an ideal, and with the natural closure of solidarity and allegiance established on this foundation'.[4] He believes that, although historicisation is important in everyone's definition of a sense of identity, it is particularly significant for diasporic people who have been cut off from continued and shared points of identification. This is why, he argues, identities of 'forced' or 'free' migrants especially, need to be situated and understood within 'those historically specific developments and practices which have disturbed the relatively "settled" character of many populations and cultures'.[5] For diasporic communities across the globe, so important is this connection that, as Nilou Mostofi highlights, 'the crux of [their] identity lies in the "collective memory, vision, or myth"' of a historicized past whereby by 'holding onto, remembering and narrating the past, the immigrant can reassure himself or herself of his or her sense of identity'.[6] This remembrance is often nostalgic, and visualises the past as an unchanging paradisiacal space to which individuals feel a strong bond and belonging.

This is the case for the global diasporic Iranian community. Since it was the revolution that led to the migration of millions from Iran, some argue that 'the history of Iranian diaspora starts with the Islamic revolution of 1978–1979'.[7] For diasporic Iranian communities, which consist of people from a culturally, ethnically and linguistically diverse background, the revolution and its interruption of the normal flow of life can be seen as the single most important collective point of identification. This is not to suggest that this is the only point of historicisation, as diasporic Iranians draw on many cultural and social elements as shared points of identification. However, the revolution as an historical event is one of the few shared elements that transcends the socio-political, religious, linguistic and class differences across various global diasporic Iranian communities. Many Iranians who live outside Iran as the consequence of the revolution, regardless of their individual background, collectively identify with the disruption of the revolution. This is also reflected in much diasporic Iranian literature, in which the revolution serves as a key point of arrival and departure, the single most important event around which historicisation or the maintenance of a sense of historical connection to their fellow Iranians revolves.

Although the revolution is a shared experience, its reflection varies according to the experiences of individual writers. While some focus nostalgically on the pre-revolutionary era, others deal with the interruption of the revolution and post-revolutionary periods.

Still others take the revolution as the point of departure, and address its exilic consequences. Some even take readers across Iranian history from pre-revolutionary Iran through to the revolution and eventual exile.

Pre-revolutionary nostalgia

Since the revolution interrupted and changed Iran's socio-cultural landscape permanently and profoundly, pre-revolutionary Iran often holds a nostalgic grip, and acts as a shared point of historical identification for many Iranians on which they draw to create a sense of continued identity. 'The trauma of the Islamic revolution and subsequent immigration has left Iranian immigrants nostalgic for a homeland that no longer exists, for a constant regeneration of "the way things were"', observes Mostofi, 'and for a construction of an identity that [. . .] incorporates their past lives and histories'.[8] For those who experienced it, this is often remembered as carefree, but, with the air filled with political build-up, peppered with a hint of danger, with the mysterious presence of the Shah's notorious secret police, SAVAK, and the pressures leading to the revolution. This era is memorable and cherished by many first-generation migrants who will forever remember the landscape of Iran as such.

This period forms the backdrop of many novels and memoirs. For instance, this is the setting for *bildungsroman* novels like Mahbod Seraji's *Rooftops of Tehran* (2009), a touching novel that takes us into the world of 17-year-old Pasha, as he falls in love with his neighbour Zari, but whose romance is cut short when they become involved with the SAVAK. Similarly, Zohreh Ghahremani's *Sky of Red Poppies* (2010) follows teenager Roya as her friendship develops with politically involved Shirin, leading to near-fatal consequences with the SAVAK. Anahita Firouz's *In the Walled Garden* (2003) follows Mahastee, a young wealthy woman married to one of Iran's elite real estate owners, as a forbidden love is rekindled with her childhood crush, Reza, who is now a Marxist, the enemy of the very class that she represents. Exploring a similar theme, Simon Sion Ebrami in *Veiled Romance* (2012) tells the dangerous story of another forbidden love between Leila and Cyrus set against the backdrop of the revolution. Rahimeh Andabilian's *The Rose Hotel* (2012) takes us into the lives of a family who run a hotel in the city of Mashhad prior to the revolution, and whose lives are permanently shifted as the result of the revolution. *The Lemon Grove* (2012) by Ali Hosseini also deals with the revolution and its interruption of the lives of identical twin boys Ruzbeh and Behruz, resulting in their separation, as one goes to America and the other remains to fight in the ensuing war. *The Caspian Rain* (2007), *Moonlight on the Avenue of Faith* (2001) by Gina Nahai, Zohreh Ghahremani's second novel, *Moon Daughter* (2012), and *Javady Alley* (1984) by Manny Shirazi, as well as Firoozeh Kashani-Sabet's *Martyrdom Street* (2010) all explore the mother–daughter relationship set in pre-revolutionary Iran. The pre-revolutionary period is also the backdrop to Nahid Rachlin's *Married to a Stranger* (1983), which follows the coming of age of a young woman as she discovers her own sense of identity after marriage. Similarly, the pre-revolutionary Iran of the 1950s sets the backdrop to I. J. Safreh's *Beyond the Third Garden* (2013), which tells the story of the encounter between an Iranian boy, Reza, living in an orphanage, and an Iranian woman, Paree, married to a British man.

This era is also the setting of many memoirs. In *The Blindfold Horse* (1988) for instance, Susha Guppy takes the reader back into the streets of Tehran from the 1940s through to her departure for Europe. Similarly, Sattareh Farman-Farmaian's *Daughter of Persia* (1996) recalls life as a princess in the quarters of her father's palace until she too left Iran permanently after the revolution. Gholam-Reza Sabri-Tabrizi, in his memoir *Iran: A Child's Story, a Man's Experience* (1989), nostalgically recounts his childhood in pre-revolutionary Iran. In *French Hats in Iran* (2013), Heydar Radjavi recalls growing up in the city of Tabriz in the 1940s. Recounting more recent memories, Roya Hakakian's *Journey From the Land of No* (2004) takes us on a more modern journey through Iran just before the revolution from the perspective of a young Jewish teenage girl dwelling at a time of social upheaval that became the revolution. Both Azar Nafisi in *Things I've Been Silent About* (2010) and Fatemeh Keshavarz in *Jasmine and Stars* (2007) candidly explore their life and family relationships leading up to the revolutionary era. In *The Apple Tree Blossoms in Fall* (2012) Armineh Ohanian, too, remembers her life prior to the revolution and eventual exile.

Although these books present diverse experiences from a cross-section of Iranian society, each in their own way contribute to the maintenance of a historicised sense of identity as they preserve and collectively remember shared sights and sounds of pre-revolutionary Iran.

Zohreh Ghahremani, the author of *Sky of Red Poppies* and *Moon Daughter*, explains this best on her blog. Before embarking on a ten paragraph reverie of how the simple phrase 'jingling of gold rimmed tea glasses' that she read in a book filled her 'mind with a hundred visions of her past in Iran', she writes:

> oceans away from the land that I love, my Americanized lifestyle helps me to bury the past so deep inside that I don't even think about it. That is, until someone, or something triggers my memory and then it all comes back vividly, as if it were only yesterday.

She concludes:

> Yes, that simple sound of thin, gold-rimmed glasses shaking in a tray and jingling as they hit one another has stayed within me for decades, only now it's no longer buried for it has emerged to remind me of all the [. . .] lazy summer days, the late afternoon tea in the garden, or the sad tea passed around at funerals. Decades later, my estekan [glass] has changed to a larger, thicker one, and my lonely glass no longer finds a companion to jingle against. Just when I thought the past was all behind me, those tiny gold-rimmed glasses have come back through the pages of a good book to remind me of who I am and how far I've come [. . .] It doesn't take much to bring back those wonderful memories. All I need is the familiar ring of a few words, the echo of a sound, or the dusty smell of a faraway place and there I am, flying back on the magic carpet of memories. I would give up all the privileges of my new life for just one moment of a life that is lost forever. It's a sweet fantasy and I cherish it while it lasts: There I am, back where I belong, back to a time when all I needed to get over my troubles was a good glass of tea.[9]

Ghahremani's expression is a clear reflection of the significance of historical engagement and nostalgic remembrance of pre-revolutionary Iran. By the same token, many Iranians of a certain generation identify with shared elements from pre-revolutionary Iran. As one reviewer of *Rooftops of Tehran* recounts on Amazon.com the book reminded him of life in pre-revolutionary Iran. He writes:

> Mr. Seraji's captivating words, interweaving history, love, heartache and humor managed to reawaken many latent memories that I had chosen to bury deep. He managed to tug on shreds of strings of a Perso-American rug that is me.
>
> [Through the book] I traveled to my childhood (pre and post 1979 revolution) until I was 13... I felt, in a way, that I was robbed from experiencing my life in Iran... Pasha filled in the void. [...] I lived a life that I could have had, vicariously-sadly-happily-remorsefully and so-on through his characters. It was a completing experience.
>
> The political undertones [...] hit home even more as I felt terror the characters. Mr. and Mrs. Mehraban, felt parallel to my mother's constant unease and fear of death and persecution for writing her stories and plays and poems during the early days of the Islamic republic regime. [10]

Another reviewer writes about their experience of *Sky of Red Poppies*: 'When I was reading *Sky of Red Poppies*, every night, I was taken to another time (the time that I was 16–17 years old). [...] I cried, smiled, and enjoyed the book.'[11]

These accounts are often utopian paradisiacal, unchanging memories of a shared idyllic past through which many can form and maintain an historicised sense of identity and belonging. As Sabri-Tabrizi tells us in the introduction to his memoir, these narratives play a significant part in maintaining the almost forgotten collective Iranian experience and memory. He writes:

> Leaving one's homeland and all relatives, friends and objects that one has become used to during childhood, creates a mental vacuum. This vacuum is filled partly with new impressions, experiences and the cultural wealth of other countries. To fill the other part one uses the imagination and begins to recreate, perhaps out of intellectual necessity, one's own past memories. This is a kind of rediscovery which is indeed essential for human existence and identity, especially when one is surrounded by an alien social and political atmosphere.[12]

He concludes the introduction by saying: 'The way of life described here is almost vanished today, but I hope that I have been able to preserve a little of it in my description of the life of one ordinary Iranian family in these years.'[13]

It is not, however, only by recounting specific historical eras that groups and individuals constitute a continued sense of collective identity. Reference to specific cultural tropes and elements play an equally significant part in the process. While this chapter outlines how reference to historical eras are utilised in maintaining a shared sense of Iranian identity, other chapters identify specific cultural and historical tropes and elements that are used in a similar manner. Chapter Two, for example, focuses on the use of Persian literature as a site for the maintenance of an Iranian identity. Similarly Chapter Four examines the trope of the home and homeland and examines how it is drawn upon to define and challenge certain aspects of Iranian national identity.

However, for many Iranians maintaining a connection to pre-revolutionary Iran has other implications than simply as a nostalgic reverie. As Mostofi argues, for many diasporic Iranians the Islamic revolution, and the image that the West has of the revolution, is a negative one. Consequently, historical engagement with pre-revolutionary Iran and its tropes becomes a means of asserting and maintaining a certain kind of identity. As Mostofi comments, 'Iranian diasporic consciousness constitutes an identity based on a "historical consciousness" where some valorise cultural traits and cultural cohesion.'[14] It is to this end that many Iranians choose to associate themselves with the pre-revolutionary era, calling themselves 'Persian' in order to identify with a cultural heritage, rather than 'Iranian' which has nationalistic connotations. By emphasising a connection to the pre-revolutionary era, diasporic Iranians assert themselves positively, disassociating themselves from identification with the Islamic regime of Iran. This is clearly reflected in their literary expressions. When Sattareh Farman-Farmaian, for instance, entitles her book *Daughter of Persia* instead of *Daughter of Iran* and poses for the front cover proudly, she is announcing her connection to that historical and cultural background rather than to the more recent negative political implications that Iran carries in the West. Farman-Farmaian is particularly self-conscious in narrating her story, telling her readers the intention of her writing: 'If my recollections can contribute to greater understanding between my Western and Iranian friends and add something to the awareness of the rich diversity of human cultures', she writes, 'I will feel that I have succeeded in doing something tangible.'[15] Similarly, Sabri-Tabrizi tells of how he draws on history and memory to offer a positive sense of historical recognition. He tells us, 'I used my inner rediscovery of my childhood memories, or rather self-awakening, as a bridge between a child's memories and a man's experience and between Eastern and Western cultures.'[16]

Revolutionary disconnections and exilic connections

Historicisation, however, does not always rest on positive memories of a nostalgic past. Rather it can be of the trauma of a shared historical dystopian experience. For the Iranian diaspora, as much as they construct an historicised sense of belonging on the back of nostalgically shared memories of pre-revolutionary Iran, they also all share the disruptions caused by the revolution, difficulties of life in post-revolutionary Iran and eventual exile. The historical significance of the revolution and the consequent interruption of life is also reflected in their literature. As Hossein Tirgan tells us in the introduction to his book *Goodbye Iran* (2013), which recounts a story based on the true events in the lives of two young men, Hamid and Hossein, as they escape Iran after the revolution:

> All my life, I believed that to study history was to study the past fruitlessly. Then, after high school, history came crashing unbidden into my world. I saw with my own eyes the fall of the Shah of Iran and the change of the governing regime of my country [. . .] I then realised that history was not only a thing of the past, it was something constantly developing, unfolding right in front of us all. Suddenly, I understood that we are all part of it, every one of us, whether we give our consent to be involved or not.[17]

He goes on to tell us how the Islamic revolution, as an historical event, affected the Iranian population:

> History put its mark on every Iranian as the new government rolled out its agenda [. . .] Decades later, I can now see how this one particular historical event impacted my own life, the lives of more than seventy five million Iranians who live in today's Iran, and the lives of more than five million Iranians who live outside Iran.[18]

Tirgan is not alone in seeing the significance of the revolution as an historical event. Indeed, a survey of books by diasporic Iranian writers, particularly the memoirs, reveals that accounts of the revolution and eventual exile outnumber nostalgic reveries of pre-revolutionary Iran. For instance, it is the revolution that forever interrupts Afschineh Latifi's life as she recalls, in *Even After All This Time* (2005), her father's execution soon after the revolution, leading her mother and siblings into eventual exile. Similarly, it is the revolution that disrupts Marina Nemat's life, as she tells us in *Prisoner of Tehran* (2005), leading to her imprisonment at the age of 16. By the same token, it is in response to post-revolutionary conditions that Cherry Mosteshar and Sousan Azadi wrote their memoirs *Unveiled: Love and Death among the Ayatollahs* (1995) and *Out of Iran: One Woman's Escape from the Ayatollahs* (1987). And it is also the revolution that interrupted the lives of Tara Baharampour and Banafsheh Serov, as they recall their experiences of having to migrate as teenagers to other countries in their memoirs *Under Starless Sky* (2008) and *To See and See Again* (1999). More recently, in her memoir *The Lonely War: One Woman's Account for the Struggle of Modern Iran* (2014) Nazila Fathi, too, recounts her life leading up to and after the revolution into modern Iran. As she tells us in the introduction 'the revolution changed every aspect of our lives.'[19] For second generation diasporic Iranians, too, such as Azadeh Moaveni who wrote *Lipstick Jihad* (2005), and Said Sayrafiezadeh who wrote *When Skateboards will be Free* (2009), it is also the revolution that has disrupted their connection to their cultural background.

Fiction writers, too, emphasise the disruption caused by the revolution and its aftermath. In *Interruptions* (2008) Masud Alemi demonstrates how the events of the revolution, and a case of mistaken identity, interrupt an innocent man's life, leading him to unfair imprisonment. Similarly, Farnoosh Moshiri, in all her four novels, *The Drum Tower* (2014), *Against Gravity* (2005), *Bathhouse* (2001), and *At the Wall of the Almighty* (2000), deals with the dark consequences of the revolution on individuals. *The Ruby Tear Catcher* (2011) by Nahid Sewell also recounts the disruption to Leila's life after the revolution, and her eventual exile. In *The Fortune Catcher* (1997) Susanne Pari follows Layla's return to Iran after the revolution, and the disruption that the regime causes to her marriage to the love of her life. In *Septembers of Shiraz* (2008) Dalia Sofer tells the story of a rare-gem dealer, Amin, who is arrested soon after the revolution, and follows his family's struggle as they come to terms with their situation.

These narratives, both as memoir and fiction, construct a site for the shared sense of historical identification based on the interruption in the form of the revolution and the difficulties of the post-revolutionary era and eventual exile. The representation of a variety of experiences of the same event further contributes to the expansion of the realisation of similarities between diasporic Iranians who come from different social, political and religious backgrounds. That the gay Iranian man captured innocently in *Interruptions* has similar experiences to the young Christian girl, Marina Nemat, of *Prisoner of Tehran*, for instance, minimises the socio-political, religious and even gender differences and hostilities that those people might have experienced in Iran. The realisation of the similarity of experiences expressed through these narratives contributes to the construction of diasporic Iranian communities, maintaining their connection to the past on a basis of understanding rather than difference.

Furthermore, the recounting of the dystopian historical interruptions caused by the revolution can be seen as a site for the healing of its trauma. In later chapters, this book will explore in detail the psychologically therapeutic effects of engagement with, and recounting of, individual and collective histories, and how that in turn can lead to maintenance and reconstruction of identities.

Whether through recounting nostalgic remembrances of pre-revolutionary Iran, the disruption of the revolution, or through the narration of individual trauma caused by the revolution, this literature is a site through which diasporic Iranians can maintain a sense of continued and historicised identity, as Hall puts it 'constructed on the back of a recognition of some common origin or shared characteristic with another person or group'.[20] The literature that reflects this can be read as 'a consolidated effort to preserve the [diasporic] community's sense of identity'[21] allowing the diasporic Iranian community to 'connect to one another through this collective remembrance'.[22]

Dangerous nostalgia and fantasies of unhappenings

While for a diasporic community recollection of the past can be positive in reasserting and maintaining identity by constructing a sense of belonging to a shared historicised past, it can also be potentially dangerous if that identification becomes a primary means of identification. Ashcroft argues:

> acts of memory are always vulnerable to nostalgia, which, rather than stimulating change can paralyse transformative action. In its most extreme form, [they] could be described as a 'fantasy of unhappening' the desire to reverse history, to retrieve some essential authentic cultural identity that existed before.[23]

If texts that reminisce about an unattainable past, or dwell too much on the dystopian interruption of the past, become the only means through which individuals or communities can maintain a sense of historicised identity in diaspora, then they could contribute to deepening a sense of loss for migrants. Potentially, this could hamper them from living in the present and integrating into their new setting. As Mostofi points out, Iranian migrants 'pine over a home they can never become a part of because the Iran of their memoires no longer exists, [but] they reside within a state they must adapt to for survival'.[24] Although in some cases recalling traumatic events may assist with coming to terms with past trauma, at times the inability to acknowledge the past and move on can place the Iranian diaspora in an 'awkward position'.[25]

However, the greater danger of this historicised identification arises when historically specific texts become models for understanding Iran and Iranianness in the West. As Hamid Naficy points out, a typical response of diasporic people 'to the rupture of displacement is to create a utopian prelapsarian [image] of the homeland that is uncontaminated by contemporary facts'.[26] Added to this for the diasporic Iranian community is a constant grieving over the dystopian events of the revolution that interrupted their lives.

Reflections of this grief can become problematic especially when there is time delay between remembered events and the time that narration becomes part of public discourse. In recent years this has been particularly the case, when in light of current socio-political conditions and renewed interests in the United States/Iran conflict, narratives from Iran have attracted American readers again, as they 'revisit and fold the events of the Islamic revolution and its aftermath into the present one more time'.[27] Although interest in such books has been triggered by current socio-political settings into which they are received, most of those that recall a specific time period in Iran (whether they focus on the nostalgia of pre-revolutionary Iran or the disruption of the revolution and the chaos that followed) remain uncontaminated by contemporary events there.

Iranian women's memoirs, most of which are delayed accounts of the Islamic revolution, have been most susceptible to this. In most cases, despite their normally self-acclaimed historically dated setting, they are taken to be representative of current Iranian society and experience. As Gillian Whitlock observes, these books 'appear at one and the same time as unfamiliar and belated to contemporary Iranians, [but] familiar and welcome to contemporary American readers'.[28] For instance when Azar Nafisi's *Reading* Lolita *in Tehran,* chronicling life in Iran's most turbulent era between 1979 and 1997, became an instant best seller upon publication in 2004, it was immediately read as a reflection of women's oppression and complete lack of freedom and rights under the current Islamic regime. Although in her epilogue Nafisi acknowledges that the situation, particularly that of women, has changed drastically since the time of her experiences, and that women had certainly gained many more rights in the last 20 years, her self-professed time delay has often gone unnoticed, making 'her recollections of a repressed and alienated society [. . .] wholly convincing and realistic to a Western reader in these times'.[29]

The diasporic Iranian community seems aware of the dangers of such historical reminiscing that can freeze Iran and Iranianness within an historical period. They are aware of the irony of texts that maintain Iranian identity through historical recollection in the West but are also contributing to static representations of Iranians and reinforcing the historically constructed barriers against the smooth integration of Iranian diaspora. Heated debates erupt regularly on popular internet sites such as Iranian.com about Iranian identity and historic representation, in which Iranians express their opinions about issues of concern. One regular contributor to Iranian.com, Ben Madadi, writes:

> I know that Iran has a glorious past. It should make all of us proud, but we cannot live in the past. [. . .] It is time to look at the world as it is today. It has really changed. It has changed a lot. [. . .] Iran will never be what it used to, not in our lifetime, not in our children's life time and not for any foreseeable future. [. . .] Iran and Iranians, can get their act together [but] first we need to come in peace with

> our past and move forward. [. . .] We must find a basis of union, not based on the past glories of Iranian empire but based on the new realities. [. . .] We cannot live always thinking about the past. The world has changed, even Iranians have changed.[30]

Iranian writers and critics also seem aware of the weight of history and historical representation in the process of construction and assimilation and are resisting its weight. But because history, both in how it is representative and as a point of identification, plays such an important part in how Iranian identity is viewed and constructed in diaspora, it cannot simply be discounted, nor can a diasporic Iranian identity be constructed in the vacuum of the present.

This is why Iranian writers, like post-colonial writers, are using the resources of history, culture and language in a self-reflective and creative manner. This is a running theme in much of the literature by diasporic Iranian writers, which not only offers alternative perspectives on history but also allows for writers to draw on different aspects, tropes and elements of their history to project and construct desired reflections for the future.

Appropriation and interpolation of history

'The construction of Iranian national identity', observes Nasrin Rahimieh, 'has insisted upon the erasure and elision of gender, language and ethnicity.'[31] This is reflected in narratives of Iranian history in which the histories and narratives of ethnic and religious minorities, alternative political parties, and women have almost always been nearly silenced, and remained outside of the main discourse, seldom publicly acknowledged. This experience of historical non-legitimation resonated even beyond the borders of Iran, as many Iranians who moved after the revolution were collectively viewed as refugees, and within the historically constructed frameworks of pre-revolutionary Oriental exotic Persians or post-revolutionary hostage-taking fanatics.

In the context of such exclusion of alternative histories, together with Hall's belief that identities are 'constituted within, not outside representation', and that 'we must understand [identities] as produced in specific historical and institutional sites within specific discursive formations and practices, by specific enunciative strategies',[32] many

Iranians find that they have not been given the ability to fully realise their own sense of identity and historic sensibility both within Iran and abroad. In other words, due to a lack of public historical acknowledgement and representation, they have not been 'legitimised' for 'what it means to have a history is the same as what it means to have a legitimate existence: history and legitimation go hand in hand'.[33] This is why engagement with history forms a significant element of diasporic Iranian writing in English. In the process of historical reassertion, diasporic Iranian writers face a challenge akin to post-colonial writers. Even though never physically colonised, the various totalitarian regimes that have ruled Iran for centuries, the unifying and exclusive historical narratives of Iran, and the hegemonic representation of Iranians in the West both pre- and post-revolution, like colonial forces, have either not factored the multiplicity of histories in the grand narrative of history or incorporated them only 'at its edges', within a 'marginal reality'.[34] For Iranian writers engagement with history requires them to tap into the very discourse of history both in Iran and abroad, in order to rewrite history that is reflective of the multiplicity of their experiences. Like post-colonial writers, they too must engage with history, to change and challenge, not only certain elements, but also the very discourse of 'history itself'.[35] This, what Ashcroft calls 'utopia from the *past*', is 'a critical strategy designed to resist the master discourse of history'.[36] According to him this can operate in two ways. One way is through 'appropriation' of elements of a dominant culture, particularly an adaptation of its vernacular and literature, in which the dominant language is taken and made to reflect one's own cultural experience. The other is to '*interpolate* the master discourse of [...] history, engaging it on its own terms'.[37] Sometimes, the appropriation of language and interpolation of history go hand in hand.

Appropriating a new language: The vessel of flight to vast possibilities

Language, as we know, is far more than a mere tool for communication. In some cases, it can be seen as an imposition by domineering forces, 'a strategy of cultural hegemony'.[38] This hegemony is often exclusive and 'impose[s] a way of talking about the world that privilege[s] certain kinds of distinction and representations and debase[s] others'.[39] This is why for post-colonial writers and those resisting dominant forms of expression, language can be a means of resistance and challenge. It is also why in post-colonial resistance, 'colonial languages have been not only instruments of oppression but also instruments of radical resistance and transformation'.[40] In such literature, the choice to write in English is a conscious decision to employ the dominant language, appropriate it and 'make it do a different cultural work'.[41]

For diasporic Iranian writers, too, the choice to write in English is a conscious decision, a strategy that allows them to speak against the oppressive historical forces of their home and host cultures. Iranian history has, almost always, been written by male members of society and through a dominant language. This dominance has caused silence, particularly of women's voices and narratives. In diaspora, however, distanced from domineering forces, many have become aware of the historical oppression that they had faced in Iran and found a new language to express themselves.

In the opening pages of *Journey from the Land of No* (2004), Roya Hakakian, a Jewish Iranian woman, tells us why she chose to write about her experiences of the revolution and of leaving Iran, in English. As a journalist, when she receives a call from another journalist, David, asking her to write about the student clashes in Iran in 1999, she finds herself 'embittered by [her] history', unable to write an objective piece. She writes an apologetic email confessing 'the past and the events that followed the revolution had biased me forever',[42] and that she was not the best source. Instead of accepting her apology David writes 'tell me about them'.[43] But recalling and sharing memories is initially a difficult task because she feels that she does not have the right language to express herself. But, through David's encouragement, Hakakian gradually finds that English could be a new medium for expression of her untellable story. She tells us:

> To write in Persian would be daunting. Instead of re-examining the memories, I feared that in Persian, I might begin to relive them. Persian could summon the teenager at sea. English sheltered the adult survivor, safely inside a lighthouse. I did not know how to use the language of the censors to speak against them; to use the very language by which I had been denied so much as a Jew, a woman, a secular citizen, and a young poet. The love of Iran was still in my heart, yet I could not return. The irrevocable journey

> I had made was not the physical one, out of Iran. It was the journey from 'no,' from the perpetual denials. And what I had painstakingly arrived at, greater than even the new land, was a new language, the vessel of my flight to vast possibilities.[44]

It is English, this new-found language, free from the constraints of Persian and its associations, that allows her to recount and reconstruct her history in her own words. Recalling Hall's argument that identities are formed through historicisation and representation, one sees Hakakian's narrative as her way of representing and anchoring her current self through history, a history that had denied her any space in the grand narrative of events as a Jewish teenage girl, but for the narration of which she has now found a new language.

While English gives Hakakian a new language to recount and reconstruct her own history in relation to her past in Iran, importantly it also gives her a voice within the diasporic community in which she lives, one which had also denied her any sense of individuality as a Jewish Iranian woman living under the historically constructed labels of exotic/terrorist. Hakakian tells us that one of the worries that had prevented her from recounting her past had been the biased vision of her potential audience:

> who came in two kinds: the misinformed, who think of Iran as a backward nation of Arabs, veiled and turbaned, living on the periphery of oases [. . .]; and the misguided, who believed the Shah's regime was a puppet government run by the CIA, and who think that Ayatollah Khomeini and his clerical cabal are an authentic, home-grown answer to an unwarranted U.S. meddling.[45]

However, Hakakian realises that English gives her a voice with which she can speak about her experiences within her diasporic community. By writing in English, she taps into the system and takes hold of the very language with which she had been historically denied her story. This linguistic appropriation interpolates the events of history by offering alternative versions of known accounts. The interpolation transforms the historically imposed beliefs of her 'misguided' and 'misinformed' acquaintances about her as an Iranian Jewish woman living in America. As Irene Wanner writes in an online review of the book for *Seattle Times*,

'This book does us the service of removing some of the region's mythical stereotypes [...] and illuminating a real contemporary culture we would do well to know better.'[46]

Hakakian, however, is not alone. For many Iranian writers, the appropriation of the English language, and, as we will see, parts of its literature, has played a significant part in allowing them to interpolate and consequently transform grand narratives of history both in Iran and abroad. In this interpolation of history, they interject their own versions of historical accounts to transform the grand narratives, in turn reconstructing histories and negotiating future possibilities.

Recounting alternative histories and reconstructing identities

One of the key function of interpolating history, according to Ashcroft, is 'to subvert the unquestioned status of the "scientific record" by re-inscribing the "rhetoric" of events',[47] by injecting, inserting and interrupting history with marginal voices and narratives. These interpolations offer alternative versions on history and reconstruct history as history books have scribed it.

In the body of diasporic Iranian literature in English, interpolation of grand narratives of history, with marginal voices, has become a common theme. Events of an historical period are told from untold perspectives and through silenced voices. For instance, in *Paper: Dreams of a Scribe* (2004) Bahiyyih Nakhjavani, a Baha'i Iranian writer, takes us back into history and into the desolate world of a scribe in nineteenth century Persia as he tries to find the perfect paper to write his perfect work at a time when paper was rare. Similarly in their historical novel *The House that War Minister Built* (2011), Andrew and Elahe Dayton weave a narrative that follows Nargess, a resilient matriarch's clan from the 1900s into the Islamic revolution and beyond, ending on the brink of the present and 9/11 events. Anita Amirrezvani, who is fast establishing herself as an historical novelist, in *Blood of Flowers* (2007) recounts the history of a little girl who makes carpets for a living during the reign of Shah Abbas (1571–1629). The book, Amirrezvani tells us in the author's note, was researched thoroughly to be historically accurate. But it draws on various historical sources, such as Western travelogues from Persia, and the history of Persian carpets, and brings us this history through the young girl's journey. Despite its historicity, the author tells us, the book was inspired by the Iranian handicraft in her house, whose artisans were always unknown. Amirrezvani tells us she purposely did not name the narrator so that the book could be a 'tribute to anonymous artisans of Iran'.[48] Her goal had been to acknowledge those 'whose work has endured through the centuries'.[49] She goes on to describe why she used rug-making as a metaphor for the way history and life are made: 'Rug-making is [. . .] an excellent metaphor', she tells us, 'you work on a loom one knot at a time, until one day you have an entire carpet with a complex personality and history. Just like life.'[50]

Amirrezvani follows a similar theme in her second book *Equal of the Sun* (2013) where she recounts the history of a Persian Princess of the 1570s, Pari Khanoom, from the perspective of a beloved servant. The prologue makes this clear. After praising the princess, the narrator, who reveals himself as a close servant of the Princess, tells us how he is offering an alternative and unheard version of history:

> I wrestled over whether to attempt this work, since I am neither biographer nor historian. Despite the danger, the ignorance of the men around me compels me to set down the truth about the princess. If I refuse this task, her story will be misrepresented or distorted to become a tool of those in power. Court historians report only the best-known fact about how royal women have led troops into battle, deposed shahs, killed their enemies, and thrust their sons into power. They are forbidden from observing the lives of these women directly and therefore must rely on rumours and inventions.
>
> As Pari's closest servant, I not only observed her actions but carried out her orders. I realized that upon my death, everything I know about her would disappear if I failed to document her story.[51]

This story told from the alternative perspective of the servant about a woman whose story would not have been told in the history books, as we know it, interjects and interpolates the grand narrative of Iranian history.

While Amirrezvani explores voices from distant history, other writers tend to engage more with recent voices. In the first of her trilogy of novels, *The Age of Orphans* (2010), Laleh Khadivi explores several decades of Iranian history through the story of the Kurdish minority by following the story of an orphan boy to adulthood. As the book begins, the young unnamed boy loses his father and is taken away from his land, and against his will he is renamed Reza Khourdi by the officials – Reza after the Shah and Khourdi after the tribe from which he comes. Through his story, in his struggle against the Shah's regime, his search for a sense of identity, which was taken away from him when he was renamed, and his position leading up to the Islamic revolution, we encounter a very dark and alternative view of Iranian history from the rarely told Kurdish perspective.

Another interpolation of the grand narratives of Iranian history has been through accounts told from alternative political perspectives. In recent Iranian history, even prior to the Islamic revolution, activists who expressed alternative political views or hinted at discontent faced harsh punishments and were quickly removed, in order to avoid social impact. In 1968, for instance, Samad Behrangi, the author of the popular children's book *The Little Black Fish*, was found drowned in a river. *The Little Black Fish* tells the story of a little fish who defies his community's rules and ventures beyond to see what lies on the other side of the sea. Written allegorically, the book was seen as encouraging revolutionary ideas. When Behrangi died, everyone assumed that he had been murdered by the SAVAK. The government never denied the accusations, but no one dared mention Behrangi or his books in public. Similarly, in 1974, the well-known poet Khosrow Golsorkhi (Khosrow the Red Rose), an anti-government activist and leftist, was charged with trying to overthrow the government. The Shah, to teach activists a lesson on their eventual fate, strategically allowed Golsorkhi's trial to be shown live on television. But, when asked to defend himself, he broke out into poetry that attacked 'the institution of the monarchy and the Peacock Throne's supplication at the altars of outside powers such as the United States and Britain'.[52] The live feed was quickly cut off, and uncensored footage of the trial was not seen again until years later. Eventually Golsorkhi was executed, leaving a deep heroic impact on people across the country. However, the legacy of those like Behrangi and Golsorkhi was pushed into the margins of history, as people were not allowed to write about them, praise them, or possess their writing. Eventually their names were erased from the official pages of Iranian history, only passing down in oral and informal histories.

The recounting of these unacknowledged voices and histories has been one of the recurring themes of diasporic Iranian literature in English. Many narratives set in pre-revolutionary Iran interpolate the grand narratives of Iranian history by revolving around and bringing forth untold stories and voices of the political tension that existed between the government and oppositional forces. In *Rooftops of Tehran* (2009), for instance, Mahbod Seraji brings to life characters who followed in the footsteps of revolutionaries, but whose stories would never have been told otherwise. As the book begins in early 1970s, Pasha has fallen in love with Zari, a neighbouring girl, who is about to get married to a respectable young man and a friend of Pasha's, nicknamed Doctor. Doctor, however, is a political activist against the Shah. When the SAVAK eventually catch him, he disappears and is executed in jail. His parents find out about his death only when SAVAK contact them to pay the price of the bullet used to execute their son if they want his body released. Following an emotional outcry, Pasha tells us how Doctor and others like him are altogether wiped from the pages of history:

> No one will ever know the price of the bullet that killed Doctor. His parents are forbidden to speak of it. The stone on his grave must be left blank except for his name. The family can visit the grave as often as they wish, but others should not be encouraged. Doctor will not be issued a death certificate, and all documents pertaining to his birth will also be destroyed. As far as the world is concerned, Doctor never existed.[53]

Pasha's emotional outburst brings to the foreground the government's systematic erasure of the names and identities of political activists from its pages. But he takes action to rekindle his friend's memory. In a daring move, Pasha gathers all his savings and borrows more, and buys a red rosebush which he plants in the middle of the night in the alley near Doctor's house. In the morning everyone is startled by the sudden appearance of the rose bush:

> 'Who planted this?'
> 'Why?'
> 'Yes, why a red rose?'
> 'Why here? It doesn't make any sense.'

> 'Oh, a red rose! Remember the posters?'
> 'The posters? Oh, yes, the posters, I remember the posters.'
> 'Red is the color of passion and the color of revolution.'
> 'Red is also the color of love.'
> 'And the color of blood.'
> [. . .]
> 'We must take turns caring for this bush,' someone says in the crowd, as I water the plant.
> 'Yes, we must,' everyone agrees. 'For Doctor.'[54]

That the neighbours, all of whom had been traumatised by the Doctor's death, do not immediately recognise the significance of the rose, points to the fallibility of such characters in Iranian history. But as they eventually remember, and feel a sense of obligation to take care of the bush, they are safeguarding the memory of all of those like Doctor who gave up their life for a cause, but who could easily have been forgotten. In fact, Seraji's book, with a cover of the landscape of Tehran juxtaposed with a deep red rose does what Pasha does by planting the red rose. It offers an alternative history told from the perspective of many who struggled against the pre-revolutionary regime, but whose existence has been wiped out completely from the pages of history.

In her novel *In the Walled Garden* (2003), Anahita Firouz, too, offers a different glimpse of untold histories of political struggles and class differences. Set on the brink of the revolution it tells the story of a near love affair between Mahastee, an independent and glamorous aristocratic woman, and her childhood sweetheart, Reza, the son of their gardener, now an ebullient political activist against the Shah's policies. As Mahastee and Reza reacquaint, through their narratives we enter into their separate and marginal social classes: the very rich who are the ruling elite, and the lower middle class political activists. But it appears that both of these groups, in their own very different and almost contrasting ways, are trying to come to terms with the political upheaval that surrounds them. Half way through the novel, however, frustrated after a friend has been jailed, Reza suddenly breaks into a powerful philosophical soliloquy. He says:

> We have two countries; the one they've designed for us, and the one we've got. They have movers and shakers and social engineers with policies and blueprints and facades, but without that flash of

> revelation at what we are from the inside out. They don't see it, that great force of a man's private history. The springboard of ideology is the intimate clockwork of blood and upbringing and the personal rituals and daily existence ticking away. They leak out and subvert all the great forces of history. Nothing lasts from the outside, finally, unless it's willed from the inside out.[55]

Reza's speech highlights the complexity of Iranian history at the time in which the book was set. The two countries that he is referring to are the one politicians have designed, and the one where people live. Often these two realities are distanced and not reflective of each other, for what the people want is very different from what the government has designed. While political activists like Reza and his comrades fight for freedom of speech and policy changes, as we see throughout the book, the government jails them, suppressing them in the interests of its own agenda. Reza, however, believes that people's personal beliefs in a cause, and their upbringing, have the power to subvert and overcome the appearance of hegemony that the government has tried to create. Indeed, it was this subversion that eventually led to what later became the revolution. Reza's statement, in its depth and complexity, is a reminder of the importance of the individuals and their struggles in shaping current Iranian history.

On another level, *In the Walled Garden* also reveals the complexity of Iranian society and history through the narratives of two socially marginal characters. By emphasising the daily struggles and personal beliefs of these two almost opposing characters, and juxtaposing them against the backdrop of what eventually became the revolution, the novel offers a different kind of history of the revolution: a history told from the insider perspective of an aristocratic woman and a Marxist revolutionary – both of whose perspectives and voices are usually left out in the history of the revolution both in Iran and abroad. As such the novel itself could be read as a subversion of recent narratives of the revolution in Iran and abroad.

But the subversion of revolutionary voices is not limited to pre-revolutionary Iranian history. Similarly, after the revolution, lost are the voices and histories of aristocrats and the ruling elite of the pre-revolutionary period. Not only have they been almost completely ignored in the sequence of events, but they have also often been demonised by the Islamic government. This is why narratives such as Firouz's interpolate the grand narratives of Iranian history, by bringing marginal voices and experiences into focus, and giving them a history. This in turn gives them, and those of a similar background, a sense of belonging, and legitimises their experiences throughout Iranian history. This sense of legitimisation and identification with a historical background consequently provides the opportunity for many to assert themselves in their new diasporic setting against the historically stereotypical portrayals of Iranians in the West as exotics and terrorists.

This is because this historical legitimisation, and interpolation of history from alternative perspectives, shatters stereotypes. As Firouz herself tells us about the responses of the non-Iranian readers on her website, 'they didn't know that the Iran in this novel existed. Because of how Iran is shown in the media, they think it is all angry fists raised in the air. But I am getting direct feedback from the readers who say they like walking into this other world before the revolution.'[56] The direct and positive response of readers indicates that Firouz has shattered the stereotype of the Iranian revolution and offered alternative perspectives of Iranian history that are full of individual human experiences. The realisation of the humanity and multiplicity of experiences for those in the host country, in turn, makes for a more hospitable environment into which diasporic Iranians can integrate.

Although many narratives do focus on the minority accounts of those who took part in the revolution, one of those groups that has not really had a chance to be represented other than in stereotypes has been the Iranian cleric or mullah. Collectively seen as angry fanatics, particularly after the hostage crisis, Iranian mullahs and the concept of Shi'i Islam have been viewed negatively in recent Western history. Although not many have tried to revise this image, in an eye-opening account in his book *The Mantle of the Prophet* (1987), Roy Mottahedeh offers readers a rare human glimpse into the life of a mullah. Inspired by the true-life story of an ex-mullah friend of Mottahedeh's, *The Mantle of the Prophet* intertwines a lengthy account of Shi'ism in Iran with the life story of a mullah at the dawn of revolutionary Iran. What differentiates Mottahedeh's narrative from textbook accounts of Shi'i history in Iran is that it tells the story through a likeable mullah, Ali Hashemi. We learn about a mullah's life from childhood, through the system of the religious school, facing self-doubt about the rigorous teachings, until he becomes a leading teacher himself. Through Ali's story, particularly juxtaposed alongside a history of Shi'i Islam in Iran, *The Mantle of the Prophet* offers a different human history about Islam in Iran and its religious leaders, a history often unknown to readers in the West. As the author himself tells us in his 'Notes to Reader', his focus on Ali as an individual was a deliberate attempt to humanize history and to represent 'real Iranians, not archetypes'.[57]

Additionally, Mottahedeh's focus on rituals and teachings of the Shi'i seminaries attempts to shift the historic image of the mullah for Western audiences. Mottahedeh recounts how upon meeting his ex-mullah friend at Princeton, he had asked about how one studies to become a mullah. When hearing that in 'the Shiah [sic] seminaries such as those in Qom a student began by studying grammar, rhetoric, and logic', Mottahedeh excitedly remarks 'from that moment I knew I wanted to write this book', and embarks on drawing a parallel between teachings at the seminaries and the ancient scholastic curriculum of medieval and Renaissance Europe. He concludes:

> I realized [. . .] that my friend and a handful of similarly educated people were the last true scholastics alive on earth, people who had experienced education to which Princeton's patrons and planners felt they should pay tribute through their strangely assorted but congenial architectural reminiscences of the medieval and Tudor buildings of Oxford and Cambridge. Here was a living version of the kind of education [. . .] that had produced in the West men such as the saintly and brilliant theologian Thomas Aquinas. [58]

By comparing Shi'i mullahs to the greatest educated men of Western history, Mottahedeh reconstructs the image of Iranian mullah and Shi'i Islam portrayed in popular Western versions of history. Readers and reviewers have been quick to pick up on this non-stereotypical representation. In an online review for the *Washington Review of Middle Eastern Affairs*, Catherine Willford concludes her remarks with:

> no one who reads this book will ever again be able to accept the media stereotype of the Shi'i as kill-crazy fanatics. The joy of religious mystery and the search for knowledge, reason and justice

> are shown to be the inspiration of the Shi'i faith, which has suffered much for its survival.[59]

Although Khadivi, Seraji, Firouz, Mottahedeh and other writers challenge history by offering readers alternative perspectives, their historical narrative still operates within the framework of a recognisable narrative of events. While in their writing, the very action of inserting alternative narratives interpolates the unity of the grand narratives of Iranian history and transforms the way Iranian identity is perceived, many of these narratives still operate and give prominence to the framework of dominant historical narratives that had placed them as peripheral to begin with. What this means is that although the above narratives offer us different kinds of history, they are still bound by the teleology and chronology of recognisable and dominant accounts. To use Ashcroft's words, they still fall victim to the 'trap of the empirical narrative which privileges certain species of "facts"'.[60]

One particular author, Gina Nahai, however, seems aware of this and has dedicated her literary career to what Ashcroft calls 'transforming history' by offering an 'incompatible and contesting' narrative to the dominant narrative of historical events in Iran. Of the four novels that Nahai has published since 1991, three revolve around the lives of Jewish women and their histories in Iran. What distinguishes Nahai's works from Seraji, Firouz and others, however, is her approach to historical perspective.

In *Cry of the Peacock* (2001), for instance, Nahai traces the matrilineal history of a group of Jewish women living in the ghettos of Iran through 200 years of Iranian history leading up to the revolution. But, instead of narrating their stories through known linear dominant discourses of Iranian history, she rewrites history as we know it. For centuries, Iranian Jews, both in their actual and historical existence, have been marginalised. While confined to their own quarters until Reza Shah's modernisation scheme, history books also mention their presence as marginal. Through research and interviews with Jewish–Iranian diasporic communities, Nahai draws on the collective memory and experiences of many to create an historical novel that reflects the Jewish experience in Iran. Based on an oral history, the narrative defies the linearity and teleology of Iranian history as we know it, instead constructing a history woven of myth and memories. In this way, the novel invents a mythical history of Jews in Iran through the story of Esther the Soothsayer, who could 'reach into your past, unveil the secrets of your sorrow', and her granddaughter Peacock, who lives well over a hundred years through numerous droughts and revolutions. Thus, Persian Kings come and go, the dynasty and the regime changes, but all of those events are peripheral, and are highlighted only if they contribute to the flow of life and the history of the ghetto, or if those from the ghetto contribute to what is happening outside. As such it is the novel's foregrounding of alternative histories that makes it a site for contesting Iranian history.

One specific example is how Reza Khan gained sufficient personal strength to eventually overthrow the Qajar Dynasty, consequently giving more freedom to Iranian Jews. Loosely based on facts, according to the novel Reza Khan was born in a village in northern Iran. Shortly after his birth his father dies, and his mother, unable to support him, gives him away to an uncle, who in turn gives him away to Kazim Khan, a general in the Persian Army. Although at Kazim Khan's house he has a chance for education, he is constantly aware of his humble status as 'an orphan boy, half-guest, half-servant', and does not have the self-confidence of his peers, until he meets Peacock. Peacock, who by then was dealing jewellery for a rich jeweller, and who had been serving Kazim Khan's household, becomes aware of Reza's status. In an awkward encounter, after seeing Reza teased by other children, Peacock calls him aside and predicts a glorious future for him: 'Doesn't matter that you were a peasant. You're going to be King someday.'[61] With this sentence ringing in his mind, Reza changes the course of his life and works to fulfil the prophecy. But he remains lonely and powerless. Years later, with Peacock's foresight still vivid in this mind, he searches for her again to confirm her vision,

> [Reza Khan] had no friends. [. . .] But all his life he had cherished his acquaintance with Peacock. In the days of Persia's greatest tumult, when he felt himself standing on the brink of disaster, Reza Khan the Maxim went back and found the Jew from Esfahan.
>
> 'You said once I could be King,' he told [Peacock] in her windowless room in the Pit. He had been struck by those words, had felt his insides boil with excitement every time he remember that encounter [...]
>
> 'You must tell me what you know,' he insisted. 'Tell me my future.'

> Peacock smiled. All through her childhood, in times of hardship and disappointment, her mother had whispered to her Esther the Soothsayer's prophecy made on the day Peacock was born. Now Peacock repeated the words for Reza Khan:
>
> 'A man shall come, riding from the north, with blood on his hands, and the wrath of God in his eyes.
>
> 'He shall sit on the Throne of the Sun, and with a sweep of his hand he shall reach across the empire to free our people.'
>
> Reza Khan the Maxim felt the veins in his temples about to burst.
>
> 'How do you know I am that man?' he asked.
>
> Peacock put her fingertip to his forehead.
>
> 'It says so right here – where Cain bore his mark.'[62]

Intrigued, Reza Khan becomes more persistent, and ten years later overthrows the Qajar Dynasty, becoming the first king to give Jews some freedom in Iran.

Nahai's representation of historical events as such constructs a narrative that contests the dominant discourse of Iranian history and 'has the potential to become the way in which the past is understood'.[63] In this way, the novel empowers the Jewish Iranian historical identity as it provides them with a site of 'struggle for authority over the past',[64] by transforming the discourse of Iranian history as we have been made to believe, interpolating the narrativity of history. This engagement is not 'simply to contest the message of history [...] but also to engage the medium of narrativity itself, to re-inscribe the "rhetoric", the heterogeneity of historical representation.'[65] This act, according to Ashcroft, 'stands as one of the most strategic and powerfully effective modes of cultural resistance'.[66] Narratives that interpolate and challenge dominant discourses of history not only provide a sense of historical legitimisation for those who had been reduced to historical labels or altogether left out of the pages of history, but also provide them with 'a vision of the future grounded in the past'.[67] This is why books such as *Cry of the Peacock* have the ability to empower diasporic Jewish-Iranians communities, to assert themselves against historically imposed stereotypes, allowing them to project and construct a vision of themselves for the future.

Tapping into the past and negotiating the future

Interpolation of history, however, does not always necessitate the recounting of grand narratives of history through distant voices and figures of the past, or the total reconstruction of the teleology of events. One simple way of interpolating history could be by the recounting of very personal accounts that overcome historically tainted stereotypes that have formed one's sense of identity. Although this sounds simple, there is a challenge in narrating alternative personal histories for those who do not have adequate personal understanding of the past because they were never given the opportunity to historicise themselves. In order to interpolate and recount an alternative history, there first needs to be an understanding of the past. Hall too believes this, as he argues that the close relationship between history and identity does not necessarily equate to a 'so-called return to roots but [also] a coming-to-terms-with our "routes"'.[68] Here engagement with roots/routes dynamics, which invokes an origin in an historical past, is not about a mere obsession about our identities as 'who we are' or 'where we came from'. Rather it is about 'using the resources of history, language and culture in the process of becoming or "what we might become" rather than "being"'.[69] Thus, the invocation of history becomes almost like a Nietzschean genealogy of descent which aims to

> identify the accidents, the minute deviations [...] the errors, the false appraisals, and the faulty calculations that gave birth to those things that continue to exist and have value for us [...] to discover that truth or being does not lie at the root of what we know and what we are, but the exteriority of accidents.[70]

In this process, historical probing becomes a way for understanding ourselves: 'how we have been represented and how that bears on how we might represent ourselves'.[71] It is through this understanding that history can be interpolated where engagement with it, as much as being a connection to the past, can also become a space for negotiation of the representation of a desired 'transformed future'.[72] This is an important step in literature that resists dominant narrative and discourse. As we recall, a key feature of post-colonial utopianism is 'the intersection of the anticipatory consciousness with cultural memory, transforming [...]

through a vision of the future grounded in a memory of the past'.[73] Ashcroft believes that literature is the best space where this type of transformation and negotiation can play out, because literature 'at its very core [has] the capacity to imagine a different world. This vision of the future depends on a "vision" of history.'[74] As such, tapping into history and memory through literature is not about 'recovering a past but about the production of possibility – [it is] a recreation, not a looking backwards, but a reaching out to a horizon, somewhere "out there"'.[75] In this way, engagement with history becomes a way to negotiate a desired state of being in the future.

For many diasporic Iranian writers, too, tapping into and drawing on elements of history is about projecting and negotiating a new vision of the future in response to historical representation both in their host and home countries. However, this is very challenging, particularly for second-generation migrants, most of whom have never been to Iran, and those who were very young when they left Iran. For them the challenge lies in gaining a comprehensive and alternative view of Iranian history, in order to counter those historical perceptions embedded in family memories and filtered through social and media networks. For many, understanding starts with investigation into the culture and history of their Iranian heritage, and sometimes ends with a physical journey back to Iran to experience the culture. The accounts that emerge from these intellectual and physical journeys often provide a means for the narrators to challenge and reconstruct how they have been represented historically, and to determine how they wish to represent themselves in the future.

In the opening pages of her memoir *Saffron Sky: A Life between Iran and America* (1999), Gelareh Asayesh tells us why, after 14 years of absence from Iran when she left as a child, she decides to go back when she feels that her sense of Iranian identity is tainted with rumours and historical fear. 'The girl I used to be when I left Iran is like an island in an eve-encroaching sea, the victim of 14 years of erosion. By now, there is little of her left.' Whatever she has left, she tells us, is tainted with a sense of fear of the revolution instilled in her by the media and her family: 'For them as for me, the Islamic Republic of Iran is like a dark and murky wood, hung about with a rumor of fear.'[76] It is only in deciding to travel back to Iran that she begins to truly understand her own historical past, which eventually enables her to come to terms with her personal duality.

Similarly, Azadeh Moaveni, the daughter of an Iranian immigrant family, born in California, self-consciously demonstrates this need for historical understanding in her return memoir *Lipstick Jihad: A Memoir of Growing Up Iranian in America and American in Iran* (2005). In the first pages of her book, like Asayesh, Moaveni recounts her struggle for self-assertion in the United States, battling against a set of historically imprinted images. She recalls how, as a second-generation migrant who had only been to Iran at a very young age, she had constructed her own self-identity against an internalisation of historical projections.[77] She writes:

> As a girl, raised on the distorting myths of exile, I imagined myself a Persian Princess, estranged from my homeland – a place of light, poetry, and nightingales – by a dark, evil force called the Revolution [. . .]
>
> Growing up I had no doubt I was Persian. Persian like a fluffy cat, a silky carpet – a vaguely Oriental notion belonging to history, untraceable on a map. It was the term we insisted on using at the time, embarrassed by any association with Iran, the modern country, the hostage-taking Death Star. Living a myth, a fantasy, made it easier to be Iranian in America.[78]

The above paragraphs demonstrate how Moaveni had comfortably internalised a sense of identity based on a set of historical imagery. Her insistence in using the term 'Persian' to refer to herself disassociates her from the political and negative associations of Iran in the West. However, Moaveni is quick enough to point out that self-assertion based on vague notions of history had not been an effective way of maintaining a sense of identity. She goes on to demonstrate how the negativity and oppressiveness of the hostage crisis, and its inevitability in their lives, had also informed much of how Iranians were viewed and viewed themselves, as well as how they tried to construct an identity devoid of historical association. She writes:

> The hostage crisis had forever stained our image in the American psyche, and slowly I saw how this shaped so much of what we did and strove for as immigrants [. . .]
>
> Iranians coped with this oppressive legacy in various ways. Some [. . .] willed it away by losing any trace of a Persian accent,

> and becoming so professionally successful that they entered a stratum of American society sophisticated enough to understand and appreciate their presence and contribution. Some [...] sought strength in numbers and found a colony in Los Angeles. They seemed unfazed by their growing reputation for vulgarity and obsession with image; better to be associated with a penchant for BMWs than revolutionary Islam, they figured.
>
> [...] But the image of that Islam-intoxicated, wild-eyed hostage taker was still a shadow that dogged all of us. Whether we were monarchists or not, whether we took some responsibility for what happened in Iran or blamed others, the shame of the revolution placed enormous pressure to be successful, but discreet about being Iranian. As though to make up for this image's awfulness we had to be ever more exceptional, achieve more, acquire more degrees, more wealth, make more discoveries – to become indispensable. All this effort was needed to clear up our nationality's good name; being average, obviously, would not cut. Redemption became our burden.[79]

This paragraph demonstrates how thousands of Iranians in diaspora have responded to the negative historically imposed images of the hostage crisis.[80] But here I find the word 'redemption' most interesting. Although Iranians have struggled to integrate into their adopted communities, for the majority, as Moaveni also observes, their integration has come at the price of the redemption of their historically tainted Iranian identity. However, Moaveni is quick to point out that integration does not necessarily need redemption of a past identity, but rather it needs transformation and an understanding that 'a vision of the future depends on a "vision" of history'.[81] She describes her own realisation of the necessity of historical understanding, rather than mere redemption, through her own experiences. When in college, she sees her situation and historical conflict reflected in Andy, an Hispanic classmate's, struggle of self-assertion. As she watches, Andy gradually transforms and empowers himself through developing an understanding and acceptance of his ancestral culture and history instead of its denial.

> As I watched Andy grow into himself [...] I also began to envy him. He was surrounded by brilliant Chicano professors who

> encouraged and understood him; who plied him with illuminating books that spoke directly to his experience. He saw his anger and confusion mirrored in poetry [...] In time, awareness and pride replaced ambivalence and shame; [. . .] he had unlocked his internalized resentment of his identity. I saw this evolution not only in Andy but in many other students of color who educated themselves about their communities and their past, and found strength and support in the process. The notion of finding power in your otherness [. . .] was incredibly compelling. So was the explosive possibility that I could be confident about who I was, the idea that being Iranian didn't have to be about silly emotional culture clashes with my mother, but a sense of self anchored in history [...].[82]

It is through this encounter with Andy, and her realisation of the need for historical engagement and understanding in the process of self-assertion, that Moaveni decides to embark on her own journey into history. After her encounter with Andy, she decides that:

> Maybe there was something to be gained by studying history dispassionately, without the flushed distortions of family memory and cultural tropes. Within two years I was totally immersed in the Middle East [...] In the process of all this academic probing, Iran was demystified – it became a subject I could learn about on my own, a civilization that I could approach from whatever direction I chose. It stopped being only the emotional place and set of rigid norms only Maman could use to pull at my heartstrings. [. . .] As I discovered contemporary Iranian poetry some of which I could read on my own, I began to feel, for the first time in my life, that Iranianness was not an obstacle to my independence. For the first time I stopped resisting it. [. . .] Once I discovered the joys of my own private Iranianness, I was reluctant to dilute it with anything reminiscent of the years of adolescent conflict.[83]

By gaining an objective insight into how Iranians have been represented historically, Moaveni, as Hall suggests, uses the 'resources of history, language and culture in the process of becoming' Iranian in America 'rather than being' Iranian–American. It is this transformation of the stereotypically historically imposed image of herself within the frameworks of exotic/terrorist, and historically frozen nostalgic and family inherited images of Iran, that interpolates the grand narratives of history that have formed her sense of identity, and leads to her eventual personal transformation about her Iranian identity. By the end of her journey she knows that her claim to Persian culture is far richer than carpets and cats. At the same time she also gains an understanding of the history of the revolution as well as the complexity of current Iranian society, and can no longer claim it to be a hostage-taking Death Star.

This realisation that by drawing on elements of the past one can transform one's future offers her a utopian vision with alternative possibilities of social change. After all, as Ashcroft tells us, 'it is by narrative, by stories we tell, that we have a world and it is by utopian thinking, utopian forms, utopian narrative, that we may have a conception of a radically changeable world'.[84] It is this insight that allows Moaveni to open up to the possibility that Iran has changed drastically, contrary to what her family, the media and books had told her. But more importantly it is this realisation that gives her courage and freedom to make the eventual decision to travel to Iran as a journalist and represent her country to the West afresh by breaking down historically imposed stereotypes.

However, while for Moaveni and second-generation migrants like her, an engagement with history requires an initial cognitive process and academic research, for the majority of first-generation migrants, particularly for women and those of minority background, who had experienced Iran first hand and had come into exile as the result of the revolution, the process of engaging with and reconstructing themselves through historical understanding is much more complicated. For them, the reflection of their identities beyond the historically imposed image of exotic/terrorist, anchored in something else, first requires a coming to terms with and understanding of their neglected histories and identities in Iran by tapping into the derelict private and collective histories of their homeland and by 'rethink[ing] the very codes and norms that consign them, as woman and other, to the margins'.[85] This is another inherent issue that runs throughout the body of diasporic Iranian literature and with which I will deal in this book.

As we have observed and will continue to see throughout this book, the narratives emerging from the diasporic Iranian community are playing a significant part in the way diasporic Iranian communities are coming to terms with their own historical and cultural identities. Each voice rooted deep down in a history of revolution, exile and resettlement, is in its unique way contributing to the way diasporic Iranian cultural identities are understood, reconstructed, maintained and negotiated. As such, and as we will see throughout this book, these narratives are a myriad of hope. As Nazila Fathi tells us in the end of the introduction to her memoir *The Lonely War*, 'History has many narrators.' While she believes that this book is her contribution to the accounts of history, she writes, 'I hope that other Iranians will add their voices to mine, just as I have contributed my tale to the river of stories flowing from Iran. Mine is the story of hope and perseverance of a nation that has never surrendered to tyranny.'[86]

CHAPTER 2

SUFI POETRY – 'UNIVERSAL AND PROFOUND'

'If jazz is the cadence of American culture', writes Hamid Dabashi, 'then Persian poetry is the pulse of Iranian culture, the rhyme and rhythm of its collective memory.'[1] He continues,

> It is said that what Muslims do is not memorize the Quran but Quranify their memory. If that is what Muslims do, then that must be what Iranians do too with their poetry, when they remember their past as the poetic resonance of their presence – in fact, of their presence in history.[2]

Growing up, I was witness to this kind of poetic historicisation in my own life. As the daughter of a banker, posted from country to country, two books travelled with us and never left my parents' bedside table. One was a copy of the Quran and the other a copy of the thirteenth century mystic Jalaluddin Rumi's *Masnavi*. My father, an ex-clergyman turned banker, read both books almost daily. Yet, despite our belief in Islam and the Quran as our book, of the two, my father would always read to us from the *Masnavi* and rarely from the Quran. We would often cuddle in bed on Sunday mornings and listen to my dad read. With little ties to an Iranian community, especially in Hong Kong where there were very few Iranians, these sessions were our only connection to the history and culture of Iran, and they left a lasting impression on me. They made me feel that I belonged to a rich historical tradition, a tradition I wanted to maintain and promote, a tradition that outweighed all negative associations I heard about Iran.

Later, when I began seriously expressing myself creatively in English, time and again I found myself drawn to Persian poetic traditions as a source of inspiration. Sometimes, if I wanted to express a particular longing or nostalgia I would refer directly to lines that had inspired me. Other times I would draw from a concept or idea that I had come across in the body of poetry and reframe it to make it reflective of my own experiences. Trained in English literature and aware of its various trends, sometimes I would blend elements of Persian literature with those of English literature and create a fusion of words and ideas that expressed my hybridity.

When I became interested in diasporic Iranian literature, I realised that many diasporic Iranian writers who wrote in English also engaged, in very similar ways, with elements of Persian poetry. Book after book revealed that for many diasporic Iranian writers, as it had been for me, and as Dabashi observes, using elements of poetry was a way to historicise a sense of identity. Its use was sometimes driven by a sense of anxiety of separation and disconnection from an historical past, an anxiety caused by the migratory experience. Just as it had been for me, manifested nostalgically, reference to Persian poetry could also be a way of maintaining a connection with a cultural past. However, it was also about using that tradition to reflect into the future, to adapt, change and transform its elements, to make it do a different cultural work. In this way, Persian poetry could be a vehicle through which writers reconstruct and negotiate their diasporic identities.

This chapter highlights the interaction of Persian poetry with diasporic Iranian literature in English and investigates the various ways writers draw on it as a form of expression. When seen in light of Hall's concept of cultural identity and historicisation of identity, engagement with various elements of this literature can be seen as a way to maintain a connection to the Iranian cultural and historical past. However, for Iranian writers, the use of Persian poetry within a diasporic setting has enabled the construction of a hybrid third space of expression that is reflective of the unique diasporic Iranian experience. This use and adaptation of elements of Persian poetry, situated against history and dominant forms of expression that had silenced many, and viewed through a post-colonial lens, can be read as critiquing and challenging existing traditions in a way that adds to both the Persian and English literary traditions. This new form of expression creates a new space that can be seen as reconstructing and negotiating aspects of Iran and the Iranian sense of cultural identity.

Situating poetry in Iranian society

Poetry is, and has always been, an inherent part of the Persian discourse of communication, with an identifiable and historical, unchanging and continuous presence in the Iranian understanding of cultural identity. So prevalent has been this type of expression that, as Fatemeh Keshavarz observes, it is even used in communication with children. In her memoir, *Jasmine and Stars* (2007), she recalls how her mother drew from Sa'adi's poetry to punish her:

> When I was about seven or eight years old and had done something very displeasing to my mother, she would press her lips together and look very stern. Next she would search her mind for a really bad punishment. Then she would settle for something relatively light like not allowing me to go out to play with the neighbour's kids for the next hour. The justification for her softness always came in Sa'adi's words: 'Trying to discipline a rascal is balancing a walnut on top of a dome!' She would not paraphrase or explain, just say the words aloud to herself. I did not know every single word in the poem but understood what she meant. This was true of all the other lines I heard people say around me on a daily basis. I understood them a little better every day as I grew older. In the meantime, these short quotes worked like little bridges connecting us with one another.[3]

This type of poetic encounter is not rare in Iran. Travelling in taxis, the seemingly unrefined taxi driver might suddenly break into poetry to reflect on the situation of the country; the grocer might respond with a poem; even the doctor might try to ease pain with poetic words of wisdom. Iranians even rely on poetry in their fortune. It is common practice for one in doubt or in need of advice to open up a page of Hafez's poetry and ask for guidance in the words of the poem.

The significance of poetry in Iran as a marker of cultural identity has deep historical roots, which go hand in hand with the spiritual nature of classical Persian poetry. So important has Persian poetry been in the Iranian understanding of their cultural identity that, as Ahmad Karimi-Hakkak tells us in *Recasting Persian Poetry*, 'the nature and significance of poetry in modern Iran cannot be understood without a close reading of the conditions that gave rise to it and the processes that determined its shape'.[4]

Seyyed Hussein Nasr traces the shape of Persian language and poetry today back to the time of the Arab-Islamic invasion of Persia in the seventh century, and argues that 'the current Persian language and the literature written in it were born from the wedding between Islam and the soul of the Persian people'.[5] The invasion, according to Nasr, 'affected deeply all facets of life of the Persians' including their social, political, artistic, religious and even linguistic dynamics. But, despite this, in contrast to the lands to the west where Arab domination brought 'Arabization', so that many countries from Egypt to Morocco speak Arabic to this day, in Persia (or what is now Iran) Islam spread without its citizens becoming Arabized. Contrarily, after the invasion, the Persian language developed and became infused with the vocabulary of Quranic Arabic, forming 'a major Islamic language while also making major contributions to Arabic'.[6] Out of this union, Persia became an important centre of Islamic thought, 'an intellectual and spiritual microcosm of the entire Islamic world'.[7] This left a profound mark on Persian literature, as it 'became the vehicle for most schools of Islamic thought and spirituality and exercised an influence in the rest of the Islamic world far beyond Persia's geographical border'.[8]

Scholars and historians believe that it was the union of Islam with Persian culture that gave birth to Sufism or Islamic mysticism. As Abdol-Hossein Zarrinkoub argues, it was traces of Persian Zoroastrianism coupled with Islamic thought that gave rise to Persian Sufism. He writes:

> [I]f mysticism is taken to be – as it usually is – an expression of man's belief in direct connection with the godhead, the well-known ethical concept of the Zoroastrian – for whom every particular deed of daily life, good or bad, is the joint product of man and either the principle of Good or of Evil – might also be considered an unconscious expression of pantheistic type of mysticism. Thus, while the late Sassanian period prepared Zoroastrian minds for a

> new faith introduced by the Muslim conquest of Persia, the converted Zoroastrians of the early Islamic period were able to retain some of their former ethical tenets in the Sufi philosophy.[9]

Sufism, according to J. Spencer Trimingham, consists of

> those tendencies in Islam which aim at direct communion between God and man, [. . .] a sphere of spiritual experience which runs parallel to the main stream of Islamic consciousness deriving from prophetic revelation and comprehended within the *shari'a* [Islamic law] and theology.[10]

Sufism is an esoteric dimension of Islam, and is to be distinguished from exoteric or external Islam. According to Titus Burckhardt:

> [W]hereas the ordinary way of believers is directed towards obtaining a state of blessedness after death, a state which can be attained through indirect and, as it were, symbolic participation in Divine Truths by carrying out prescribed works, Sufism contains its end or aim within itself in the sense that it can give access to direct knowledge of the eternal.[11]

This means that while generally Sufis attempt to 'observe the "rule of the heart"', the ulema, the arbiters of Shari'a law, 'concentrated on the external acts'.[12]

Here I refer to Sufism because Sufi philosophy has to some degree influenced Persian poetry traditions. According to Zarrinkoub, 'Sufi philosophy found a most hospitable soil in the domain of Persian poetry',[13] and, as such, has had great significance in the direction of Persian poetry and literature. In fact, like Zarrinkoub, Nasr believes that the influence of Sufism completely changed the shape of Persian literary tradition. As he writes, 'if Sufi poets had not appeared on the literary stage, Persian literature would have remained for long centuries no more than a court literature limited to a panegyric character'.[14] Indeed, so profound has been the union between Sufism and Persian poetry, that Nasr calls it 'a cultural miracle in the bosom of Islamic civilization, [. . .] a vast ocean which has succeeded in expressing the most inward and spiritual dimensions of Islam in a most universal language'.[15]

Persian Sufi poetry is thus reflection of the esoteric and spiritual aspect of Islam. Often referred to as poetry of divine love, its origins can be traced back to the eleventh century, and includes such a long list of poets. According to Zarrinkoub, 'every great poet of that period was a Sufi, as nearly every great Sufi of the time was a poet'.[16] Among them, some of the best known as Sufi poets, include Baba Tahir (eleventh century), Abu Sa'id Abi l-Khayr (eleventh century), followed by those such as Attar (twelfth century), Rumi (thirteenth century), Hafez (fourteenth century) and Sa'adi (fourteenth century).[17]

According to Nasr, there are several elements that distinguish Sufi poetry from other kinds of verse in Persian.[18] First is its association with 'the Spiritual Path', which is 'concerned with transformation of a man's entire being – for without becoming a new being one cannot see things in a new way'.[19] This poetry enables us to 'become what we should really be, what we are already *'ind Allah*, that is "in God," to become ourselves'. This means that it directs us to change and transform by breaking boundaries that our ego and environment have placed upon us. Its aim is to bring us closer to our true selves so that we can 'become ourselves [. . .] that archetype or essence which is our very "self" and inner reality'.[20] Iranians, even today, believe in the transformative nature of this poetry, and often turn to the poetry of the masters if they feel lost and confused.

The second aspect, related to its transformative quality, is its highly symbolic nature. Because Sufism is concerned with the hidden aspects of one's being, as well as metaphysical experiences for which there may be no physical equivalent, Sufi poetry, too, is often enveloped in metaphors and symbols that hide certain truths for readers to unravel. As such 'one penetrates into the language to be carried by it to the inner meaning'.[21] As Al-Ghazzali, one of the greatest Sufi poets, writes: 'We mean by metaphor or analogue (mathal) to render meaning (ma'na) into the external form (surah). So if one sees its inner meaning, he finds it true. But if he sees only its external form, he finds it deceiving.'[22]

The significance of metaphorical description is connected to another distinguishing aspect of Sufi poetry, its 'depiction of paradise'. It is through symbolism and allusions that Sufi poetry 'creates a kind of celestial atmosphere for the soul to breathe in'.[23] The celestial quality of this poetry, if understood beyond its symbolism, attempts to connect the reader to divine reality. Thus, in the body of Sufi poetry across the centuries, the garden, rose, wine, lovemaking and ecstasy, are symbols and allusions that point to this celestial atmosphere.[24] These symbols often create in readers a sense of nostalgia or longing for that paradisiacal space, the ecstasy of union and connection with the divine.

Another quality of this poetry, according to Nasr, is that it has a 'therapeutic effect' as it provides the soul with nourishment. He writes, 'the mystical poetry has created a kind of world into which the human soul can withdraw for nourishment and protection, and a kind of complement to the external world'.[25] In fact in Iranian tradition, so accepted is this therapeutic effect of poetry, that if someone is feeling depressed, people do not refer them to the doctor, instead they tell them to go and read poetry in silence.

This literature, in its essence, is utopian, for as Jacqueline Dutton argues with regard to the utopian aspects of Islamic poetry, it not only 'present[s] a description of the physical incarnation of the ideal place, but it [also] explore[s] the relationship between the cultural aspects of social dreaming and nature, as well as the role of human agency or free will, in the conception of the utopian vision'.[26] This vision, although 'depicting the desire for a better way of being, built on the Islamic foundation of the ideal of paradise attainable through the realization of God's immanence in all creation',[27] is also very much rooted in the physical realm, and indeed draws on rich imagery, allusions and elements of the physical world in its description. It is the duality of this literature, which refers to both known physical and spiritual elements of human life and condition, that allows for the construction of an imaginative future or the remembrance of an idyllic past.

It is these qualities of Persian Sufi poetry, passed down generationally, that have made it such a significant element of Iranian cultural identity and discourse, an element, according to Nasr, 'of utmost importance [...] for Persian culture and the nourishment of the Persian soul'.[28] However, more important than its unique elements, Persian Sufi poetry is considered a site of shared identification, an element of cultural identity, among Iranians of various ethnic and social backgrounds because it has become a symbol of cultural resistance and pride. As a cultural tradition, Persian Sufi poetry has surpassed, survived and retained its most distinguishing attributes despite the socio-political changes that have affected Iran over the centuries. The very fact that after the Arab invasion, Persia managed to retain its own language and developed a literature that is unique to its culture has always been a source of historical pride for Iranians. As such, according to Jahanshah Rashidian, this literature 'fosters Iranian identity by establishing Persian as a common language of all Iranians'.[29]

Persian literature has also overcome the great rift that has always existed between Sufism and conservative Shi'i leaders of Iran. Looking back at Iranian history, there has always been tension between traditional Muslim leaders and various Sufi traditions. According to Abdol Karim Lahiji, the source of tension between these two schools can be summed up in their difference of thinking. He writes, 'the Sufis were more tolerant of freedom of speech and freedom of religion. The {shari'a} people were more aggressive and less tolerant of the other interpretations of Islam.'[30] As Vanessa Martin also observes, Sufism has always been to some extent frowned upon by orthodox Islam, because 'with its supposition of individual union with God, and in its more extreme form of pantheism, the presence of God in all things, it undermined the orthodox concept of divine transcendence'.[31]

However, the tendency of Sufism towards a more open-ended approach, always challenging established authority, lay or religious, has made it 'the object of suspicion of both orthodox Islam and the state'.[32] Although an in-depth understanding of the rift between Sufis and Shari'a laws in Iran needs another study of its own,[33] it is important to note here that although tensions have always existed between Sufis and Islamic leaders in Iran, this hostility has grown more since the revolution. The current Islamic government, particularly, has been extremely intolerant of alternative schools of Islamic thought. After the revolution, leaders of various Sufi orders were forced to leave Iran and have established centres across the world for diasporic communities. Those who remained in Iran, to this day, face a constant struggle with the regime. Their centres are shut down and their gatherings are often invaded by the morals police.

As a result of this tension, Persian poetry has also suffered. As Abdul Kasem reminds us about the rules of Shari'a:

> the status of poetry depends upon the content of the poem a poet composes. If his composition is to praise Allah and His messenger then that is fine. Any other type of poetry (like philosophical, love, romance, patriotism, nationalism, free and secular thinking... etc.) are completely illegal or *haram*.[34]

This is why in the early days after the revolution, most poetry, particularly Sufi poetry, was pulled off the bookstore shelves. With constant symbolic allusion to ecstasy, love, lust, music, dance, wine, love making, male/female relations, and normally accompanied with risqué miniature-style imagery of men and women drinking wine together, these books were declared *haram* or illegal by authorities and censors. While symbolic references to ecstasy in the poetry were deemed corrupting to the mind, even blasphemous, it was believed that this kind of poetry, which constantly turns the attention inwards, could be debilitating. This stemmed from the idea that 'poetry protects the soul artificially, makes it lazy and prevents it from going out and achieving practical ends in the world'.[35]

Yet, despite the fact that Sufi poetry was frowned upon by the Islamic government, it continued to form an indelible part of Iranian literary discourse and cultural identity. No one stopped reading or reciting poetry because the government told them to do so. In fact, after the revolution, Sufism and Sufi poetry, with its aspirations to mysticism and the spiritual aspects of Islam, became a more favourable point of identification for many Iranians who did not agree with the government's forced Islamicisation of the country. As Rashidian observes, 'a growing majority of Iranians, specifically among the youth, is motivated to demarcate their self identity from the one which is imposed by the regime'.[36] As such, many Iranians maintain a connection to shared elements of their culture that predate the revolution, and are devoid of particular nationalistic identities that the state wishes to impose on its people. Persian poetry, it seems, has been one of the most significant historical and cultural elements that has formed Iranian cultural identity beyond a strictly nationalistic or political one. As Azar Nafisi explains in an interview, her father always reminded her that throughout history Iran has been invaded numerous times, rulers have come and gone, houses and cities have been destroyed, but 'one thing we have kept that gives us our Iranian identity [. . .] is our poetry and literature'.[37] Similarly, as Zohreh Ghahremani tells us at the end of her novel *Sky of Red Poppies,* in a section entitled 'A Note about Poetry', 'poetry is a common denominator for us, an integral part of our culture'.[38] But perhaps Nasr sums up the importance of poetry in the Iranian cultural identity best when he writes that Sufi Persian poetry has become 'the supreme expression of what is most universal and profound in the Persian soul'.[39]

Poetic encounters in Diaspora: What we were...

It is in the above context that the importance of Persian poetry for and within the works of diasporic Iranian writers in English can best be understood. While poetry is the epitome of cultural identity for many Iranians across the divide in Iran, it seems as though for those living beyond the borders it plays a much more important part in maintaining and forming their sense of identity. This, needless to say, has to do with the separation caused by migration.

As Hall argues, an important aspect of cultural identity rests on 'one, shared culture, a sort of collective "one true self", hiding inside the many other, more superficial or artificially imposed "selves", which people with a shared history and ancestry hold in common.' Here,

> cultural identities reflect the common historical experiences and shared cultural codes which provide us, as "one people", with stable, unchanging and continuous frames of reference and meaning, beneath the shifting divisions and vicissitudes of our actual history.[40]

Recalling the concept of historicisation, there is a necessary connection between the way we define ourselves and the connections that we maintain to a series of continued and shared elements of our cultural identity and history. However, for those who have migrated, there is often a disconnection from this continuation, a fragmentation. Cut from other sites of cultural identity, in their new setting they are left with only a few markers of cultural belonging. As Andrew Davidson and Kuah-Pearce Khun Eng describe it, 'migrants experience a sense of deterritorialization and dislocation where the break with the country of origin with its familiar social practices and cultural icons means these are no longer available to these migrants in their adopted country'.[41] As a result, many migrants 'consciously seek to retrieve and reproduce some of these social practices and cultural icons',[42] that serve as reminders of their sense of belonging and cultural identity. This act of remembering and drawing upon certain elements of a cultural past, according to Hall, 'offer[s] a way of imposing an imaginary coherence on the experience of dispersal and fragmentation, which is the history of all enforced diasporas'.[43]

Although diasporic Iranian communities are made up of people of varying religious, political and ethnic backgrounds and beliefs, many choose Persian poetry as a shared element through which to maintain and connect with their historical past and others of Iranian background. In fact, so important is poetry for diasporic Iranians that when Zohreh Sullivan conducted a survey of a large number of Iranian diaspora about what it means to be Iranian and the elements that constitute their sense of identity, in every response except two there were 'recurring references to the love of poetry "essential" to Iranian identity'.[44] For diasporic Iranian writers in English, there are several ways in which they draw upon this literature to maintain a connection to their historical past.

Poetic openings

One of the most manifest ways diasporic Iranian writers engage with Persian poetry is by the transference of verses or stanzas of Persian poetry into their work in English. In line with the Persian discourse of communication, in which poetry is infused, it is common practice in Iranian prose books that an author opens his or her book with a verse or poem that is reflective of the intention or content of the book. Looking at the body of work by diasporic Iranian writers in English, many have maintained this tradition. For example, Afschineh Latifi begins her memoir *Even After All This Time* (2005) with a poem by Hafez:[45]

> Even after all this time
> The sun never says to the Earth
> 'You owe me'
> Look at what happens with a love like that
> It lights the whole sky.

Her memoir draws from this poem to compare her mother's unconditional love to that of the sun of which the verses speak. The memoir, thus, is a tribute to her mother who had selflessly and without complaint raised her three children by herself in exile after her husband had been executed.

Similarly, Sattareh Farman-Farmanian begins every chapter of her book *Daughter of Persia* (1996) with a borrowed reflective poem about the theme of each chapter from masters of Persian poetry. When describing the 'Fall of the Reza Shah', for instance, she begins with a couplet by Sa'adi: 'When a man prospers, people sing his praise / When he falls, they trample his neck'. In a chapter about her 'Setting Out' from Iran as a young woman she borrows the words of Khayyam to explain her feelings: 'Strange, is it not, that of the myriads who / Before us passed the door of darkness through / Not one returns to tell us of the Road / Which to discover we must travel too.' She also draws from the words of Sa'adi to console herself about her migration and her need to adapt to her new country in 'The Land at the End of the Earth', which she begins with 'Do not give your heart to one mistress / nor your loyalty to a single place / for countless are mistresses / and extensive are lands and seas.'

Gholam-Reza Sabri-Tabrizi, too, begins his book *Iran: A Child's Story, A Man's Experience*, which, according to him, is 'a bridge between a child's memories and a man's experience and between Eastern and Western cultures',[46] with these famous lines by Sa'adi that speaks of the universality of human experiences:

> The sons of Adam are limbs of each other
> Having been created of one essence.
> When the calamity of time afflicts one limb [member]
> The other limbs [members] cannot remain at rest.
> If thou hast no sympathy for the troubles of others
> Thou art unworthy to be called by the name of man [human being].

Shirin Ebadi, the Iranian Nobel Peace Prize winner, opens her memoir *Iran Awakening* (2006) with lines from Rumi that reflect the grandeur and universality of her work:

> Sadness to me is the happiest time,
> When a shining city rises from the ruins of my drunken mind.
> Those times when I'm silent and still as the earth,
> The thunder of my roars is heard across the universe.

Similarly, Farnoosh Moshiri begins *Bathhouse* (2003), the story of a young girl imprisoned in the early days of the revolution in a deserted bathhouse, during the time when there were rumours that if you looked closely you could see Ayatollah Khomeini's image on the moon, with the following verse from Rumi: 'When the full moon comes out, look around.' Anahita Firouz also draws on Rumi's words in the opening pages of her romantic love story *In the Walled Garden* (2003), which explores the relationship of two marginal characters set against the rapidly changing social landscape of Iran just before the revolution. It begins, 'The dust of many crumbled cities/settle over us like a forgetful doze, /but we are older than those cities. . . ./and always we have forgotten our former states.'

In *The Fortune Catcher*, Susanne Pari sets the tone of the book, in which a blind fortune-teller informs Leila of a future she tries to escape, with a poem by Hafez, 'Seeking a refuge from the cruel bettering of Fortune, We have come.' Susha Guppy, too, begins her memoir *The Blindfold Horse* (1988), a nostalgic reverie about Iran, with a poem from Hafez, 'Sit down by the side of the stream/And in the rushing of water/ Witness the transience of life.'

Although there are numerous other examples, some drawing on more modern verses, the above examples demonstrate the variety of ways Iranian writers engage with elements of poetry to express their intentions and sentiments. This kind of engagement allows the author to maintain a connection to their Iranian identity through reference to traditional Persian modes of expression, despite the distance and language difference.

Nostalgic sentimentality

What has made Persian poetry, especially Sufi poetry, particularly appealing for diasporic Iranians as a means to maintain a connection to their past, is the fact that this tradition does not necessarily shackle itself to any form of nationalistic sentimentality. This is important for Iranians abroad, many of whom have been forced to leave the country due to disagreements with the current regime, and who, in their expression and maintenance of their Iranian identity, want to disassociate themselves from the current nation state of Iran. This is why, as Mostofi observes, 'the Iranian diasporic consciousness constitutes an identity based on a "historical consciousness" where some valorise cultural traits and cultural cohesion through poetry, history, and geography'.[47]

That Iranians want to maintain a sense of connection and identity to their cultural heritage rather than to the nation state is nothing new. As scholars such as Shahrokh Meskoob argue, maintenance of a connection to a cultural heritage for Iranians began with the Arab invasion, when the most important source of their pre-Islamic history was 'remembered, imagined, and reconstructed, for the most part, in the mytho-historical narratives, such as Ferdowsi's *Shahnameh* (Book of Kings)'.[48] Although

Meskoob puts forth this argument about maintaining an Iranian identity through reference to cultural elements in the face of Arab invasion, other scholars, such as Mostofi, argue that the Islamic revolution resulted in a similar response from many Iranian immigrants who have also maintained 'a diasporic nationalism – for the purpose of maintaining their cultural heritage'.[49] Out of this diasporic experience, however, came a new 'remembered, imagined, reconstructed mytho-historical narrative' of the past and the meaning of culture. As Mostofi puts it:

> The trauma of the Islamic revolution and subsequent immigration has left Iranian immigrants nostalgic for a homeland that no longer exists, for a constant regeneration of 'the way things were,' and for a construction of an identity that not only incorporates their past lives and histories but also represents the experiences of their new lives.[50]

With Persian Sufi poetry being one of the most significant tropes for pre-revolutionary nostalgia, one of the mytho-historical narratives that defines Iranian cultural identity, it is no wonder then that diasporic Iranian writers draw upon it to maintain their sense of cultural identity. Added to this, there is the fact that Persian Sufi poetry also provides a language with which many diasporic Iranians can express their nostalgic sensibilities. As Nasr argues,[51] one of the distinguishing elements of this poetry is its highly nostalgic sentimentality. Although in Persian Sufi poetry nostalgia refers to the concept of 'divine nostalgia', which expresses a desire for the beloved, or God, its expressions, as J.T.P de Bruijn points out, are 'derived ultimately from emotions experienced in the human psyche in the situation of its earthly existence'.[52] This means that this love is normally depicted through physical allegory and symbols, which were and continue to be a shared point of identification among Iranians. Among these, a physical separation from a home or loved one, for instance, symbolises the separation of man from God. It is this element of the poetry that speaks directly to the sentiments of many Iranians in diaspora, and is why many diasporic Iranian writers draw upon its nostalgic elements and allegories to express their own nostalgic sentimentalities for the way things were.

One of the most common ways to engage with this nostalgic sentimentality is through a direct reference to some famous lines of

Persian poetry. Although there are numerous Sufi poets whose memorable words of divine nostalgia are often quoted and referred to by Iranians across social, religious and ethnic divides, among them, the first section of Rumi's *Masnavi,* known as the *Nei Nameh* or *The Tale of the Reed,* is by far the most known and widely quoted. It reads:

> Listen to the song of the reed,
> How it wails with the pain of separation:
> 'Ever since I was taken from my reed bed
> My woeful song has caused men and women to weep.
> I seek out those whose hearts are torn by separation
> For only they understand the pain of this longing.
> Whoever is taken away from his homeland
> Yearns for the day he will return.
> In every gathering, among those who are happy or sad,
> I cry with the same lament.
> Everyone hears according to his own understanding,
> None has searched for the secrets within me.
> My secret is found in my lament
> But an eye or ear without light cannot know it.' [53]

These verses, which vary in translation, embody the very essence of Sufi and mystic Persian poetry and its axis of divine nostalgia and longing for the beloved. According to Firoozeh Papan-Matin, these lines speak of 'the account of the separation of the lover, personified as the reed, from the Fatherland, the reed-bed, where it had belonged in the presence of God, the beloved'.[54] As such they represent a spiritual longing for return to the maker. However, beyond an allegorical and spiritual realm, they also refer to the more concrete realm of physical and emotional experiences of separation from one's roots. Thus, the painful laments of the reed can be read as the displaced person's cries for their beloved homeland.

These lines, repeatedly and effusively recited at various diasporic Iranian events, have also been ones that many writers draw upon in different ways to express their nostalgic sentimentality. For example, Manoucher Parvin in *Avicenna and I* (1996) directly quotes these lines to express his character's nostalgic yearnings. As the novel begins, Professor Pirooz, a middle-aged Iranian academic living in New York, is facing a mid-life identity crisis. His loving partner has just been murdered. Yearning for love, and feeling spiritually disconnected, Pirooz begins to feel nostalgic for his native land of Iran. He complains about his condition to everyone he sees but no one understands him. To alleviate his pain, he wishes to return to Iran. But at the peak of the war between Iran and Iraq, Pirooz is at first reluctant. However, through a series of unexpected events, and as the result of spiritual callings in his dreams by the famed first century Persian philosopher-physician Avicenna, he finds himself in the Iranian city of Hamedan where Avicenna is buried. Yet, he still finds himself unhappy. Having been called in his dream by Avicenna himself to visit the mausoleum at a certain hour of the night, he takes a cab to reach the destination of his calling. Sitting in the cab in the middle of night, to attend what seems to be an imaginary rendezvous, he has a moment of uncertainty. At that very moment, however, the taxi driver suddenly starts reciting the verses of *Ney Nameh.* Hearing the words, Pirooz suddenly finds the courage to continue his journey. Consequently, it is at the mausoleum that very night that he meets the love of his life. Alongside her, he stays happily in his homeland, the very land for which he was yearning. Eventually he finds spiritual fulfilment through his relationship with his wife and through the customs in his homeland. By the time the book ends, the happy couple have a child, Avicenna reincarnated.

The fact that all of this comes to Pirooz upon hearing the most famous and traditional lines of Persian poetry highlights the significance of this tradition for the Iranian soul. But that all the changes that take place in him lead to the creation of a child, especially one who carries the soul of one of Iran's most revered intellectuals, points to the fact that this tradition is not merely about looking back nostalgically. Rather, it is also about offering hope for the future, a future in which traditions will live on. This offers a new mytho-historical narrative for diasporic Iranians, a new utopian discursive space of expression 'for a construction of an identity that not only incorporates their past lives and histories but also represents the experiences of their new lives'.[55]

Gardens of paradise

While Parvin and other writers demonstrate this nostalgic sentimentality through direct reference to specific lines of Persian poetry, others draw upon certain significant poetic tropes to express themselves. Although diasporic Iranian writers in English use a vast variety of tropes, one of the most recurring elements has been the garden. The garden is a significant and special element in Persian poetry, reference to which permeates across the body of work by various poets. We see the garden, for instance, depicted as a setting in the twelfth century poet Nezami's *Haft Peykar*, as well as in his romantic *Layli o Majnun* and *Khosrow o Shirin*. Similarly, we see the garden and various references to it abundantly throughout Rumi's work. Significantly, Sa'adi names two of his books of poetry *Bustan* (*The Orchard*) and *Gulestan* (*The Rose Garden*).

In all these works, although the garden may be a physical setting, it is also an allegorical space referring to man's relationship with the divine. If we recall, one of the distinguishing elements of Sufi Persian poetry is its allegorical reference to known earthly physical elements to connect the reader to hidden aspects of their being and the universe. As Julie Scott Meisami observes, for Persian Sufi poets:

> allegorical imagery was the natural result of the need to find a language through which to express the inexpressible, and in it, allegory is a stylistic means for the depiction of spiritual *invisibilia* through the portrayal of the *visibilia* of nature.[56]

In this depiction gardens were chosen because, as a lived-in and experienced part of nature, they provided the poet and the reader with an understood earthly point of reference to depict the invisible. This is so because, as Meisami observes:

> Through the gardens he builds (in physical or in mental space) man expresses not only his conception of and his longing to recapture that ideal state, but also his perception of his relationship with nature: of the design of the cosmos and of his own place in it. The earthly garden functions both as an object of man's contemplation and his setting for important human activities; it differs from a natural landscape by virtue of being an artefact, constructed according to design (a fact no less true of literary gardens than of real ones) as well as by the frequent opposition of the garden world to the wilderness beyond it (gloomy forest or desert waste), the abode of forces hostile to man

> and to order. In proportion as its design and constituent elements are seen as reflecting principles of cosmic order and beauty, the garden itself becomes an ideal place wherein such principles may be observed; garden poems, as well, function as places of learning and discover as well as of recreation and delight.[57]

References to gardens resonate especially well with Iranians because of their historical significance in ancient Iranian culture, which predates even the Islamic invasion. According to Meisami, the importance of the garden, both as a lived-in, experienced space, and as a space that reflects an ideal state of metaphysical connection between man and the divine, dates back to the time of Zoroastrianism. Elaborate gardens built at that time were not only spaces of leisure, but also 'enjoyed a deep symbolic significance'.[58] Referred to as *pairidaeza*, from which the word 'paradise' was later derived, the symbolic association of the garden also heavily influenced Islamic thought and its lyrical tradition.

However, it is not only in history that Iranians have had a special affinity for the garden. For many Iranians, until recently when the country's economic instability started pushing people into high-rise apartment blocks, gardens played a central role in their lives. Many remember growing up in the safety of the walled garden of their homes, plucking flowers, climbing trees, and looking out onto the hostile streets. They still remember sitting out in idyllic afternoons in the garden, watching the stars appearing as the world got ready to rest. Others remember sleeping under the starry skies in the security of their garden, wondering what lay above them in the heavens.

This is why for many diasporic Iranians the absence of the garden is a significant reminder of their diasporic life and a symbol of their loss of identity. In her memoir *Lipstick Jihad,* Moaveni demonstrates the sense of loss associated with the absence of the garden in her own diasporic family. She writes:

> The trauma of dislocation varied, of course, by generation and gender. [...] But the loss everyone felt together, among the most acute, was the loss of gardens. Trees, flowers, the garden courtyard occupy a hallowed space in Iranian culture. [...] In California, the absence of gardens seemed the bitterest part of our reconstructed lives.[59]

To compensate for this loss, she recalls how both her grandfather and father obsessed over trying to recreate a garden, even if it was merely a patch with some vegetables. When her grandfather's garden did not turn out as he had envisioned, she recalls, he turned to poetry until his only means of communication gradually became Persian poetry that he carried from memory, poetry that connected him to his Iranian identity and past.

Within the body of work by diasporic Iranian writers, references to gardens, particularly through the allegorical language of Persian poetry, are also employed to describe the difficulties of migratory life. Tara Bahrampour, for instance, opens her memoir *To See and See Again* (1999) with this garden poem by Rumi:

> Outside, the freezing desert night.
> This other night inside grows warm, kindling.
> Let the landscape be covered with thorny crust.
> We have a soft garden in here.
> The continents blasted,
> Cities and little towns, everything
> Become a scorched, blackened ball.
> The news we hear is full of grief for that future,
> But the real news inside here
> Is there's no news at all.

This poem forms a base for her ensuing chapters, where she draws upon its words as her titles, to metaphorically follow her father's migration. The first section, called 'Soft Garden', traces her father's family history back to his grandfather and the feudal farming system in Iran, up to his departure for the United States. Like Rumi's Soft Garden, the ancestral land is safe and privileged. As she recalls her father's description, 'nothing ever today could be as good as those early days [in the farm]'.[60] The next section, entitled 'The Landscape', however, contrasts the safety and security of the 'Soft Garden', and the ancestral homeland. Here she follows her family's difficult and weathered life in the United States as her hybrid family (Iranian father and American mother) try to make ends meet. In the 'landscape' unlike in the 'soft garden' of the ancestral homeland, life is tough for her father and family. The last section of the book, 'The Garden Again', marks her revisiting Iran years later as a young adult, where she is reacquainted with the customs, landscapes and rituals of her ancestral homeland.

Similarly, Irish-Iranian Marsha Mehran[61] opens her book *Pomegranate Soup* (2005), about three Iranian sisters who try to settle and find new life in Ireland after immigration, with a garden poem. However, instead of drawing on traditional Iranian verse, she uses the words of one of Iran's contemporary Iranian poets, Forough Farrokhzad's 'Conquest of the Garden':

> Everyone knows,
> Everyone knows,
> We have found our way
> Into the cold, quiet dream of phoenixes
> We found truth in the garden
> In the embarrassed look of a nameless flower,
> And we found permanence
> In an endless moment
> When two suns stared at each other.
>
> I am not talking about timorous whispering
> In the dark
> I am talking about daytime and open windows
> And fresh air and a stove in which useless things burn
> And land which is fertile
> With a different planting
> And birth and evolution and pride.
> I am talking about our loving hands
> Which have built across nights a bridge
> Of the message of perfume
> And light and breeze.

Like Bahrampour, Mehran draws on the metaphor of the garden in the poem to reflect the three sisters' migration and settlement in Ireland, as they struggle and eventually establish themselves, introducing Iranian culture to the Irish by setting up a unique and successful Persian restaurant. We see this reflected in the final pages of the book when the sisters have, after much effort, finally settled in and found a new sense of permanence in their new garden. The book ends with one of the sisters, Marjan, observing a harvest celebration:

> The sun began to set over Clew Bay as Marjan leaned back with her tea to watch members of the acrobatic circus troupe, dressed in jumpsuits of green and gold silk, cartwheel across the modest wooden amphitheatre. The impromptu show was a dance based on the festival of Lughnasa, that harvest celebration of ancient Celts, which marked their new year. Marjan marveled at the similarities between this ancient ritual and her own version of the pomegranate myth.
>
> Unlike the classical Greeks, for whom the fruit symbolized the inescapable cycle of bitter death, with remorseful Persephone returning to the underworld for her sixth months of required winter, Marjan liked to believe the old stories of Persian soothsayers, who held a different vision of the tart fruit's purpose in life. She liked to remember that above all else, above all the unfortunate connotations of death and winter, the pomegranate was, and always would be, the fruit of hope.
>
> The flower of fertility, of new things to come and old seasons to be cradled.
>
> [...] that was how she would like to think of that particular sweetness. The myriad seedling that could only, really, be the flower of new beginnings.[62]

That the book ends with the possibilities of re-growth, symbolised through the seeds of the pomegranate and fertility festival, offers a sense of hope for the future. A new future that despite carrying the sentimentality and nostalgia of the old, symbolised through the garden and pomegranate, also offers the possibility of new and fertile futures.

In expressing their sentimentality towards their homeland and their childhood through garden imagery, however, some choose to write their own garden verses. In his poem 'To the Aged Mulberry Branch', for instance, Esma'il Kho'i represents his nostalgic memory of the garden of his childhood through a single memory of a mulberry tree:

> A long string trails
> To a torn kite
> Hanging
> From a branch of an aged mulberry tree

Whose afternoon umbrella of shade
Spans over the hubbub of the barefoot children of the alley

My goodness!
My entire childhood –
Summer-like –
Caught in the snapshot of this memory!
Look:
Dusty earth,
Dusty sky,
Dusty sun
And dusty children
Picking up dusty mulberries
With dusty hands
From dusty earth
To blow on
And place in their mouths!
And a torn kite
On the branch of an aged mulberry tree...[63]

Kho'i's poem expresses the duality of emotions for diasporic people, caught between nostalgic memories of childhood and a desire to move beyond the memories in the new country. For Kho'i, an exilic poet living in America, the mulberry tree expresses his most nostalgic memories of an idyllic life, an image that sums up his childhood identity. However, in telling about this space, the narrator is not involved in all the playfulness. We know that he is not a child any more eating dusty mulberries. We feel this through the image of the kite, which gives us a sense of separation, a lack of intimacy with the space, with almost a desire to fly away. Yet, the kite, like the poet, is torn, caught 'on the branch of an aged mulberry tree', rooted, unable to leave that memory in the past and move forward.

As Mostofi tells us, 'immigrants maintain a longing for their homeland and a desire to either return or preserve their nostalgia as a form of identification'.[64] For diasporic Iranian writers, elements of Persian poetry and Sufi literature, and their various interpretations, play a significant role in the maintenance of that shared sense of cultural identity. The belief that cultural identity is usually rooted in a shared unchanging historical past, and the nostalgia associated with it, is what

Hall argues is the most common understanding of what actually constitutes people's sense of cultural identity. Migrants often associate with the unchanging nature of cultural identity because, according to Hall, they 'offer a way of imposing an imaginary coherence on the experience of dispersal and fragmentation, which is the history of all enforced diasporas'.[65]

What we have become...

However, neither Hall nor all Iranian writers agree that cultural identity has to be defined as something unchanging and rooted in the past. Hall believes there is another way of understanding cultural identity in which, as much as acknowledging the relationship with the past or what we were, it is seen as accommodating and reflecting 'what we have become'. As he writes, 'cultural identity, in this second sense, is a matter of "becoming" as well as of "being". It belongs to the future as much as to the past. It is not something which already exists, transcending place, time, history and culture.'[66] Although cultural identities have histories, he believes that, like everything else historical, they undergo transformation:

> far from being eternally fixed in some essentialised past, they are subject to the continuous 'play' of history, culture and power. Far from being grounded in a mere 'recovery' of the past, which is waiting to be found, and which, when found, will secure our sense of ourselves into eternity, identities are the names we give to the different ways we are positioned by, and position ourselves within, the narratives of the past.[67]

This is also the case for Iranian writers' engagement with Persian poetry. Although for many Iranians, Persian poetry and some of its distinguishable elements constitute a central and unchanging aspect of Iranian cultural identity, one upon which they draw to maintain a sense of historicised identity, for some these traditional elements do not accommodate the complexity of the diasporic Iranian experience and sense of cultural identity. In adopting this position, some writers draw upon, challenge and transform existing literary traditions to construct a new discursive space that is reflective of their new realities.

There are various ways in which diasporic Iranian writers are challenging and drawing upon these elements, to make them reflect their own current condition. For example, adaptation of Persian poetic forms, which have always been praised for meticulous structure, can be seen as an act against its unifying dominant structure. In a way this act challenges dominant modes of expression and emphasises the diasporic Iranian writers' 'need for a lively heterogeneity of styles and speaking positions in their work'.[68] To do this Iranian writers have taken on varying strategies.

Re-inscribing poetry, reflecting realities

One way to make this tradition do different cultural work has been to transform the meaning or context of a traditional poem or verse. In her novella *The Heart's Desire* (1995), for instance, Nahid Rachlin adapts a well-known Persian poem into English prose to reflect contemporary diasporic issues. The novel begins with a quatrain from the eleventh century Omar Khayyam's *Rubaiyat*:

> Ah, Love! could thou and I with Fate conspire
> To grasp this sorry Scheme of Things entire,
> Would not we shatter it to bits – and then
> Re-mould it nearer to the Heart's Desire!

As the book begins, Karim, an Iranian man married to an American woman, Jennifer, has returned to Iran with their young child for a visit right after the revolution. During this short stay, however, he begins to fall in love again with the landscape, culture and customs of his Iranian heritage, where 'everything about the sights and sounds of Iran penetrated Karim deeply as if hollows had been carved inside him during the years of his absence and were now being filled'.[69] Although his heart's desire is to stay in Iran permanently and use his skills for the betterment of his country, he is conflicted between this and his obligations to his job as a college professor, and his wife and child, the only elements in his life that have given him a sense of solid identity. But some time into their stay, his entire sense of identity is suddenly shattered. First, at the height of the aftermath of the US hostage crisis, he is fired from his job in the United States. Then, when in search of a job in Iran, his marriage, too, suddenly, falls apart. When he and his uncle are out of town on business, Karim's mother takes his son to the city of Qom and enrols him at a religious school without Jennifer's permission. Jennifer chases after them and sneaks her son away. However, with nowhere else to go, she turns to her son's young physician and upon his insistence she moves in with him and begins an affair. Ashamed and unable to stay in Iran, she quietly leaves the country with her son. But Karim, who has lost his passport, cannot leave the country for at least six months until his new passport is reissued. During this time, their relationship collapses and they separate; Karim achieves his dream and remains in Iran.

Initially the connection between the opening poem and the content of the novel might not be clear. However, if we draw our attention back to the poem, one can argue that the book is indeed the poem that has been transformed into prose to reflect issues relevant to diasporic Iranian experiences today. As Dutton examines Khayyam's *Rubaiyat*, the body of work from which the opening quatrain of *The Heart's Desire* is taken, she observes that it 'indicate[s] a utopian vision of a better future, shaped by human agency'.[70] Drawing upon the indicated quatrain as an example, she concludes that:

> The *Rubaiyat* does not present a description of the physical incarnation of the ideal place, but it does explore the relationship between the cultural aspects of social dreaming and nature, as well as the role of human agency, or free will, in the conception of the utopian vision.[71]

Elaborating on Dutton's point it can be argued that it is this very element of the quatrain that Rachlin draws upon and reconstructs in prose form that reflects the utopian desires of a diasporic Iranian man through Karim. While within the verses of the poem there are no indications of what exactly that ideal place or what the heart's desires may be, in the novella Rachlin transforms this ambiguity into one that reflects a diasporic person's desire to maintain a sense of attachment to his cultural roots and identity. As the novel begins, we realise that although Karim has established an American identity for himself, his real desire has always been to return to Iran after the completion of his education, to help his countrymen. Yet, the course of life in the United States, particularly his job and family, had diverted him from attaining this dream. However, when things around him that prevent him from achieving his dream start to collapse, he is able, as the poem indicates, to re-mould the situation to his Heart's Desire.

However, in transforming this quatrain into prose, Rachlin has done more than challenge traditional Persian verse to open up a new discursive space for the expression of diasporic Iranian realities. Written in English, it also has the potential to reconstruct the way diasporic Iranians are perceived by the members of their host country. As we know, many diasporic Iranians were discriminated against after migration as the result of political tensions between Iran and the West. This discrimination resulted from dominantly negative descriptions of Iranians and consequently hampered their integration into their host societies. In *The Heart's Desire*, too, Karim tells of the discrimination he had faced in the early days after the revolution and the hostage crisis. However, the novella operates like a Persian Sufi poem and transforms the readers' perception of the reality of events. If we recall, one of the distinguishing elements of Persian Sufi poetry has been its transformative quality on the reader's perception. As James Roy King tells us in his essay 'Religious and Therapeutic Elements in Sufi Teaching Stories', in mystic Sufi tales, the author 'retells familiar stories and meditates at length on their meaning'.[72] These tales often operate by calling our attention to structural realities, and according to King 'they also challenge normal thought patterns, defy cultural proprieties, and suggest that problems can be approached from surprising angles'.[73] As such, he argues that the structural narrative of a Sufi poem is much more productive than one could imagine, in that it gives the readers much more than they had anticipated.

The Heart's Desire operates in the same way as Sufi Persian poetry by challenging the expected structural realities of events, particularly for Western readers. Although *The Heart's Desire* is about Karim's story, it is told through the dual perspectives of Jennifer and Karim. In this structure, it is Jennifer's perspective that gives us much more than we expect. Throughout the novel we hear Jennifer's story, her sense of alienation in Iran as a foreign woman. We also come to sympathise with her as a woman who has made the mistake of having an affair but who now has no way of turning back. We feel her sense of hopelessness and confusion. But, in a self-conscious manner, the novel seems to almost set Jennifer up in Iran to mirror Karim's condition in the United States as she gradually comes to understand some of his feelings reflected in her own situation in

Iran. After the confusion and affair that followed her son's enrolment at the religious school in Qom, Jennifer has an epiphany:

> [Karim] was unhappy in the United States and she would be unhappy living in Iran. At the beginning when she married Karim she had been delighted to immerse herself in his culture, but now in Iran it was as if she were impersonating someone else, just being here, conforming to the rules. And Karim had never become a true American, or his sense of identity could not be so easily threatened in a crisis. She *felt* for the first time, what before she had only understood in a cerebral way, what Karim had been through in a culture alien to him in so many ways. Tears rolled down her cheeks. She sat at the edge of the bed and breathed deeply a few times, trying to calm herself.[74]

One of the elements of Sufi poetry, as King suggests, is its emphasis on moving beyond assumptions and hypothesis in 'confronting reality'. This means that instead of theories and assumptions, Sufi poetry and the Sufi path often tries to direct the truth-seeker into experiencing a situation with all of their being. King believes that such 'contact with reality can be healing and transforming', and it is one of the main emphases of any Sufi tale or poem.[75] Viewed through this tradition, in *The Heart's Desire* Rachlin sets up Jennifer so that she confronts the reality of life in Iran, as Karim would perceive it in the United States. While in this encounter, Jennifer herself is transformed in terms of her own impressions of Karim, and can now easily accept his situation, her contact with reality also transforms Western readers, who identify with Jennifer's situation, and thus, through her, understand Karim. Such transformation is significant in how Iranian identity is perceived in the West. Through understanding Jennifer's point of view, they can no longer label Karim through historically imposed stereotypes.

Negotiating poetry: Reflecting modern sentimentalities

While Rachlin transforms Persian poetry into prose to construct a new discursive space for the reconstruction and negotiation of a diasporic Iranian identity, other writers take up the task of transforming Iranian poetry and poets into a new setting to reflect a new set of realities altogether.

Manoucher Parvin's *Dardedel: Rumi, Hafez & Love in New York* (2003) is one such book. A novel-in-verse, it tells the story of a recurring character in his other books, an Iranian migrant academic, Professor Pirooz, who, fed up with his life, travels from New York to Phoenix and wanders into the desert by himself in the middle of the night, hoping to die. As he pours his heart out to nobody, two cactus plants engage him in conversation, and they happen to be the reincarnations of the poets Hafez and Rumi. The two cactus poets save Pirooz and urge him to go back to New York, where they reappear in different forms as different people and continue to engage with him.

Dardedel, beginning with its very title, is a story that reflects the deep-seated importance of poetry in the maintenance of the Iranian identity in diaspora. The word *dardedel*, as Parvin tells us in the introduction to the book, is a Persian word which, translated into English, means 'a heart-to-heart talk, and so much more than talk'. *Darde* means 'ache of'. *Del* means 'heart'. 'But put together they mean *one* and *another* sharing the most private, sincere and important things', which

> unchains us from the burdens of our isolation and loneliness. By uniting our soul with another soul, our deepest thoughts and feelings are set free, without the shame of judgment or the fear of betrayal. It is this absolute trust that makes dardedel so special and sacred.[76]

In this case, the problems that bother Pirooz, about which he needs to have a heart-to-heart talk, are the problems that bother most Iranian migrants: displacement, lack of connection, and hostility between his home and host cultures that place him in an awkward social situation. It is these issues that Pirooz shouts out in the middle of the night in the desert:

> 'I am a refugee tonight,
> With two new friends whose arms stretch to the unknown
> Ask me not why I'm in this otherworldly place alone
> Thinking of death – my death
> Ask me not about cause and consequences
> Or other imponderable questions.
> But ask me what I want and I will tell you that I am starved

> As you are perhaps starved, to be loved and listened to,
> Just like the canaries who scream from their fancy cages,
> Just like the homeless who scream from their cardboard boxes.'
> 'My dear saguaros,' Pirooz confesses,
> I need to dardedel with you tonight.
> [. . .]
> 'so now listen to me,' Pirooz begs,
> 'As you would listen to a sombre cello:
> My home has disappeared behind years of exile,
> I can barely mourn for losses I can barely recall.
> My mother tongue has been conquered, word by word by English,
> So that I have neither one language nor two, but two halves.
> My two homes are at war, tearing my mind and heart apart.
> I am a teacher dedicated to teaching truth,
> Yet I am afraid to teach the truths I know,
> For fear I may lose my welcome, even my job
> So I must teach the Norm, the damn Norm,
> As if it was the word of God.
> I must dissimulate, dissimulate, dissimulate,
> To no end, until I am a foreigner even to myself,
> Until I'm an accent even to myself.
> That's why I've come to your desert, my dear saguaros,
> To die and be myself.'[77]

What saves Pirooz from hopelessness is the surprising response that he gets from the two cacti who reveal themselves as his revered poets Rumi and Hafez. In the two now displaced poets, he finds the companions to *dardedel* with:

> And so they dardedel,
> This mortal man who wants to leave this world,
> These two wise spirits stuck in hot American sand,
> Uprooted and reborn, like so many Persian immigrants in exile.[78]

After a night of *dardedel* with the poets, having been convinced by them to live for at least another year, Pirooz leaves the desert with a hopeful perspective on life. Upon his return to New York, he sets about learning new things and changing his lifestyle to live a different and fuller life. His regeneration of hope through an encounter with two of the greatest Persian poets reveals the significance of Persian poetry in revitalising a sense of identity for the Iranian diaspora. Parvin himself tells us in the introduction of the book that 'Persians feel at home in poems.' Thus Pirooz's salvation through an encounter with the masters of Persian poetry, who in their language of divine nostalgia, understand his laments of separation from his beloved homeland, further emphasises the ability of Persian poetry to accommodate Iranians wherever they may be.

Although Parvin demonstrates this diasporic salvation through Pirooz, writing the book has also been therapeutic for him as the author. In the introduction Parvin tells us about his own life and the emptiness he felt despite his success as what he calls an 'accented' academic in the United States. He reveals 'as I climbed the academic ladder I felt emptier at each rung. Emptiness, like a cancer of the soul, invaded me, established roots in me, and grew in me.' The antidote to this emptiness, he finds in both writing and reading poetry, and as he tells us:

> this book [. . .] is my dardedel with you [. . .] in [it] has been a healing effort – a dardedel free of all literary restrictions, personal fears and pretensions, a dardedel where science and spirituality clash, where modernity and history clash, where the soul of man is mended, if only on paper temporarily.[79]

Writing in verse, as he tells us 'in honor of Hafez and Rumi and the other epic poets of my homeland', this book becomes his way of saving himself through poetry, a way for accepting his own diasporic condition. He ends his introduction with a poem, which reflects the essence of the book as a *dardedel*:

> There is a pinch of Eastern culture and mysticism
> A dash of tenderness resurrected from industrial ashes,
> A touch of science and technology related to the fate of man,
> Drops of liquid soul from Hafez and Rumi,
> Blended with the love story of all love stories,
> Into a poem of poems, and,
> I pray, a dardedel of self-realization between you and me.[80]

While on this level, *Dardedel* reveals the significance of poetry for the Iranian soul, on another level it is making an attempt to revitalise Iranian poetry and poets by recontextualising them as more accessible to modern Iranian readers in diaspora. When Pirooz first accidentally encounters Hafez and Rumi as cacti in the desert, they have been made redundant and literally deserted in the modern American world. Despite their wisdom, the two poets sleep all day and count stars at night to keep busy as they recall their own poetry. Their redundancy in the American desert reflects their condition and accessibility as poets for many Iranians, particularly second-generation migrants who are not familiar with the Iranian culture. But the encounter between the poets and Pirooz changes the situation. After his encounter with the deserted poets, their perspective of life changes. As they realise the healing effect that they have had on him the poets feel intrigued by things that are going on around them in the modern world, of which they are unaware. Hafez, who in his life never travelled outside his city of Shiraz, desires to experience the world, and decides to go to New York:

> I do respect the old wisdom, the old reasonings and answers.
> But man faces new questions - so he must invent new answers!
> . . . Hafez shouts. 'I want to go to New York!'
> [. . .]
> 'I know it and I know it that Pirooz needs me in person.
> Our old books may be of no help to him any more.
> And, I confess, I need him in person, too, Rumi Jaan.
> How much can I gain by reciting the Koran or my own *Divan*,
> Neither containing the knowledge of modern times?
> Even in death I refuse to be bound by irrelevance
> Or the glorified past!
> I know it and I know it that I must go where life has journeyed,
> Where science and art and faiths and law have journey
> While we stood still, our feet bound in sand and death.
> I must go before I cannot go, and as Pirooz has said,
> I must wake up before I can never wake up.'[81]

Soon after these words, Hafez is transported to New York as a taxi driver to experience city life, to learn new things, and to keep Pirooz company. Rumi, left alone in the desert, eventually joins them. The surreal reincarnation of great Persian poets as taxi-drivers and various modern day New Yorkers, challenges the very notion of classical Iranian literature as an indisputable marker of Iranian cultural identity. Not able to fit into this modern world with their own ancient systems and philosophies, the poets soon adapt the new culture of the times. Although they continue to write poetry, their poetry is in line with the issues and concerns of the modern era. Rumi, for instance, begins to rap, and through this he introduces himself and the poetry of his past life. Such change in the great poet's attitude and styles points towards a necessity to break free from the unchangeable traditions and ideas that have bound us, formed our identity and prevented us from integration, even if it means having a modern take on classical Persian poetry to reflect our time and condition. This modern take on Persian Sufi poetry reflects the needs for change in traditional modes of thought in order to accommodate new realities.

In transforming Persian Sufi poetry and poets into a modern context, Parvin is doing more than simply challenging traditional perceptions of Persian literature and opening up a new discursive space reflecting the diasporic Iranian experience. Parvin's transformation operates as a decolonising apparatus for the way Iranians and Iranian culture have been perceived within Western culture. By physically transporting deserted Iranian poets and poetry into mainstream American life, and integrating them completely into the culture, he is centralising the marginalised aspect of Persian poets and poetry as a significant aspect of cultural identity for the Western reader. This is an important step in reconstructing and negotiating diasporic Iranian identities within their Western context. Although poetry is such a significant aspect of Iranian cultural identity, its importance has often been ignored or understated in mainstream representations of Iranian culture in the West. Centralising poetry as an important part of Iranian cultural identity for a Western audience allows for the opening up of a space for the reconstruction and negotiation of a new diasporic Iranian identity, one that replaces the historically imposed images of the exotic and terrorist.

Parvin is not alone in doing this. Many Iranian writers are aware of the need to centralise this aspect of Iranian culture and have made a point of bringing it to the fore, and sharing aspects of Persian literary tradition. Fatemeh Keshavarz, for instance, has dedicated her entire memoir, *Jasmine and Stars: Reading More than* Lolita *in Tehran* (2007), to this task. Keshavarz self-consciously sums up her life in a literary memoir as a means of reconstructing the Iranian identity in diaspora. She outlines the reasons for writing her memoir in the first few pages through an ancient universally known story recounted by Rumi. She recalls the tale in which an elephant is brought into a city at night, where no one has seen one before. The townspeople are insistent to know what this creature is. So, they begin to feel their way around in the dark. Each touches one part of the elephant's large body, reducing their understanding of the animal to their minimal and partial encounter in the dark. Rumi, according to Keshavarz, concludes the tale by saying '"if they each had a candle, they would all be looking at the same beast"'.[82] Keshavarz soon draws a parallel between this tale and how the Middle East, particularly Iran, is viewed in the West. She believes that, particularly after 9/11, people in the West want to know about the Middle East as a 'matter of life or death'. In this attempt, like the townspeople in the dark, people reach out to anyone, 'tourists', 'scholars' and particularly 'eyewitness narratives' with the hope of learning anything they can about the Middle East. But the problem is that most of these views, like each person's interpretation of the elephant, is partial, and 'the feel-in-the-dark method of describing life in Iran [. . .] hampers the critical ability to question the narrow and slanted vision provided by the popular media'.[83]

In her memoir, Keshavarz hopes to shed light on some important elements of Iranian culture that are missing in the existing narratives about Iran but which form Iranian identity in diaspora. Through an 'in depth critical understanding' of literature about Iran, which claims to provide an insiders' account into Iranian life and culture but which in reality she believes is like 'tapestry or mosaics' with holes or missing pieces, she hopes to create 'an alternative approach for learning about an unfamiliar culture'.[84] What she feels is missing in this tapestry of narratives, particularly, is a representation of the rich and ancient literary culture that shapes every aspect of Iranian life and identity but which has been underrepresented in many tales about Iran, particularly in those written by certain popular diasporic Iranian writers. So her alternative approach is to fill in the gaps and to introduce this aspect of Iranian culture through a 'literary and cultural analysis' with the hope that she will 'plant the seeds of interest in learning about aspects of Persian and Muslim life not yet known to most American readers'.[85]

One of the ways in which Keshavarz fills this gap is through the representation of the importance of literature in her own life as a typical Iranian woman. Thus, every chapter that narrates significant events in her life is told through a literary anecdote that not only demonstrates the importance of literature in forming her life, but also introduces different aspects of Iranian literature to the readers. For instance, she recalls how she and her father bonded over hours of reading and interpreting classical Persian poetry, and how they drew on the expressions they read in the poems to communicate with other people. Through these personal accounts, she introduces readers to various classical Persian Sufi poets, explaining their poetry and significance in Iranian culture. But her explanation of Iranian literature is not limited to classical Persian literature, for she also introduces various modern Iranian writers and poets, and describes their importance in her life through similar stories. For example, she recalls how she met her best friend on the day she first walked into her new high school. Written on the chalkboard she saw her favourite poem by Forough Farrokhzad, one of the most controversial Iranian women poets. The person who had copied the poem onto the chalkboard immediately became her friend. The love they both shared for poetry, and Farrokhzad in particular, forms the basis of their life-long friendship. Here, once again, Keshavarz uses the opportunity of a personal anecdote to introduce Farrokhzad as one of the most important figures of modern Iranian literature.

However, for Keshavarz the reference to the Iranian literary tradition is much more than a mere introductory lesson about its significance to the lives of Iranian people. Rather, her engagement is also a critique of what she calls New Orientalist narratives, which are 'exaggerated and oversimplified at best and fully distorted at worst'[86] in their representation of life in the Middle East, particularly when it comes to the representation of Iranian women, culture and literature. She announces this critical intention self-consciously early in the book by explaining 'when speaking of meaningful instances in my personal experience, I add my literary/cultural analysis', focused 'mostly on a harmful rhetoric infusing our modern popular culture through the lens of a New Orientalist narrative'.[87] One of the examples on which she bases her criticism of New Orientalist narratives, as the title of her memoir also suggests, is Azar Nafisi's *Reading* Lolita *in Tehran* (2004), a book that she believes presents the view that '"we [Iranians] lived in a culture that denied any merit to literary work"'.[88] Although revolving around the healing power of (Western) literature for seven of Nafisi's students over several years in a private book club, *Reading* Lolita *in Tehran*, ironically as Keshavarz argues, fails to acknowledge or reflect the importance of Iranian literature in the lives of ordinary Iranians, like the women who attended her book club. Instead, Keshavarz believes, it paints the picture that 'all good things in the Muslim Middle East belong to the past [. . .] all that are left in the culture that once produced giants such as Attar [classical Persian Sufi poet] are domineering runts'.[89] While, according to Keshavarz, the book does mention the names of great Iranian poets like Attar, they are portrayed as if 'they are a thing of the past'. Quoting Nafisi, 'there was such a teasing, playful quality to their words, such joy in the power of language to delight and astonish [. . .] I kept wondering: when did we lose that quality?' Keshavarz puts forward her own response, 'the answer is rather simple, we have not lost them'.[90]

The works of authors such as Parvin and Keshavarz not only reveal that this literature is still alive and a significant aspect of Iranian cultural identity, but they also ensure that this aspect of Iranian culture lives on through the English literary tradition. By entering the very tradition that had been used to formulate the Iranian identity in stereotypical images of the terrorist and exotic, they transform it. One of the most significant strategies of post-colonial resistance in challenging domineering representation, as we know, has been that it 'takes the dominant language and uses it to express the most deeply felt issues of post-colonial social experience'.[91] This form of expression 'becomes the key to transforming not only the imitator but the imitated'.[92] The fact that Parvin's Rumi, for instance, begins to rap in English, the very language that has often been used earlier to discriminate against Professor Pirooz, transforms both elements of Persian literature and the landscapes of English literature. This is significant, as it has the potential to open up new discursive spaces of expression and cultural exchange that are no longer bound by our limited historical perceptions. To put it in Ashcroft's words, 'the engagement of post-colonial writing is one which had transcultural consequences, that is, dialectic and circulating effects which have become a crucial feature of the world we experience today'.[93]

As we have seen so far, Persian poetry is an important marker of Iranian cultural identity, which heavily informs the works of diasporic

Iranian writers in English. While, by drawing on its nostalgic sensibilities and tropes, diasporic Iranian writers are maintaining a sense of historicised identity, they have also been engaging with it to reconstruct and negotiate a new sense of diasporic identity for themselves. However, diasporic Iranian writers are also drawing upon elements of Persian literary tradition as a form of critique of certain aspects of Iranian society, as well as the Western setting in which they are now residing.

However, despite the importance of this literary tradition in Iranian cultural identity, until recently, it was a predominantly male-centred and male-constructed tradition, in which women's presence, as both authors, and central characters, has been almost minimal. While in the Iranian literary tradition, women usually only existed as symbolic images that aided a male hero's quest, in the Western representation of Iran, until recently, Iranian women's representation never went beyond silences and veils. But this has been changing. This is why, in what follows, this book will examine the emerging and shifting presences and voices of women in diasporic Iranian literatures, paying special attention to the way their contribution is continuously changing not only how Iranian women are represented and representing themselves both in Iran and abroad, but also how their contribution is shifting the very nature of elements of both Persian and English literature as we have traditionally known them.

CHAPTER 3

THE MEMOIR – 'DOUBLE-EDGED' NARRATIVES

My maternal grandmother, who had seven children, one of whom was stillborn, lived a happy life. When we started going to school, she would often play with us when we were doing our homework. My cousins and I would sit with her after school in our primary years, and draw squiggly lines that would later form parts of our understanding of the Persian alphabet. But as we moved on from lines into alphabets, my grandmother stopped playing with us. She no longer helped us. It would only be years later that I discovered the reason she stopped was because we had, at eight years old, surpassed her literary knowledge. My grandmother lived well into her 70s, completely illiterate. She had, all her life, depended on others to read things to her. It always fascinated my cousins and I to know why her parents had not insisted on her education, when she herself had made sure all her children received adequate schooling. When I was a teenager, I asked her why she had not been encouraged to go to school. She looked me in the eye and told me that parents of her generation did not like girls to receive an education because if they did learn to read and write they would start communicating. They would start writing and sharing things. Families did not like this. What happened in the family was to stay in the family.

I did not fathom the cultural and societal gravity of my grandmother's statement until years later when I studied English literature and became exposed to narratives by women from across the globe. It was then that I noticed the missing voices of Iranian women in literature and realised that many women of my grandmother's generation, and prior, had never had a chance to express themselves. In their illiteracy they had not authored any books. When they did appear as the subject of men's books, it was often in passing, and as symbolic characters who aided the male hero in his quest. Even Sufi Persian poetry, for instance, the literature loved by everyone in Iran, was mostly a strictly male-dominated form. It was not only in Iran, however, that women's voices and stories had remained absent. When Iranian women did appear in Western literature, their presence was marred by Oriental mystery, passive subjects of Western male gazes, often victims of patriarchal societies.

My initial awareness of the historically missing voices of Iranian women in literature coincided with a revolutionary rise in Iranian women's memoirs in English post-9/11. While between 1980 and 2001 there had been only 16 memoirs published by Iranians abroad in English, at least 50 more have been published since then. This sudden increase in the number of Iranian women's memoirs has brought with it a whole new genre of writing. Although their books are often placed alongside other Middle Eastern Muslim women's autobiographies on bookstore shelves, they are distinctively different. Not only do they often speak of a specifically Iranian experience from a woman's perspective – something that is radically new in Iranian history and society – but they are also received within a historically conflicted atmosphere between Iran and the United States, where most of these memoirs are particularly popular. This has given them a unique position within both the literary history of their home and host cultures.

Perhaps the position of these memoirs can be understood best by answering two key questions, which are often asked of the famed Iranian writer Gina Nahai. In an anecdotal piece, Nahai tells us that at every book signing she is asked by readers 'why so many memoirs?' and 'is there a market for all those books?'[1] Nahai herself answers these questions briefly by saying that there are so many women's memoirs because these women 'live in a place and a time when they can speak the truth without fear of morbid consequences [and] they are getting published [...] because [...] publishers think there's a market for all those books.'[2] Although her response sums up well some of the factors for the sudden increase in Iranian diasporic memoirs, the reasons are far more complicated and have far-reaching historical, personal, social and political roots and implications for both writers and readers. As Gillian Whitlock argues, there is a great interconnection between the 'ebbs and flows [of] history', and 'networks of consumption, pleasure and agency that carry life narrative'.[3]

This chapter examines the reasons for the sudden rise in the number of Iranian women's memoirs in relation to the ebbs and flows of history, particularly in light of imposed silences, stereotypes, and traumas of their home and host countries, and explores their significance within the networks and patterns of consumption into which they are received. Especially important here is the social and cultural contextualisation of these books historically in relation to the American interest in captivity narratives, American Orientalism and declaration of 'war on terror' after 9/11, as these have had a profound effect in the way diasporic Iranian women's memoirs are constructed and consumed. However in this context the memoir form itself, and what it offers both writers and readers, becomes very important. What is significant here is the relationship between narrativity and subjectivity, or what Suzette Henke calls 'scriptotherapy', and Kelly Oliver 'bearing witness'. This relationship between narrativity and autobiography not only determines how these books are constructed, but also the way they are consumed.

'Why so many memoirs?'

The popularity of the memoir among diasporic Iranian writers today can, ironically, be traced back to its lack of historic popularity in Iran. As Farzaneh Milani observes in her seminal book *Veils and Words* (1992), in Iran the autobiographical form, as we know it today, which leads to the revelation of private and personal information, had not been a favourable form of expression. Therefore, perhaps the question that should be asked first is 'why not so many memoirs?' Milani believes that several factors have contributed to the historical scarcity of the memoir form in Iranian literature.

One of the reasons for the unpopularity of the autobiographical form among Iranians, according to Milani, has been the 'fear that the information revealed by them can be used, or rather, misused against their authors'.[4] This stems from the strict censorship of the almost-totalitarian regimes that have ruled over centuries of Persian literature and culture. As she puts it 'a manifestation of the strength of totalitarian regimes, religious fanaticism, and chaotic, and ultimately repressive historical periods, this tradition of official censorship is important in any study of Persian literature'.[5]

Milani goes on to argue that although censorship has always been externally imposed, gradually it has also become part of the Iranian discourse of communication. People gradually began to self-censor for fear of the consequences of revealing too much information. Emerging out of this has been a cultural tradition of strict censorship of disputes, scandals, or involvement of family members with criminal and political activities. This is why, according to Milani, proverbs such as 'hefz-e aberu [to save face], Hefz-e zaher [to protect appearances], Ba sili surat-o sorkh negah dashtan [to keep the face red with a slap]',[6] play a central role in Iranian family dynamics, even today. Consequently, 'avoiding voluntary self-revelation and self-referentiality, most Iranian writers have turned their backs on autobiography'.[7] This is not to say, however, that Iranians have never written about their lives. Throughout recent Iranian literary history one does encounter so-called autobiographies. But these are normally written by public male figures, in an impersonal manner, avoiding self-importance, and revolving around their public office, lacking any private depth.

While for Iranian men, at least for those with public presence, there was the choice to write about their life, until recently that chance never existed for Iranian women. Milani relates the lack of women's public voice to the concept of veiling. She writes, the majority of Iranian women 'were suppressed physically and verbally by the conventions of the veil and public silence'.[8] Traditionally Iran has been a highly gender-segregated society in which men belonged to the public sphere and women to the private.[9] In this culture, women's domain 'was a private world, where self-expression, either bodily or verbally, was confined within the accepted family circle'.[10] Within this tradition, propriety demanded that 'a woman's body be covered, her voice go unheard, her portrait never painted, and her life story remain untold'.[11] Milani blames this segregation for the lack of autobiographical accounts by women. She writes:

> Erased from the public scene and privatized, the Iranian woman has for long been without autobiographical possibilities. Textual self-representation of individuals is not divorced from their

> cultural representation; and in a culture that idealizes feminine silence and restraint, not many women can or will opt for breaking the silence. Most will not name the formerly unnamed, move beyond the accepted paradigms of female self-representation. In a sexually segregated society where access to a woman's world and word is limited, and the concept of honour is built around woman's virginity (proof of her inaccessibility) women's autobiographies, with their assertive self-attention and self-display, cannot easily flourish, and they have not.[12]

It was this social dynamic, coupled with the general lack of women's education until Reza Shah's modernisation in the 1930s, that until recently led to the absence of women's autobiographical voices in Persian literature. Despite this, however, some brave and educated Iranian women had attempted to write autobiographies. For instance, the highly rebellious and educated Princess Taj-al-Saltaneh (1848–96), the daughter of Nasser-e-din Shah, did write a memoir. However, it was not published until 86 years after her death.[13] One of the first Iranian women to transgress this boundary and write about her very personal life openly, for circulation while she was still alive, was the controversial and celebrated poet Forough Farrokhzad (1935–67), whose autobiographical poems reflected her unconventional life.[14] Women like Taj-al-Sultaneh and Farrokhzad, however, were few in Iranian history. Unlike them, the majority of Iranian women upheld the social conventions of silence and segregation because they knew that 'public disclosure of any [...] aspects of a woman's life was considered an abuse of privacy and a violation of societal taboos [...] for which punishments [...] were many and varied'.[15]

Added to this has been the trauma of the revolution, which not only brought stricter censorship policies, but also tightened gender dichotomy. As Haleh Esfandiari argues in *Reconstructed Lives: Women and Islamic Revolution*, a book that played a part in her later imprisonment in Iran:

> the Islamic revolution had a marked and transforming impact on all areas of Iranian life. But for women, its consequences were especially profound – legally, socially, professionally, psychologically, both in the home and in society. [...] The state set out deliberately and

> consciously to reconstruct and redefine the place of women under the law and in the public and the private spheres.[16]

Such transformation, however, was not towards more freedom. If, prior to the revolution, women's inability to write about their life experiences had mostly been due to family and self-censorship, after the revolution the state's censorship of their voices was added to this. The Islamic revolution had a traumatic impact on many Iranian women's lives. While those who stayed had to live with everyday oppressions, silences, and even impositions on the way they dressed, those who left faced the trauma of exile.

It is in response to the absence of autobiographical accounts, particularly women's narratives, that diasporic Iranian writers have chosen the memoir form as a favourite medium of expression. Distanced by time and space from the dichotomous society that had held many in silence, diasporic Iranian writers are 'free, at last, to shape the boundaries of [their] own story'.[17] But the memoir, as opposed to other forms of expression, has been particularly favoured because of what it offers both its writers and its readers.

Memoir as scriptotherapy

In *Shattered Subjects: Trauma and Testimony and Women's Life Writing*, Suzette Henke argues:

> Autobiography has always offered the tantalizing possibility of reinventing the self and reconstructing the subject ideologically influenced by language, history, and social imbrication. As a genre, life-writing encourages the author/narrator to reassess the past and to reinterpret the intertextual codes inscribed on personal consciousness by society and culture. Because the author can insatiate the alienated or marginal self into the pliable body of a protean text, the newly revised subject, emerging as the semifictive protagonist of an enabling counternarrative, is free to rebel against the values and practices of a dominant culture and to assume an empowered position of political agency in the world.[18]

This is what Henke calls 'scriptotherapy': 'the process of writing out and writing through traumatic experiences in the mode of therapeutic reenactment'.[19] This therapeutic potential has to do with the very form of the memoir. It is a utopian mode and space, offering writers endless possibilities to express realities of a distant, sometimes dystopian, traumatic, or at times nostalgic, past that would have otherwise not been expressed. I use the term utopian here because the memoir is one of the few forms that allows candid expression of ideas that would otherwise not have a chance to be heard. As Ashcroft argues:

> utopias are not so much concerned with the future as much as with sketching the present and our ways out of it. [. . .] The issue is not what is imagined, the *product* of utopia so to speak, the imagined state or utopian place, but the *process* of imagination itself.[20]

For the memoir, too, although the result might be a representation of a dystopian memory, it is the process of writing, the very act of narrativity, that allows it to operate as a therapeutic space of expression. As Kelly Oliver argues with regard to the psychology of oppression, individuals and groups who have been tortured, traumatised and discriminated against have been objectified, and their sense of identity and agency has been taken away. One of the means through which such people can regain that sense of identity is through the process she calls 'bearing witness to oppression and subordination'.[21] She believes that those affected can heal themselves and 'repair damaged subjectivity by taking up a position as speaking subjects',[22] and being recognised by others as sharing with them the same human feelings. In this process, the memoir, because of its emphasis on recalling and engaging with very personal experiences, often traumatic, provides the perfect formal space through which this kind of private/public interaction can play out. As Whitlock, too, acknowledges in *Soft Weapons*:

> autobiography is fundamental to the struggle for recognition among individuals and groups, to the constant creation of what it means to be human and the rights that fall from that, and to the ongoing negotiation of imaginary boundaries between ourselves and others.[23]

According to her, one of the significant elements of the memoir is that it can mediate 'between the public and private'.[24] It 'is a cultural space where relations between the individual and society are thought out intensely and experienced intersubjectively'.[25] Psychologically, for many, breaking boundaries between private individual experiences and society at large can be an important process in reconstructing and even negotiating any kind of personal or group identity. This is why the memoir or autobiographical narrative can be a powerful form of scriptotherapy.

This is also why the memoir can be seen and used as a site of resistance by post-colonial and diasporic writers who want to foreground forgotten narratives and transform the way they are perceived. The memoir allows for the voices of the marginal to regain their agency and subjectivity through very personal and remembered experiences, by transcending boundaries of public/private, dominant/dominated, colonised/coloniser and offering multiplicities of alternative social narratives to the grand narrative of history. It becomes a space where, by drawing on the past and looking into the future, identities can be negotiated. As Whitlock observes in the introduction to *Intimate Empire: Women's Autobiography*, 'autobiographic writing can suggest the multiplicity of histories, the ground "in between"'[26] where the oppressed can regain their sense of subjectivity, thereby resisting and dismantling totalising discourses, practices, and institutions that had objectified them.

Reconstructing the self: Bearing witness to trauma and silences

It is in this way that most post-revolutionary diasporic Iranian women's memoirs serve as a form of scriptotherapy, as individual exercises of healing and reconstruction from trauma and oppression. One of the most recurrent issues with which diasporic Iranian memoirs engage has been the issue of silence. The majority bear witness to the pathos of silence and self-censorship that has ruled Iranian society and family throughout history. As we know, Iranian society has always operated on the basis of a dichotomy of public/private domains, resulting in a kind of self-censorship. Although these practices operated mostly on the dynamics of the public/private domains, as Milani believes, 'external restrictions sustained over time eventually generate[d] internal ones'.[27] Over time, this created a kind of individual/family dichotomy, a form of self-censorship that separated the individual, especially one who had been in a potentially shameful or harmful situation, from the rest of the family by a veil of silence. However, such silence fails to recognise the trauma of the oppressed person, so that as 'these private, sacred precincts protect, they also imprison', because 'the sophisticated mechanisms that shield the inner self from exposure and intrusion also amputate and silence part of the self'.[28] Nafisi observes the operation of this silence in her second memoir, *Things I've Been Silent About*:

> There are so many different forms of silence: the silence that tyrannical states force on their citizens, stealing their memories, rewriting their histories, and imposing on them a state-sanctioned identity. Or the silence of witnesses who choose to ignore or not speak the truth, and of victims who at times become complicit in the crimes committed against them. Then there are the silences we indulge about ourselves, our personal mythologies, the stories we impose upon our real lives. Long before I came to appreciate how a ruthless political regime imposes its own image on its citizens, stealing their identities and self-definitions, I had experienced such impositions in my personal life – my life within my family. And long before I understood what it meant for a victim to become complicit in crimes of the state, I had discovered, in far more personal terms, the shame of complicity.[29]

This veil of silence has always ruled Iranian families and, in various ways, has formed one of the major underpinning themes of diasporic Iranian women's memoirs. While this has deep historical roots, one of the most recently experienced silencing and traumatic issues that has affected the majority of Iranian women has been the revolution and its aftermath.

In her essay 'From Tehran to Tehrangeles: The Generic Fix of Iranian Exilic Memoirs', Gillian Whitlock argues that most diasporic Iranian women's memoirs 'share experience and articulation of the revolution as a traumatic event, as a wound inflicted during a key period in the author's personal development'.[30] Looking at the body of diasporic Iranian women's memoirs, whether exilic narratives of aristocrats or royalty, or return stories of second-generation daughters of the revolution, or even recent prison memoirs, it is clear that the lives of each and every one of these writers has been affected dramatically by the revolution. While the restrictive Islamic codes of conduct had relegated many to the margins of society, eventually forcing some into exile, the revolution had also been discriminatory against many minority groups. It is to this sense of oppression and discrimination that many have responded in their memoirs. Perhaps the oppression felt as the result of the revolution is best summed up in the words of Azar Nafisi who, in *Reading* Lolita *in Tehran*, complains 'of a loss, the void in our lives that was created when our past was stolen from us, making us exiles in our own country',[31] where 'they invaded all private spaces and tried to shape every gesture, to force us to become one of them, and that in itself was [a] form of execution'.[32] This is why, as Whitlock observes, these memoirs 'constitute a "gathering of the wounded," a working through revolutionary trauma, and the disclosure of memory marked by the events of the revolution: the loss of home and culture, shaped by the nostalgia that scars life in the diaspora'.[33]

The memoirs of first-generation migrant writers who experienced the revolution and its aftermath first hand vividly bear witness through painful personal accounts to alienation, loss, dismay and ultimately exile. This reflection of loss can be seen from the earliest and more obscure memoirs emerging in the late 1980s to better-known accounts published post 9/11. For instance, in *Out of Iran: One Woman's Escape from the Ayatollahs* (1987), one of the first memoirs by an Iranian woman in English, Sousan Azadi bears witness to the personal subordination that she faced following the revolution. As a great-grand daughter of a Qajar King, she narrates her life through her husband's death from cancer to her difficulties with her in-laws regarding child custody, through the Islamic regime, her imprisonment and her eventual escape through Turkey into Canada. This book, republished 13 times by two different publishers between 1987 and 2003, begins with the narrator recalling the discrimination her family faced immediately after the events of the revolution. She begins:

> The *taughout.* Satan. A ruler who has transgressed the limits of his authority. Such was Ayatollah Rhollah Khomeini's title for Mohammad Reza Pahlavi, King of Kings, Shah of Iran. And we, the Shah's loyal subjects, were condemned by Khomeini as the *taughouti,* the followers of Satan [. . .] We were the rich of Iran, the ruling elite, the nation's leaders. We didn't want to accept a vengeful religious leader as our new master. In his view, because we were Westernized, we must have been immoral. I have known what it is like to be hated just because I wanted basic rights as a woman in a Moslem country. Within three years I found myself an

> unwilling exile, purged by a society that I barely recognized as my own [. . .].[34]

Azadi's opening paragraph bears witness to the oppression that she and her family had faced following the revolution, something she would not have been able to express had she been in Iran. By explaining her own position, and ideological beliefs, Azadi uses the autobiographical form to become a speaking subject, to reinvent herself anew, not as a *taughouti* but as an educated, honourable member of Iranian society who had been discriminated against by the oppressive forces of the regime. Azadi is not alone in wanting to reinvent herself against the discriminating label of *taughouti*. In her memoir, *Unveiled: Love and Death Among the Ayatollahs* (1995) Cherry Mosteshar too tells us about the discrimination she had faced as the result of her social position. From a similar background to Azadi, Mosteshar also tells us:

> there was a day, before the revolution of 1979, when I had been one of the richest young women on our street in wealthy North Tehran. With the coming of the Islamic state I was transformed into evil Taghouti. [sic] [. . .] I was marked as a traitor in my native Iran even before I had a chance to be anything other than my parents' rebellious youngest child.[35]

Here, similarly, the memoir form allows the narrator to reconstruct her own sense of subjectivity against the historically imposed image of the *taughouti*. In both cases, it allows them to become speaking subjects by bearing witness to the discrimination they had faced from the newly established regime. To put it in Henke's words, the autobiographical form provides them with a space in which they can 'rebel against the values and practices of the dominant culture and to assume an empowered position of political agency in the world'.[36]

For those who encountered the revolution as children, the memoir allows them to tap into their childhood memories, recount and bear witness to horrific events of that era, perhaps understanding them more now as adults than they did as children. Afschineh Latifi, in *Even After All This Time* (2005), for example, recounts the traumatic story of her father's execution, a high-ranking colonel under the Shah's regime, and follows her family's harsh journey into exile. Similarly, Banafsheh Serov, one of the first Iranian-Australians to write a memoir, in *Under a Starless Sky* (2008) remembers her family's illegal and dangerous escape after the revolution through Turkey and eventually to Australia. Roya Hakakian, too, in *Journey from the Land of No* (2004) recalls the discrimination her family faced as a Jewish family after the revolution, causing their eventual journey to the United States.

Recalling these traumatic experiences as adults can be healing, as it not only allows them to bring to the fore repressed memories but it also offers them a sense of closure. As Eve Zibart writes in an interview with Hakakian, 'the word is the expression of the essential self, and the manner in which we re-create our universe'.[37] About Hakakian she writes, she 'thought she had understood pretty well the upheaval of the late 1970s and early '80s in her native Iran [. . .] but once she began to write about that time, the act of writing both clarified and reshaped those events'. Indeed Hakakian confirms the therapeutic effects of writing as she tells us that once she started writing 'everything came into focus and I was able to make sense of things I thought were unconnected'.[38]

While for most of these writers writing a memoir is a kind of scriptotherapy without the narrator acknowledging it openly, for a few writers it is the therapeutic effect of writing that has attracted them to write a memoir. For instance, in Marina Nemat's *Prisoner of Tehran* (2007), which deals with her imprisonment and forced marriage to her interrogator at the age of 16, Nemat overtly addresses the therapeutic effects of writing in regaining her subjectivity. *Prisoner of Tehran* opens with her arrival in Canada, drawing upon an ancient Persian proverb. She writes, 'there is an ancient Persian proverb that says: "The sky is the same color wherever you may go."'[39] But she quickly breaks that well-know proverb, recreating its meaning as she continues:

> But the Canadian sky was different from the one I remembered in Iran: it was a deeper shade of blue and seemed endless, as if challenging the horizon [. . .] the vastness of the landscape astonished me. [. . .] We had to build a new life in this strange country that had offered us refuge when we had nowhere to go. I had to concentrate all my energy on survival.[40]

This opening establishes and acknowledges that it is distance from Iran that has allowed Nemat to survive and bear witness to the traumas of her imprisonment, for, as Paul Sheehan observes, 'had she written this book in her native Iran, she would have been executed by the state'.[41] But these lines also set the tone of the entire memoir. Set in a new land with an endless horizon we immediately know this is a personal narrative of survival, healing, reconstruction, new beginnings and possibilities. This self-consciousness, which becomes even more obvious as the narrative proceeds, forms a running theme throughout Nemat's memoir. For instance, later in the memoir she clearly reveals the reason why she had, after nearly 20 years of silence, and after becoming a 'proud middle-class Canadian', decided to speak. She writes:

> This is when I lost the ability to sleep.
>
> It began with snapshots of memories that flashed into my mind as soon as I went to bed. I tried to push them away, but they rushed at me, invading my daytime hours as well as the night. The past was gaining on me, and I couldn't keep it at bay; I had to face it or it would completely destroy my sanity. If I couldn't forget, perhaps the solution was to remember. I began writing about my days in Evin – Tehran's notorious political prison – about the torture, pain, death, and all the suffering I had never been able to talk about. My memories became words and broke free from their induced hibernation.
>
> I believed that once I put them on paper, I would feel better – but I didn't. I needed more. I couldn't keep my manuscript buried in a bedroom drawer. I was a witness and I had to tell my story.[42]

Although this reveals Nemat's writing as a conscious therapeutic exercise to keep her sanity, her emphasis on the fact that without sharing her manuscript her healing is not complete points to her realisation of the need for intersubjective recognition to fully reconstruct her sense of subjectivity. Both Oliver and Henke argue that it is by being recognised by others that those oppressed can regain their sense of subjectivity. When someone, like Nemat, writes a memoir, a significant part of their healing takes place only when they are read and acknowledged by others.

The fact that Nemat has the urge to share her manuscript with others bears witness to something beyond her own personal story and desire to be recognised. In reading these memoirs, we must keep in mind that they are not narrated nor should they be read exclusively as one woman's experience. Rather, through the narration of their individual stories, they are also bearing witness and responding to larger, often generational, historical and socio-political oppressive forces. As Oliver argues, those traumatised 'do not merely articulate a demand to be recognized or to be seen [...] they bear witness to a pathos beyond recognition and to something other than the horror of their objectification'.[43] Seen in this light, these memoirs, too, though articulated in and through personal accounts, should be read as witnesses of horrors beyond personal desire for recognition. They are witnesses to a larger discriminatory socio-political and historical pathos and their narratives are a way of obtaining recognition of those groups and individuals who had been marginalised and objectified under various oppressive forces.

While, without a doubt, the revolution was an historical event that created an apparent oppressive force, there are many other socio-historical issues to which diasporic Iranian memoirists are responding. One of the most dramatic forms of silence has been that of ex-prisoners, particularly between the prisoner and his or her family. Ex-prisoners, especially female political prisoners, have had an invisible existence. Fuelled by a kind of usually self-imposed rigid censorship that dichotomises public and private, their silence frequently stems from fear that personal information revealed can be used or misused against them and their families. For many, fear of exposure is magnified as it entails risk of further persecution for them and, again, their families. In listening to political prisoners who have now come forward to speak, one common experience has been they had received threats during their imprisonment. Unable to speak about their experiences publicly, ex-prisoners are frequently doubly oppressed as they are received into silent families who are fearful of knowing what has happened, and are afraid of the consequences of knowledge. Ex-prisoners often complain about being received into shrouds of silence upon their return. Zarah Ghahramani, a young political activist who was imprisoned for a month in Evin during the student protests of 2001, and who recounts this ordeal in her memoir *My Life as a Traitor* (2007), reveals the silence into which she walked after being released. In an interview she speaks of her experiences after being picked up by her father from the side of the road where prison guards had dropped her off blindfolded:

> He came, and we hugged and cried and all that, and then we went home. My sisters came over, and my father made breakfast for us, like when we were kids. It was all really normal. I was expecting

> them to ask me what had happened, where I had been, but we just had normal, everyday breakfast. Then I went to have a shower and I saw my face for the first time after a month. It was really scary. I hardly stopped myself from screaming, wondering what my family was going through seeing me like that, and not even saying anything. It was really frustrating for me – I really wanted to talk. But when I think about it now, it was the best thing they did. It was hard enough for them, what happened to me. I'm sure they didn't want to know any more.[44]

While the very act of writing is liberating and therapeutic for those who have experienced such silence, for some writing has become a deliberate and conscious attempt to break down the walls of silence. In *Prisoner of Tehran*, for instance, Nemat seems driven to write in a deliberate and self-conscious attempt to bear witness to this particular social pathos of silence. When she is freed from prison after two years, like Ghahramani, she is received into a web of silence. Instead of asking her about what has happened, she is made to dress in fine clothes and attend parties. No one, not even in her family, asks, acknowledges, or wants to know what happened. But unlike Ghahramani, frustrated by this silence, she confronts her grandmother:

> 'Why doesn't anyone ask me anything about the last two years?' I asked.
>
> 'The answer is very simple. We're afraid to ask because we're afraid of knowing. I think this is some kind of a natural defence. Maybe if we don't talk about it, and maybe if we pretend it never happened, it will be forgotten.'
>
> I had expected my homecoming to make things simple again, but it hadn't. I hated the silence surrounding me. I wanted to feel loved. But how could love find its way through silence? Silence and darkness were very similar: darkness was the absence of light and silence was the absence of sound, voices. How could one navigate through such oblivion?[45]

However, Nemat too would have lived with these stories in her own heart, as she had for 20 years, had it not been for the sudden realisation that there are many such women whose voices needed to be heard. The decision for her to break this silence came after a life-changing encounter with another ex-prisoner. Early in the memoir, after establishing her personal reasons for writing, Nemat tells of an event that redirected the course of her narrative. In 2005 in Canada, she meets a girl, Parisa, who had been an inmate at Evin at the same time as her. Parisa reveals that she had not until that night 'talked to anyone about her prison experiences' because '"people just don't want to talk about it"'.[46] It is this silence to which Nemat responds in her writing:

> This was the very silence that had held me captive for more than twenty years.
>
> When I was released from Evin my family pretended that everything was all right. No one mentioned the prison. No one asked, 'what happened to you?' I ached to tell them about my life in Evin, but I didn't know where to start. I waited for them to ask me something, anything that would give me a place to begin. I guessed that my family wanted me to be the innocent girl I had been before prison. They were terrified of the pain and horror of my past, so they ignored it.[47]

After this meeting, she writes, 'if I had doubts about speaking out, they vanished'.[48] It is Nemat's recognition of Parisa, and the similarity of their silence, coupled with the significance of Zahra Kazemi's death (the Canadian-Iranian photojournalist who was captured and beaten to death in Evin in 2003) that makes her break her silence. This decision allows her to speak and heal herself, and consequently, through her own narrative, bear witness to the larger socio-political situation that had affected others in similar condition. Nemat's last words in the postscript reveal her intentions:

> I knew what I had gone through in Evin was still happening behind its walls, but seeing Zahra's picture, and her beautiful smile gave this knowledge, a painful and shocking power that cut through me. [. . .] The world had now taken notice because Zahra was a Canadian. If the world had paid attention, if the world had cared, Zahra would not have died; many innocent lives would have been saved. But the world had remained silent, partly because witnesses like me had been afraid to speak up. But enough was

> enough. I was not going to let fear hold me captive any longer. [...]
>
> I had a story to tell. Zahra had given Iran's political prisoners a name and a face; now it was my turn to give them words.[49]

Memoirs like Nemat's, which highlight the oppressive silences of others through their own personal stories, recuperate silenced experiences on multiple levels. On a personal level, they allow for the narrator to bear witness to the trauma that they had faced. Narration, thus, becomes a form of scriptotherapy, a way of gaining personal recognition and regaining subjectivity. On another level, these narratives operate on a social level and bear witness to something beyond the narrator's need for personal recognition. They bear witness to a social and historical pathos of silence, and allow for the recognition of the voices of those who otherwise might not have a chance to express themselves. As such they are important milestones in helping those who have been oppressed historically to regain their subjectivity, as they 'render human the dehumanized and convey the fullness of voice and presence to those denied their rights'.[50]

Return narratives: Therapeutic negotiations of belonging

For the diasporic Iranian community, as with most communities in a similar position, one of the most traumatic experiences has been the process of exile and resettlement. Adult migrants, having grown up in Iran, often have a sense of belonging and community, enough for memories of childhood to help them maintain a sense of identity, even if that shared memory is of a traumatic period. But those who migrated as children, or those who were born to migrant parents, often do not have enough personal memories to be able to construct a continued sense of belonging to Iran. For these people, their only maintained sense of Iranian identity is derived from early idyllic childhood memories, nostalgic reveries from their parents and relatives, or from contradictory and often negative images shown in the media in their new home. For them, there is great conflict in their sense of continued identity, belonging and allegiances. For this generation, the formation and negotiation of a kind of diasporic hybridity has been a great trauma in the way they construct a sense of identity. As Tara Bahrampour tells us in her memoir *To See and See Again*:

> those young enough to have adjusted to America but old enough to still remember Iran seem to have the most difficulty choosing their cultural allegiances, perhaps because they were too young to have made their own decisions about staying in Iran or leaving.[51]

Similarly, as Azadeh Moaveni demonstrates in *Lipstick Jihad*, 'growing up Iranian in America had been arduous and awkward. We had little consciousness of assimilation, because we were in denial of our permanence in America [...] mentally still in between.'[52]

This 'dispersal and fragmentation' of identity, and the split of allegiances between two cultural identities, as Stuart Hall reminds us, is part of the history of all diasporic experience. But Henke believes that testimony to this identity crisis through the autobiographical form can be effective 'in working through episodes of psychic fragmentation'.[53] For this group, writing becomes a way of negotiating a sense of hyphenated identity by bridging the cultural differences between their home and host cultures. However, in this process, not many of these young writers remember Iran very well. To negotiate this sense of duality they must first gain an understanding of their home country and culture. While for some this has involved an academic process of learning more about Iran, many more have bridged this gap through a return trip to Iran. As Bahrampour writes in her memoir:

> No one could give me a full picture. People might tell me stories about what Iran was really like, but they were not talking about 'my' Iran. We had left at the end of my childhood, and like childhood it had frozen in my mind into a mythical land. Once we landed in America, I lost the power to separate Iran from my memories of what it had been. The only way to do that would be to go back and see it for myself.[54]

This is why in recent years the return memoir has become popular for second-generation diasporic Iranian writers. These memoirs, of which there are several, such as Tara Baharmpour's *To See and See Again*, Gelareh Asayesh's *Saffron Sky: A Life Between Iran and America* (1999) and Azadeh

Moaveni's *Lipstick Jihad: Growing Up Iranian in America and American in Iran* (2005), are all accounts of a personal quest to negotiate a sense of cultural identity. As Stuart Hall reminds us, cultural identity is 'a matter of "becoming" as well as "being." It belongs to the future as much as to the past.'[55] What the return memoir allows these women to do is to negotiate a space in which instead of carrying the burden and trauma of cultural hybridity, they can understand and celebrate their own unique hyphenated cultural identities through the process of understanding, and by coming to terms with their alienated home cultures. As Moaveni tells us:

> As life took its course, as I grew up and went to college, discovered myself, and charted a career, my Iranian sense of self remained intact. But when I moved to Tehran in 2000 [. . .] it, along with the fantasies, dissolved. Iran, as it turned out, was not the Death Star, but a country where people voted, picked their noses, and ate French fries. Being a Persian girl in California, it turned out, was like, a totally different thing than being a young Iranian woman in the Islamic Republic of Iran. [. . .] So, I learned for myself, as I endured a second, equally fraught coming of age – this time a Californian in Iran. I never intended my Iranian odyssey as search for self, but a very different me emerged at its end.[56]

In these memoirs, it is often through the process of the return and writing about it that the narrators come to embrace their hybridity. Frequently, through this process, the trauma of duality is transformed into a celebration of multiplicities and unique cultural identities in a world where identities are no longer bound by a sense of nationalistic belonging. As Amy Motlagh observes:

> while first-generation authors are still invested in the depiction of a national story and the possibility of a return to power in the home country, members of the second generation [. . .] sense the fragmentary nature of the world they live in and simply want to claim that fragmentariness as their own condition.[57]

Towards the end of her memoir, Bahrampour demonstrates this as she writes:

> We had not fit into any mold; compared to Iranian kids in Iran or American kids in America, we had had a sense of being untethered in the world. We had travelled all our lives; we were seasoned experts on jet lag and layover. [. . .] Our futures too were uncharted. With no model to follow, we could imagine ourselves anywhere in the world.[58]

For many diasporic Iranian writers, these memoirs serve a purpose additional to simply being discursive spaces through which they negotiate their own sense of personal identity. For many second-generation diasporic Iranians, and those who migrated as young children, adding to the trauma of having to navigate and construct a sense of identity at the intersection of two cultures has been the troubled relationship between their home and host countries. As such they operate on a social level through which the narrators also negotiate a social sense of identity within their diasporic environment.

As I have shown, the situation of diasporic Iranians within their host communities, until recently, has been one of ambivalence and virtual invisibility, fuelled by the still-looming resonances of the revolution, the hostage crisis and hostile political relationships between Iran and the West. As Moaveni complains:

> as a teenager I felt there was nowhere to turn, and I often felt invisible, alone with my two irreconcilable halves. Sometimes I felt like we didn't even exist, even though I had proof we did. [. . .] We weren't reflected anywhere – not on television, not on radio. [. . .] It was too overwhelming to dwell in a home wracked with inter-cultural turmoil, within a larger community wrapped up in the awkwardness of arrival, to attempt to bridge my two identities.[59]

It is this need to negotiate a social identity and existence within their host communities that also leads to the popularity of such memoirs. As Oliver argues, subjectivity is constituted intersubjectively so 'that we come to recognize ourselves as subjects or active agents through recognition from others'.[60] But the lack of recognition, and even at times negative recognition, both of individuals and a community, oppressed diasporic Iranians within their host communities. They often had little sense of positive intersubjective recognition in their new homes. As Oliver believes, this sort of 'oppression creates the need and demand for recognition'.[61] This demand can range from the desire to be 'recognized by their oppressors, the very people most likely not to recognize them', to 'demands for retribution and compassion' from the dominant culture. The memoir, particularly one that speaks of the perils of hybridity and misrecognition of a community, then, is in effect a space where negotiations for this kind of recognition are taking place. As Henke believes, 'in the very act of articulation, the trauma story becomes a testimony, a publicly accessible "ritual of healing" that inscribes the victim into a sympathetic discourse-community and inaugurates the possibility of psychological reintegration'.[62] What this means is that these narratives are, like post-colonial writing, negotiating a space of belonging for diasporic Iranian communities through recognised discourses of dominant cultures that had failed to recognise them to begin with. In effect, these memoirs can be seen as sites of resistance from a dominant and stereotyped perspective, and as spaces for negotiating and forming a new kind of identity. But, as will be discussed, the process of negotiating this kind of belonging is highly dependent on recognition, in this case recognition by readers and in turn through the publishing market. Although this recognition does have positive influences for diasporic Iranians, it is also very complicated and could paradoxically lead to other forms of misrecognition, oppression and silence.

As we will see these texts can be taken up, decontextualised and interpreted within various post 9/11 discourses and causes, turning a personal narration of healing into a political manifesto or a social commentary about the masses of Iranian and Muslim women. In this case these texts can be interpreted as supporting ideologies of particular groups that 'advocate certain foreign policies towards the Middle East and purport to defend women's rights',[63] and be seen as 'complement[ing] the current military agenda of the US foreign policy',[64] in the name of feminist causes.

'Is there a market for all those books?'

In *Soft Weapons,* Whitlock argues that after 9/11 'Muslim life narratives have been taken up variously in the recent past, in a time of crisis when recognition of viable speaking subjects in the public sphere has become an urgent issue'.[65] According to her, these autobiographical accounts are often approached 'emphatically identifying in and through trauma and in terms of human rights campaigns for social justice that play to Western traditions of benevolence'.[66] There is no doubt that this tradition has greatly benefited the reception and recognition of books by Middle Eastern, including Iranian, women. The events of 9/11, which created an avid readership interested in consuming these narratives, has for the first time recognised Middle Eastern women's voices and given them the opportunity to bear witness to personal trauma. Considering the historical background of silences and oppressions of Iran and the difficult diasporic conditions out of which many of these narratives arise, this type of recognition could be very beneficial for the narrators. As we have already seen, for those traumatised and oppressed, narration or writing could be a way of being 'recognised by their oppressors, the very people most likely not to recognize them', or even a form of 'demand for retribution and compassion' from the dominant culture. Furthermore, this interest and recognition has provided a space through which diasporic Iranians could also negotiate spaces of belonging and their sense of diasporic identities. This reciprocal relationship between Iranian narrators and their readers has led to the publication of over 65 memoirs by the Iranian diaspora over the last three decades.

However, the reception of and interest in Iranian women's accounts has deep historical roots, which mean that, although it does provide a space of expression and recognition, it also has a predefined scope of reception. As Amal Amireh and Lisa Suhair Majaj argue in the opening of their book *Going Global: The Transnational Reception of Third World Women Writers,* 'the efforts of feminist scholars inside the academy to correct the limitations of a Eurocentric feminist movement and to make space for... [other] women to speak of their own experiences instead of being represented as the "Other" seemed to be coming to fruition'.[67] However, they feel that this 'gesture of inclusion [has] not [been] innocent, but instead often functioned to contain our voices within a predefined space'.[68] This predefinition stems from the historical and socio-political backgrounds and interests into which these books are received. As Whitlock observes, these books have been 'hostages to publishers, the taste of the reading public, and shifts in the political, cultural and social life of the nation'.[69] What this means is that often, instead of being spaces for affirmation of a sense of identity, these memoirs appear to re-affirm certain preconceived perceptions about East/West relationships, in particular, about Middle Eastern women, driven alongside socio-political interests. This has made them 'easily co-opted into propaganda'.[70]

In this context the question that I believe should be asked is not 'is there a market for those books?' but rather *why* is there a market for all those books, particularly in the last decade? What are the effects of this demand on their production and consumption? And do these demands affect interpretation and limit the voices and intentions of authors? In fact, one of the most crucial questions that I believe should be asked, one that Whitlock also puts forth in her study of diasporic Iranian memoirs, is 'what is at stake when memoirs by Iranian exiles trade as best sellers in these times?'[71]

The rest of this chapter answers these questions and analyses the diasporic Iranian memoir, not just as a personal healing device, but rather as a popular piece of public discourse. Here we investigate the value of the memoir form for its readers and pay attention to the popularity of the form and the Western fascination with the 'Other' historically, particularly in relation to the exotic Orientalist imagining of the Middle East by the West, the recent conflicted history between Iran and the United States after the American hostage crisis in Iran, as well as the more recent events of 9/11.

However, the popularity of diasporic Iranian women's memoirs today has an additional cause dating further back than most scholars have recognised. Their popularity today can be linked to the popularity of the American captivity narrative and America's encounter with the native Other. This, however, is not a claim that diasporic Iranian memoirs are replacing or directly congruent to the captivity narrative genre. The American captivity genre in its traditional form has certain conventions and is representative of a particular era of American history. However, we can see that certain elements of the captivity genre, which is essential to the landscape of the history of American culture, literature in particular, continue to engage the imagination and interest of American readers. These elements include a particular set of assertions of race, gender and culture dichotomy and hierarchy, which not only reflected the condition of the American encounter with the native Other, but which also continue to inform America's encounter with the global Other in an age of multiculturalism and transnationalism.

Captivity narratives, American Orientalism and Iranian women's memoir

Scholars of American literature often view captivity narratives as 'one of America's oldest literary genres and its most unique'.[72] The origins of these narratives date back to the early days of settlement, when European settlers made contact with the unknown natives of the land. Consequently 'stories of captivity by an alien culture began to excite the public imagination'.[73] According to Alden Vaughan and Edward Clark, early literature of American colonisation is dotted with tales of seizure, torture, adaptation and eventual escape or release of the European settler/explorer by the natives of the land. But it was not until the late seventeenth century that the captivity narrative became a popular and distinct genre, when Mary Rowlandson's *A Narrative of the Captivity, Suffering and Removes of Mrs. Mary Rowlandson* (1682), which sold a minimum of a thousand copies with four editions in the first year of publication, became the first American bestseller.[74] Over the last 400 years, there has been a string of accounts by other women that follow on from Rowlandson's account of captivity by the native Other. These narratives often operate by asserting a certain kind of social hierarchy and a dichotomy between us/settlers/Europeans and them/natives of the land.

However, the captivity narrative, though maintaining some of its elements, has not been static throughout history, and has always been closely linked to the socio-political atmosphere of the times. As Catharine Stimpson, the series editor of Christopher Castiglia's *Bound and Determined*, explains in the introduction of the book, 'the laws of this genre are very clear'. She tells us that the narratives are often told in such a way that they 'maintain the established interlocking hierarchies of race and gender'.[75] Often, they appear 'during the periods of gender and racial tension in the United States that challenged these hierarchies – for example, during the colonial confrontation with Native Americans and during the Civil War'.[76] She goes on to explain that these accounts usually tell the story of a brutal, murderous group of savages who capture 'a frail, vulnerable white woman'. Traditionally, these savages are American Indians or, in some cases, they are black. According to her, they 'threaten to rape and enslave the white woman. White men must kill them in order to rescue the woman and restore her to civilized society.'[77]

This interlocking system of racial and gender hierarchies has informed much of American history and its literature. However, as Brian Edwards points out, we cannot claim 'too neat a continuity between the captivity narratives of the eighteenth and twenty first centuries'.[78] Shifts have occurred inevitably in American society that have affected the way these hierarchies are perceived. One way in which we can better understand this, Edwards suggests, is through 'something we can call tentatively American Orientalism'.[79] Edwards characterizes American Orientalism, like the Orientalism described by Edward Said, as having a 'dual focus on the putatively exotic other and his customs'.[80] But he quickly adds to this by arguing that American Orientalism is much more complicated, for it does not only revolve around the relationship of us/them. For Americans there has been the issue of a 'European other' who is 'always present in the background or foreground, as a model, negative or not, of imperial political presence'.[81] Moreover, he argues, the United States' global hegemony in the mid-twentieth century, at the wake of globalisation, transnationalism and multiculturalism, further complicated the situation, so that the dichotomy and hierarchy that informs Orientalist discourses can no longer be neatly divided by a racial boundary.

Twentieth century United States of America was a post-modern nation, as Melanie McAlister points out, 'in which territory, community, and political affiliations were reconfigured'.[82] In this society, Iranians, Arabs, Asians and Latinos – all those who were essentially the Other – were as American as the descendants of early settlers. In this new America, migrants, like Iranians, had integrated and had gradually become part of the fabric of American society. Consequently, racial barriers that defined American superiority became more porous. In this America, as Dominic Tierney puts it, 'to be American is not to hark from a particular ethnicity, but to profess a creed of liberal ideals rooted in the ideas of John Locke: freedom, individualism, democracy, limited government, the rule of law, and free expression'.[83]

In this new America, the captivity narrative continued to exist, but it, too, changed its shape to reflect the complexity of the new society. These narratives no longer told of domestic encounters and threats of captivity from the native Other. Instead, they told of American adventures in a globalised, international world, where American citizens were being held hostage by Others in exotic and distant locales. These American citizens were no longer the Puritan Anglo settlers, but a cross-culture of a variety of people who were all part of the American nation. Their encounter and capture in other countries was no longer simply a threat to the racial hierarchies that early Americans had assumed as the creed of their nation state, but the capture of, and threat to, these multi-racial Americans was a threat to the very ideological core that distinguished America from other nations.

Throughout America's encounter with the Other on an international scale, the Middle East and the Muslim Other has greatly excited the American imagination. Although this relationship between Middle East, Islam and America is far more complicated than could be addressed in this book, it is important to note that there has been great enthusiasm by the American media about the encounter of Americans with the Middle Eastern Muslim Other. As Douglas Little argues in *American Orientalism*, 'few parts of the world have become as deeply embedded in the U.S popular imagination as the Middle East'.[84] One of Little's arguments revolves around the way this encounter has been represented in American media, 'reflected in everything from feature films and best-selling novels to political cartoons and popular magazines'.[85] Among these, 'tales about the capture and rescue of hostages have been told and told again – in novels, autobiographies and, later, in movies and TV'.[86] There have been frequent 'sensationalistic accounts in the mainstream press that would reincorporate a period two centuries or more ago in the vocabulary and logic of the period'.[87]

Although the way in which the American encounter with the Middle East and American captivity in the region is characterised has its roots in the early days of post-Columbian American history, according to McAlister it reached its 'television-age apotheosis only with the Iranian [hostage] crisis'.[88] The American hostage crisis, as it unfolded, was one of the most widely covered stories in American television history, gaining as much attention as civil rights, Vietnam and Watergate.[89] The representation, reception and interest in the American hostage crisis in Iran, as McAlister believes, was all very much informed by the captivity narrative. As she argues, 'the discourse of terrorist threat formed in the context of the Iran hostage crisis depended on the underlying structure of [early American] captivity narrative'.[90] The sensationalistic media coverage of the 444-day event, as Catherine Scott also observes, 'echoed Puritan captivity stories of confrontation with the "other," [with] fears of innocents being violated, and the call upon heroic leadership to rescue both the hostages and the nation from threats to American identity'.[91] In this saga, Iranians replaced native Americans, and 'the hostages in Iran, like those early captives came to represent an entire nation in its conflict with another culture; the public concern over their captivity was part of a larger story about national identity, foreign policy, and racial constructs'.[92]

The Iranian hostage crisis and its aftermath gave rise to a frenzy of books, television shows and movies that dealt with threats to American national and cultural identity. Among the books, however, one that most closely replicated the earlier captivity narrative in an Iranian setting was Betty Mahmoody's still-best-selling memoir, *Not without My Daughter* (1987). Set in Iran, after the hostage crisis and in the early days of the Islamic government, it claims to tell the true story of Betty, an American woman's captivity in Iran at the hands of her own husband, and her eventual dangerous escape to the United States. Mahmoody's narrative, emerging at a time when the hostage situation was still fresh in the psyche of American readership, resonated elements of the captivity narrative in a modern setting, and reminded people of the hostility and cultural differences that existed between the United States and Iran.

However, accounts such as Mahmoody's became popular not only because they were timely and capitalized on the United States' conflicted relationship with Iran, but also because they offered glimpses into the lives of Middle Eastern women. In Western and American encounters with the Middle East and Iran, women have always been shrouded in mystery. The dichotomous structure of Iranian society had not only made it impossible for women to speak of their own experiences, but had made it even more difficult for non-Iranians to understand details of Iranian women's lives. This has been a cause of curiosity for the Western world, which desperately wanted to unravel and demystify details of the lives of veiled Middle Eastern women.

Additionally, the more recent political situation following the events of 9/11, and the particular interest in women's issues after the United States' declaration of 'war on terror', has led to a new interest in narratives by and about Iranian and Middle Eastern women. The lack of women's voices, coupled with an American mission to 'rescue' these women, as Jasmin Darznik puts it, created 'an insatiable curiosity for both the intimate details of [their] lives and descriptions of forbidden landscapes'.[93] It is within this context that recent diasporic Iranian women's memoirs have been received, consumed and interpreted. Such narratives in a time of continued conflict with Iran, like modern captivity narratives, highlight certain elements of the cultural hierarchy that American society continues to uphold.

Among the many narratives by Iranian writers, the memoir has become particularly popular for Western readers, as opposed to fictional narratives on the same issues, because of what it offers its readers. Because of its intimate nature, the memoir promises first-hand experiences from spaces that were previously inaccessible to Western readers. Heavily invested in the personal and emotional life of its narrator, it 'offers lived experiences; it professes subjective truths; and [...] it signals to the reader an intended fidelity to history and memory'.[94] This creates a personal bond between narrator and reader, which 'engages the reader powerfully, imaginatively, intimately'.[95] The memoir is, by its nature, bound by an autobiographical pact, an assumption that there is truth in the relationship between the experiences described by the narrator and the world beyond. Although this 'truth' might be variable depending on from whose perspective these accounts are narrated, there is a general assumption that the memoir has the ability to bring to the reader, to the world outside, insider truth about certain aspects of life. Middle Eastern women's memoirs have become particularly popular because of their ability to offer supposedly rare and insightful glimpses into forbidden landscapes of women's lives in the Middle East. As Whitlock puts it, these 'life narrative[s] [are] of course one of the most seductive forms for the projection and naturalization of the exotic and an offering of authentic others'.[96]

In addition to this, it is the human connection created between the narrator and the reader that has readers taking up these narrative memoirs time and again, 'emphatically, identifying in and through trauma and in terms of human rights campaigns for social justice that play to Western traditions of benevolence'.[97] It is this interest in the private lives of Middle Eastern women, embedded in historical and political influences, that, according to Whitlock, 'allows these life narratives to move from East to West rapidly and to become highly valued commodities for a "primed" readership'.[98] Among these, in the post 9/11 apotheoses of Middle Eastern memoirs, Iranian women's memoirs have been particularly appealing for an American readership because of the still-lingering bitter resonances of the hostage crisis. As

Whitlock observers, 'contemporary memoir from Iran attracts American readers again now, and it revisits and folds the events of the Islamic revolution and its aftermath into the present one more time'.[99] Emerging at the height of tensions between Iran and the United States these narratives were received by 'the curious and uninformed American readership eager to know about Iran and primed for the stories of disenchantment by exiles'.[100] It is no wonder, then, that after 9/11 there was a sudden rise in the number of memoirs by diasporic Iranian women. From 2003 to date Iranian women have published over 40 books with reputable publishers, most of which provide a delayed yet timely account of the Islamic revolution and its traumatic consequences, with the benefit of hindsight with regard to conflict between Iran and the United States.

The socio-political and historical context into which these books are received, coupled with certain expectations of the memoir form, have inevitably affected the way these memoirs are produced, received and consumed. As French theorist Gerard Genette argues, all literary works consist of accompanying elements, beyond their actual words and content, that 'mediate the book to the reader'. These elements, which he calls 'paratexts' are essentially influenced by the socio-political and cultural situation of the time in which a book becomes part of the public domain. Paratexts, according to Genette, are elements that are within and outside the book, which he distinguishes as peritexts and epitexts. While peritexts are all those elements between and on the cover of the bound copy of a book, including 'titles and subtitles, pseudonyms, forwards, dedications, epigraphs, prefaces, intertitles, notes and afterwards',[101] as well as the visual imagery of the cover, epitexts are elements beyond the bound copy such as interviews, reviews and scholarly examination, which are also heavily influenced by both the private history of the author and the public history of the situation into which books are received. An examination of the paratextual elements, according to Genette, can help critics and readers better situate and understand a book.

Paratexts have played a particularly significant part in the way diasporic Iranian women's memoirs are constructed, received and consumed. In *Soft Weapons*, Whitlock examines in detail how paratexts have affected the production and consumption of Afghan women's memoirs after 9/11. Here, I would like to draw on and extend Whitlock's argument to paratexts that surround diasporic Iranian women's memoirs.

Paratexts

If we walk into any major bookstore today in any Western country, it is the peritexts, the covers, titles and blurbs that attract us to the books by Iranian and Middle Eastern women. Upon entering these bookstores, we are confronted with rows and rows of half-veiled faces of women or of women with the veil loosely hung around their neck or body, peering out with exotic eyes. While this has become convention for books that deal with Middle Eastern women's issues, particularly for the memoir or autobiography, a survey of Iranian women's memoirs in particular, reveals how telling these covers are of the formulated space into which these narratives are received. Of the 50 or so memoirs published by Iranian women over the last 30 years, nearly half comply with this formula. These images (some reproduced in this section) are the first point of communication and interaction between the book and the potential readers.

If we look at these veiled images closely, particularly in an American setting, they are telling of an American Orientalism that affects how the books are marketed and consumed. The presence of the veil operates on several layers that invite curious readers to pick up these books. On the one hand the image of a chador-clad woman, an indistinguishable figure in the shadows, such as on the covers of *My Prison, My Home* and *Persian Girls*, appeal to the stereotypical Western imagination of Middle Eastern women. Women here are shadowy figures, hidden in the background, without any agency, just as the Western reader imagines her. The chador-clad figure is the symbol of the passive and silenced woman, and her appearance on the cover is an invitation to the Western reader to unveil her.

On the other hand, others dare to break this silence and are stepping forward to seek recognition. The veiled women, with only their eyes peering out at the viewers, as on the covers of *Unveiled*, *Out of Iran*, *Prisoner of Tehran* and *Journey from the Land of No*, *Rage Against the Veil*, *In the House of the Bibi* and *Watch Me*, are inviting and yet challenging the viewer/reader to pick up the book to enter into their mysterious, hidden world. The eyes in these images, sharp in focus, distinguish each woman from the other under the veil, a humanising strategy suggesting that the woman behind the veil 'can look back at the spectator mute but eloquent'.[102] However, what is interesting to note is that despite this

Figure 3.1 A collage of the covers of some of the memoirs by diasporic Iranian writers in English.

humanising strategy, there is a sense of generalisation, a kind of 'one woman's story is every woman's story' approach. If we look, for instance, at the covers of *Journey from the Land of No* and an edition of *Prisoner of Tehran*, it is the same eyes that are peering back at us, hinting at the similarity of these two narratives. All of these images, despite slight variation, tap 'into a [Western] fantasy of the illicit penetration of the hidden and gendered spaces of the "Islamic World"'.[103] They are 'invit[ing] and encourag[ing] the Western imperial gaze, offering Westerners a glimpse into the presumably forbidden world beneath the veil'.[104]

This invitation is almost a call for acknowledgement by the Western reader, an appeal for recognition, by women who have so far been silenced in their own country. However, the fact that the Western reader is involved in this act of unveiling and recognition operates on an acceptance of cultural dichotomy between the narrator and the reader, appealing, as Whitlock also reminds us, to the Western tradition of benevolence. It is only by the book being picked up by the Western reader that Iranian women can be recognised and thereby regain their sense of subjectivity. This recognition, however, operates on a presumption that Iranian women are oppressed, and imprisoned behind the veil, and need Western readers and values to liberate them from their social imprisonment.

The use of the images of young veiled girls – the kind of pictures usually used for passports, birth certificates, and school records in Iran – on such covers as *Living in Hell* and *The Last Living Slut*, further highlights the dichotomy and the seemingly oppressive force bearing down on women's lives in Iran. On the cover of Omid's *Living in Hell* this message is emphasised further, as the girl's face is framed, bound, almost branded with the logo of the Islamic republic, hinting at oppression under the regime.

The image of the unveiled woman with the scarf around her neck, staring straight at the camera, invites the reader into a different kind of story. These women, such as Ardalan and Saberi on the covers of *My Name is Iran* and *Between Two Worlds*, appear liberated. They have taken the chance to speak for themselves in line with Western traditions of freedom of speech. They are inviting the viewers to read about their passage from oppression to freedom. Here, their stories are not so much about the oppression, but about the process of liberation and unveiling. These women have demystified themselves by unveiling, and are offering curious readers a chance to glimpse into their lives.

Figure 3.2 A collage of the covers of some of the memoirs by diasporic Iranian writers in English.

The titles and promotional blurbs also heighten these elements by feeding off the current socio-political interests of the times in which the books are marketed. A survey reveals a set of key phrases in the titles of many of these memoirs, which are almost as conventional as the cover images. Titles such as *Unveiled: Life and Death Among the Ayatollahs*, *Out of Iran: One Woman's Escape from the Ayatollahs*, *In the House of Bibi: Growing up in Revolutionary Iran*, *Honeymoon in Tehran: Two Years of Love and Danger in Iran* and *Rage Against the Veil: the Courageous Life and Death of an Islamic Dissident,* draw on the urgency of life, death, and revolution, and debated issues of veil and unveiling. They feed into American Orientalist perspectives, and are, as Whitlock argues, 'designed to grab the Western eye and with a glimpse of absolute difference, of the exotic'.[105] At a time of America's declared 'war on terror', and Iran's presence in the axis of evil, these titles feed into this discourse, and are 'a way of positioning them for metropolitan markets'.[106] Other titles, such as Haleh Esfandiari's *My Prison, My Home: One Woman's Captivity in Iran* and Roxana Saberi's *Between Two Worlds: My Life and Captivity in Iran*, draw directly on the well-known American tradition of captivity, as they once again reframe the story of the American(-Iranian) woman caught this time in the web of extremist society. In both Esfandiari and Saberi's titles the word captivity, juxtaposed with the word Iran, reminiscent of the hostage crisis and looming hostility between Islam and the West, and Iran and America, transforms them immediately into a modern version of the American captivity narrative.

In framing the way these texts are received and consumed, epitexts, such as the media, scholarly articles and reviews, also play a crucial role. In this respect, Azar Nafisi's *Reading* Lolita *in Tehran* (2004) is particularly interesting. When Nafisi had the idea of writing a memoir-in-books about her life in Tehran between 1979 and 1997, and in particular a private book club that she conducted with seven of her students, Random House bought the concept for $30,000 in 1999 with the promise of a small print run of only 12,000.[107] However, the events of 9/11 and ensuing war in Iraq, which brought with it a sudden interest in Middle Eastern women's memoirs, reshaped *Reading* Lolita *in Tehran*'s publication so that by the time it reached print, orders from bookstores had surged to over 50,000. When the paperback was released in 2004 it sold over a million copies worldwide and remained on *The New York Times* best seller list for over 70 weeks.[108]

Figure 3.3 Cover image for Azar Nafisi's *Reading* Lolita *in Tehran: A Memoir in Books* (2004).

Peritexts, without a doubt, have played a significant role in the book's success. The cover, depicting two veiled girls bowing their heads reading something (*Lolita* perhaps) beyond our view, immediately places the book in the same category as all the other Middle Eastern women's memoirs that speak of the Muslim woman's veiled silence and oppression. The blurbs on the back intensify this effect for the readers. On the back of the paperback edition, the blurb reads, 'Azar Nafisi's luminous tale offers [. . .] us a rare glimpse, from the inside, of women's lives in revolutionary Iran', followed by praise from Susan Sontag, 'Azar Nafisi's memoir contains important reflections about the ravages of theocracy, about thoughtfulness, and about the ordeals of freedom.' The emphasis on Nafisi's 'rare' insider account of the lives of Iranian women, followed by another successful writer's affirmation of the book as offering 'important reflections' on 'theocracy' and 'ordeals of freedom', according to Catherine Burwell, not only plays on the reader's interest by 'exploiting stereotypes of oppression [. . .] in order to sell the memoir'[109] but more importantly it points to '"preferred" ways of reading and responding to such books'.[110] In this way, the blurb reframes and highlights Nafisi's oppression under the Islamic regime as its dominant theme and frames the reader's interpretation within discourses of American Orientalism, particularly at a time of renewed conflict between the United States and Iran. Thus, Nafisi's voice and her reasons for writing have already been glossed over by the publishers, and preferred modes of reading have been announced, even before the reader has opened the first page of the book.

But in framing how Nafisi's book is received and consumed, epitexts, materials outside the bound volume such as scholarly engagements and critiques, media releases, interviews, analyses and reviews, have played a more important role than the presentation of the volume itself. In the case of *Reading* Lolita *in Tehran*, scholarly essays in particular have been fundamental to the way the book has been framed, received and consumed. When *Reading* Lolita *in Tehran* appeared, it brought with it a huge wave of scholarly essays and critiques – a search for scholarly articles that deal with *Reading* Lolita *in Tehran* reveals hundreds of essays – that have received and interpreted Nafisi's account from various, and sometimes contradictory, perspectives. One of the most recurring arguments by scholars[111] is that the book generalises the position of all Iranian women as static and oppressed, only able to be saved and freed through Western intervention (in this case Western books), conforming thereby to American Orientalist discourse.

Published at the time of the United States' declaration of war on terror, they argue, the book could be seen as providing justification for military intervention in the region for the sake of women's liberation. Roksana Bahramitash, for instance, accuses Nafisi of contributing to Islamophobia, writing that 'Nafisi's selective and partial view of Iran is not innocent but seems to have a particular agenda, namely to contribute to the Islamophobia that already exists in North America.'[112] Hamid Dabashi, a prominent Iranian Professor at Columbia University, makes a personal attack against Nafisi. In his famous essay 'Native Informers and the Making of the American Empire', he compares Nafisi with colonial agents in India and accuses her of being 'the personification of that native informer and colonial agent, polishing her services for an American version of the same project', arguing 'if Edward Said dismantled the edifice of Orientalism, Azar Nafisi is recruited to re-accredit it'.[113] He concludes 'rarely has an Oriental servant of a white-identified, imperial design managed to pack so many services to imperial hubris abroad and racist elitism at home – all in one act'.[114]

Although there is no denying that Nafisi's memoir, not only in its paratexts but also in its content, does tend to take part in a self-orientalisation discourse, that is nothing new if we look at the Western-educated class of Iranian women who have been writing about their experiences in Iran over the last decade. One might say that for critics the great popularity of the book had the effect of emphasising its self-Orientalising qualities. As I will address in depth in the final chapter, Iranian women who have been educated and raised abroad with Western values have a tendency towards self-Orientalisation. This may appear unpleasant and hypocritical, especially when they claim to write to liberate themselves and others, but in this process they appear to be replicating and affirming the position of Iranian women as silent and oppressed. However, what needs to be kept in mind is that despite this tendency, they cannot be so easily marked as personal native informants or agents for a specific cause. Critics who are quick to point fingers at individual allegiances must keep in mind that often these narratives do not have a deliberate intention to pursue a certain discourse; rather, the socio-political context into which they are received can direct their interpretation in certain ways. In fact, if ever they have a chance to break this cycle through their narration, such interpretations are themselves contributing to strengthening preferred modes of reading. These readings eradicate other aspects of these works, certainly overlooking the narratives as personal accounts of healing.

While these modes of reading were very much influenced by a kind of post-911 American Orientalism, one that anchored military attack on the basis of women's issues, things began to shift after 2009 when Iran had a controversial presidential election where voters accused the government of rigging their votes. This led to major national protests, imprisonment and death of thousands. The events of 2009 brought a new angle for approaching diasporic Iranian memoirs. After the events of 2009, we begin to see fewer and fewer memoirs of the Islamic revolution. No longer do we have exotic eyes staring at us from behind the veil. Instead, a glimpse at the recent books by Iranian writers reveals accounts that deal with current protests and issues in Iran. The paratexts that surround these books also frame them within the post-2009 socio-political interest in Iran's condition for a Western audience.

It is these new social concerns, for instance, that have framed Haleh Esfandiari's *My Prison, My Home* (2010) and Roxanna Saberi's *Between Two Worlds* (2010), both of which tell of the two Iranian–American women's imprisonment in Iran. Although both women recount their experiences prior to the 2009 elections, their books are framed in line with the recent interest in Iran after the elections and emphasise a new kind of modern American captivity narrative. Haleh Esfandiari, a prominent scholar working on women's issues in the Middle East, was imprisoned in Tehran in January 2007 while on one of her annual trips to visit her 93-year-old mother. Initially robbed, in what appeared to be a coincidental roadside mugging on her way to the airport during which all her travel documents were stolen, Esfandiari soon finds herself involved with charges of leading a 'velvet revolution' and 'threat against the government'. Eventually the 67-year-old who had lived in the United States with her husband since the late 1970s is taken to Evin and put in solitary confinement for over three months, where she is questioned regularly in relation to the Wilson Cultural Centre for which she worked in the United States as the director of its Middle East section. Although she was almost incommunicado while in custody, news of her captivity in Iran travelled far and wide through her husband, also a prominent scholar of Middle East affairs. Soon her case became one of the biggest news headlines in the United States, with constant media coverage worldwide. The verbal and visual discourse that surrounded her captivity in the media replicated that of the earlier Iranian hostage crisis for American audiences as reporters, writers and analysts around the world drew direct allusions to the 30-year-old event. Esfandiari's own husband, Shaul Baksh, was among those who contributed to this comparison as he published an op-ed piece in the *New York Times*, entitled 'Our Family Hostage Crisis'.[115] Other media outlets, too, picked up this rhetoric, many emphasising Esfandiari's American nationality. CNN, for instance, ran a series of articles on their website, with titles such as 'Detained American Appears to Confess on State TV' and 'Iran Releases American after Mother Posts Bail'. Similarly the *Washington Post* published an article in which Esfandiari was identified as an American scholar from Potomac, only briefly mentioning her dual nationality. The BBC too published an article entitled 'Bush Urges Iran to Free American'.

Throughout the saga of an American woman caught in the brutal forces of Islamic extremism, there was also an emphasis on Esfandiari as a frail American woman, in the claws of an inhumane system. Every mention of her in the media, without fail, points to her as a 67-year-old grandmother of two. *Timesonline* reporter Christina Lamb, for instance writes, 'It is hard to imagine how anyone could have thought this 67-year-old grandmother visiting her frail 93-year-old mother in Tehran was a threat. But to the Iranian authorities she was the key figure in an American plot to bring down the regime.'[116] In a photo essay after her release, the *Washington Post* emphasised her sense of family values and domesticity as it captured her in reunion with her family as a loving American grandmother unwrapping Christmas presents with her granddaughters, and in another, lovingly looking into her daughter's eyes as they hug.[117]

Two years later a similar story unfurled when Roxanna Saberi, a freelance journalist working on a book in Iran, was arrested on charges of espionage in 2009. This time, however, instead of an aging grandmother, it was a 31-year-old 'American journalist of Iranian and Japanese descent', a former American beauty queen from Fargo, North Dakota, who was captured. Soon after her arrest, pictures of Saberi in her bathing suit competition popped up all over the internet in contrast to images of her chador-clad with camera in hand in Iran. Once again headlines attracted audiences by reference to an American journalist's captivity in Iran. Titles such as 'The Roxanna Saberi Hostage Crisis: Day Eight and Counting', became common Google return hits for 'Roxanna Saberi'. A similar series of events occurred for her as for Esfandiari. Once more, petitions were signed, web pages were made, politicians intervened and Saberi was eventually released.

Although both women's capture occurred prior to the controversial 2009 presidential elections in Iran, their books were released after the world had already encountered brutal videos and accounts of the post-election protests, and one could clearly see this change in the way the books were framed. By then, it was the Iranian government's human rights violations against its people that were making headlines around the world, and Evin prison had become as well-known as Abu Ghraib. There was a clear shift in the political atmosphere and world interest in Iran. Instead of interest in the silences of Iranian women who had now been seen fighting side by side with the men in opposition groups, the world became interested in Iran's human rights violations. When Esfandiari and Saberi's books came out 2010, they too were framed to reflect this renewed media interest as they promised to bring insider accounts of the condition of prisons and Iran's struggles for freedom. The blurb on the back of Saberi's audiobook for instance, reads:

> Now Saberi breaks her silence to share the full account of her ordeal, describing in vivid detail the methods that Iranian hard-liners are using to try to intimidate and control many of the country's people. *Between Two Worlds* is also a deeply revealing account of this tumultuous country and the ongoing struggle for freedom that is being fought inside Evin Prison and on the streets of Iran.

The blurb attracts a curious audience to a personal story, an insider account, one that can expose and bring to light what is going on in Evin. But at the same time, it promises an insight into the political situation of this 'tumultuous country'. This statement is immediately followed by praise from Shirin Ebadi, the Iranian Nobel Peace Prize winner, an expert on human rights violations in Iran, as she declares, '*Between Two Worlds* is an extraordinary story of how an innocent young woman got caught up in the current of political events and met individuals whose stories vividly depict human rights violations in Iran.' Ebadi's statement heightens the rhetoric of the captivity narrative, as it highlights Saberi as a young innocent woman, caught in an unforgiving political situation. Once again, by emphasising its vivid depiction of human rights violations, it is directed toward readers who wish to understand more about the situation.

Reviews and praises for Haleh Esfandiari's book also frame the book in a similar fashion on her website.[118] Lisa Bonso of the *Washington Post,* for example, writes, the book 'goes well beyond the headlines by deftly weaving personal narrative with a political history of modern Iran'. 'Experts' such as Madeline Albright, write, 'from the threads of history and personal experience, Haleh Esfandiari has woven a masterful memoir. *My Prison, My Home* is an intimate tale of bravery in the face of ignorance set against the larger tragedy of U.S.–Iran relations. Esfandiari's story – timely, suspenseful and artfully told – will fascinate experts and general readers alike.' The emphasis on Esfandiari's personal account, told in parallel to the larger political context of United States–Iran relations, places the book within a current context that is of interest for readers: not only does it promise to unravel the life of an Iranian (American) woman, but it does so in light of the recent conflicts.

Interest in post-election Iran has brought more than a new discursive frame within which diasporic Iranian women's memoirs are received. It has also brought with it newly found interest in Iranian men's narratives to the point that in the last few years Iranian men have published three well-received memoirs. The prominent Iranian journalist Houshang Asadi, for instance, published his memoir *Letters to my Torturer: Love, Revolution, and Imprisonment in Iran* in 2010, recounting his ordeal with the Iranian regimes over several decades. Similarly, Arash Hejazi, the man who tried to save the life of the famous protestor Neda Agha Soltan who was shot dead on the streets of Tehran during the post-election protests in 2009, published his memoir *The Gaze of the Gazelle* in late 2011. Reza Kahlili published his thriller spy memoir, *A Time to Betray,* in 2010.

Given the increased popularity of Iranian men's memoirs, here I want to pay special attention to paratexts that frame diasporic Iranian men's memoirs through an analysis of Reza Kahlili's *A Time To Betray: The Astonishing Double Life of a CIA Agent Inside the Revolutionary Guards of Iran.* I believe this clearly demonstrates the shifting framework in which memoirs and narratives from Iran have been constructed, received and consumed in recent years.

Figure 3.4 Cover image for Reza Kahlili's *A Time to Betray: The Astonishing Double Life of a CIA Agent inside the Revolutionary Guards of Iran* (2010).

Using Reza Kahlili as a pseudonym to avoid recognition by both the Iranian agencies and the CIA, the narrator of *A Time to Betray* tells of his life as a CIA operative inside the Iranian Revolutionary Guards, Iran's notorious secret service responsible for the clampdowns on protestors. The bold cover of this book, unlike any other diasporic Iranian memoir, speaks directly to the urgent interests of the market. The cover has a large image of the then Iranian president Mahmoud Ahmadinejad framed by the Iranian flag above and the United States flag below, and the words A TIME TO BETRAY stamped with large lettering on the Iranian flag. That an image of the most unpopular (in the eyes of both Iranians and the Western world) Iranian president since the Islamic revolution appears as the cover of a popular book is indicative of a major shift in the way these books are produced and marketed. To place Ahmadinejad's gazing image between the Iranian and American flags, positions him as the man who is leading the polarisation of the relationship between the United States and Iran. At the same time, given his unpopularity amongst Iranians following the post-election protests and horrific human rights violations, Ahmadinejad is not only presented as an enemy of the United States, but as also an enemy of his own people. As a representative of the Islamic government, he is the one who is separating Iranian people from living with values, such as freedom of speech and respect for human life, that Western/American society upholds with pride. Thus, Kahlili's book, starting from its very cover, is a challenge to the concept of us/them. As a result of the recent news from Iran, and people's opposition to the regime, a clear distinction has emerged between perceptions of the Iranian government and its people. Unlike at the time of the hostage crisis, when Iranians were collectively viewed as hostage takers, now Iranian people are no longer seen merely as anti-American fanatics. Considering the Iranian government's conflict with the American government, and Iranian people's recent opposition to the Iranian government, then the Iranian population can be seen in a favourable light by Americans, because they appear to be fighting the same enemy. The blurb on the back of the book also hinges on this dichotomy, as it promises to take us on a man's mission to infiltrate the Iranian government and help overthrow it. The blurb on the dust jacket reads:

> As Reza, a member of the elite Guards, my role was to look and act the part of a devout Muslim enforcing all the new rules laid down

> by the mullahs. A full black beard was a mandatory accessory to the Guards' uniform, and I sported one along with every other member of the Guards. Playing the part of a zealot did not come naturally to me, and there were times I had to do things I dreaded. [. . .] Back in Iran now, I knew that I would have to try and convince myself that doing these things allowed me to maintain my role – and maintaining my role allowed me to contribute to the downfall of the organisation to which I so fervently imitated allegiance.

The framing of Kahlili's book brings to our attention a new kind of captivity and freedom narrative. This is not the captivity of a single man or woman; rather it is the captivity of a nation at the hands of a regime that must be overthrown in order for its people to gain freedom. Indeed, epitexts that surround this book frame it in light of this new form of captivity narrative. In an online interview with Steffan Piper, Kahlili confirms this, telling the interviewer, 'the establishment as a whole must be changed, otherwise the regime will continue what it does best – terrorizing its own people and the rest of the world'.[119] Another reviewer, Joel Rosenberg, reads the book in the same frame on his blog, writing, 'Reza is a man clearly [. . .] on a mission: to liberate the people of Iran from one of the most evil monstrosities of our time, especially before Iran gets nuclear warheads.'[120]

This chapter so far, through examination of examples, has demonstrated how paratexts have influenced the way that Iranian life narratives are produced and consumed in light of socio-political interests. However, what we need to remember is that these paratexts have constructed specific modes of reading and frameworks within which these narratives are received. These frameworks, however, can be limiting and may lead to further silences. Recalling Oliver's argument that 'if recognition is conceived as being conferred on others by the dominant group, then it merely repeats the dynamic of hierarchies',[121] then the framework within which these books are received could be seen as repeating the very oppression that their authors are attempting to dismantle. Produced and received at the juncture of a conflicted relationship between Iran and the United States, these books can easily be framed within a discourse that emphasises the cultural and political differences between Iran and the United States. Thus, they are not only lending themselves to interpretations within existing frames of reading, such as American

Orientalism and captivity narratives, but also forming new ones, as we have seen with regard to books emerging after the 2009 elections.

New modes of reading

Not all writers and critics, however, are oblivious to the kinds of discourses associated with Iranian memoir. Some, for instance, have tried to defy these predefined modes of reading and are more self-conscious in the way their work speaks to the public. Fatemeh Keshavarz, for example, in her memoir *Jasmine and Stars: Reading More than* Lolita *in Tehran* (2007) tries to reframe the position of Iran, starting even from the cover of her book. Instead of using the conventional cover of passive exotic women gazing at the viewer, for instance, her book shows two modern Iranian girls with sunglasses, actively holding up signs, one reading 'We, women want equal rights', and the other, 'violence against women equals violence against humanity'.

This self-consciousness is reflected in the content of her book. She dedicates her entire introduction to explaining the reasons she wrote the book as a critique and response to Azar Nafisi's *Reading* Lolita *in Tehran*, a book she views as New Orientalist. After telling us of the desperation of Western readers to learn anything of the Middle East, through the memoir or autobiographical form, or what she calls 'eye witness narratives', she tells us,

> I have two specific goals. The first is to bring you an in-depth critical understanding of this eyewitness literature, which I dub the New Orientalist narrative. But the second and equally important goal is to provide an alternative approach for learning about an unfamiliar culture.[122]

She argues that she sees New Orientalist narratives such as *Reading* Lolita 'as silencing as its predecessor authored by the nineteenth-century European Orientalists'.[123] Such an account 'does not necessarily support overt colonial ambitions', she argues.

> But it does not hide its clear preference for a western political and cultural takeover. Most importantly, it replicates the totalizing – and

Figure 3.5 Cover image for Fatemeh Keshavarz's *Jasmine and Stars: Reading More than* Lolita *in Tehran* (2007).

> silencing – tendencies of old Orientalists by virtue of erasing, through unnuanced narration, the complexity and richness of local culture.'[124]

She believes that it is only by breaking down 'polarized visions' offered by New Orientalist narratives that people can really understand what is going on in other parts of the world, behind the political façade and the 'face they make when they are angry'.[125] She hopes for her book to offer a 'glimpse of the ordinary Iran, the one that smiles' with the hope of offering more human understanding between various cultures. Indeed, her entire book, a memoir interwoven with Persian literature, offers rare insightful understanding of her own life, counteracting many assumptions about life in Iran.

Others, too, such as Massoumeh Ebtekar, the spokeswoman for the students who captured the American embassy in 1980, have written memoirs in an attempt to break the stereotypes that surround Iran and Iranians as violent hostage takers. In a memoir called *Takeover in Tehran: The Inside Story of the 1979 U.S. Embassy Capture* (2000), Ebtekar, now one of Iran's leading reformist women, writes about her perspective and the perspective of those who participated in the hostage-taking. Throughout the book she argues that over the years accounts about the hostage crisis have all been from the Western perspective, reflecting 'not a single Iranian viewpoint, not a single Iranian voice'.[126] She goes on to write:

> this book – which breaks that silence for the first time in print – is intended as a long-needed corrective to the stereotypical account of which I speak, and as an antidote to the distorted images conveyed by the world media not only during and immediately after the capture of the embassy, but right up to this day.[127]

Believing that the cultural gap between developed and developing countries 'has grown wider over the last twenty years', with one of the primary sources of this gap being 'the inaccurate or even biased reporting of Western media of events that have captured the imagination of millions in developing countries',[128] she hopes that her memoir will help close that gap by offering a dialogue. She asks:

> Can the misconceptions and misjudgments which have been created by years of conscious disinformation ever be put right, I wondered, as I began the task of sifting through my notes, diaries and memories? Can the American and Iranian peoples ever hope to overcome the barriers of propaganda and fiery rhetoric that now stands between them, and finally come to understand one another? The only way – and this is the ultimate aim of my account of the fateful events of 1979 and 1980 in Tehran – to alleviate tensions between the two nations, is to engage the two diverse and different cultures in a constructive dialogue.[129]

But unfortunately, among all the books that conform to the conventions and are framed within particular frameworks to reflect the ongoing tensions between Iran and America, Ebtekar's memoir went almost unnoticed, receiving almost no attention from the media or reviewers. The lack of adequate acknowledgement of an historical memoir by an Iranian woman that could shed new light and demystify one of the most significant events in recent American and Iranian history, points to the predefinition of the space into which these narratives are received. What this means is that, despite having the freedom to speak of those events, she has effectively remained silent.

While, beyond doubt, the memoir in diaspora has, as Stephen Kaufman believes, provided Iranian women with 'the opportunity to tell their own stories, [by] taking advantage of new freedoms and an increase feeling of comfort in their new societies',[130] it seems that they cannot escape the socio-political predicaments of the diasporic society into which their books are received. As Amireh and Majaj put it in their complaint about the interest in Middle Eastern women's narratives, 'our identities [. . .] served to silence us at a time when we most felt the need to speak'.[131] Considering the complexity of these narratives, perhaps the best way that we can succinctly describe them is, in the words of Whitlock, as 'soft weapons', a term that 'captures the double-edged nature of these forms of life narrative'.[132]

CHAPTER 4

MOTHERS AND DAUGHTERS – WRITING 'BEYOND THE HOMELAND'

One of the fears I faced living abroad by myself was of returning to Iran and finding my childhood home changed or destroyed; or worse still going back home and finding my mother somehow absent. Any changes, alterations, the destruction of my childhood home, or the absence of my mother was, somehow in my mind, linked to a destruction of my sense of identity and belonging. I struggled with this fear for years. Although I did not acknowledge or understand it, this translated itself into creative expression when I wrote a novella that followed a young woman going back to her homeland, in an unknown location, where her mother had passed away and her childhood home had changed beyond recognition. As we follow her, we hear her mother's stories, secrets that the mother had told her only daughter. Although when I wrote this I would have denied any autobiographical connection, or even the hint of any truth to the stories shared between the mother and daughter, it took me years to come to the understanding and acknowledgement that this was a reflection of my fears of loss of a sense of belonging which I had attached so closely to my mother and home.

In reading books by other Iranian writers, I soon realised that the mother–daughter relationship and homeland was a recurring theme in many. Within the body of diasporic Iranian literature in English there are numerous titles about diasporic daughters returning to their home, daughters searching for missing mothers, or daughters working through a conflicted relationship with their mother and their own daughters. In these books the diasporic daughter is usually trying to make sense of her connections to her past and identity. Alongside her struggle, we are usually exposed to generations of secrets shared between mothers and daughters. As I read book after book with a similar theme, it became clear that for many diasporic Iranian writers, as for me, this theme played a significant allegorical role in the way they defined and explored their sense of identity and belonging.

This chapter examines the reasons for and implications of the recurring mother–daughter relationship in diasporic Iranian writing in English. It situates this theme within a historical context and highlights how Iranian writers are breaking down certain literary traditions to transgress silences, foreground oppressed voices and construct new utopian spaces of expression.

There are two recurring forms of transgression, or boundary crossing, in mother–daughter narratives – discursive and physical. On the one hand, there is a tendency for breaking up of identifiable singular narrative forms through polyphonic narration. This overrides dominant, often unified male-constructed narrative forms, allowing for the expression of multiple voices and experiences, and the construction of various identities. On the other hand, mother–daughter stories almost always seem to involve a physical traversal in the form of a journey, which every mother and daughter seems to have to undertake if they are to break free from the socio-political and historical boundaries that had limited their relationship. Sometimes, however, these physical journeys are not easily undertaken, since numerous obstacles prevent the departure of mothers and daughters. Consequently, many such journeys are made possible only by the intervention of some sort of metaphysical force, such as magic and dream elements.

Mothers and daughters in Iranian literary history

'If Iranian women writers, or their many mute foremothers, are to be understood and appreciated more fully, if the true impact of their writing is to be felt', argues Milani, 'then the conditions out of which the literary tradition was born have to be understood.'[1] Iranian literature, through to the second half of the twentieth century, as Milani writes, 'has long possessed a predominantly masculine character'.[2] In this tradition women have been 'conspicuously absent [. . .] as writers or critics, as makers of literary tradition'.[3] As Azar Naficy[4] also observes, Iranian women's lack of presence in the literary tradition stems historically from Iran's 'highly hierarchical and masculine society'.[5] This means that until the mid-twentieth century men authored almost all Iranian literature. When women did appear in these accounts, although they were sometimes active characters, they existed mainly to 'revolve round the male hero'.[6] In this context, in which women were absent as subjects and makers of literary tradition, the mother occupied an ambivalent position. While she played a significant symbolic role in constructing identities of male characters, particularly in relation to notions of home and homeland, she has always been invisible as an autonomous subject of representation, her existence never extending to herself as an independent character in and of herself. She existed as a symbol in relation to male characters for the construction and support of their identity 'without a private, individual self, without "interiority"'.[7]

In her essay 'The Vatan [Homeland] as Beloved and Mother', Afsaneh Najmabadi describes the literary process through which, in Iranian literature, the mother transcended individuality, becoming a symbol of a 'nationalistic discourse representing the homeland as a female body, [. . .] [which was] used to construct a national identity based on male bonding among a nation of brothers'.[8] According to her, the mother, who had always been the reassuring centre of the domestic realm, first came to connote the homeland, 'vatan', in the nostalgic writings of early Islamic writers who travelled the wider Islamic world. These wandering scholars, writers and poets produced a large body of work in which they expressed their exilic sentiments towards their birthplace and homeland, which were 'akin to the grief to the pain from the loss of mother, agony of separation from a protective bosom'.[9] This type of sentimental and nostalgic remembrance of the homeland, according to Najmabadi, 'often expressed through the remembrance of the homeland's scents and scenes, a sensuality of seeing and smelling'[10] proved productive in later nationalistic gendered associations of homeland.

A different association of the mother with the homeland was formulated by Sufi poetry, which considered one's 'vatan' to be 'an allegorical concept that denoted that which existed beyond the material and mundane – the spiritual world, the abode of unification with the divine'.[11] This correlated with the idea of 'vatan' as the mother, where 'the return to earth was also a return to the womb whence one had been born'.[12] From this perspective, the grave and earth could be like the mother's utopian and peaceful womb to which one yearns to return. As Najmabadi explains, 'the Sufi desire to reach the grave and to unite with the divine expressed a desire to return to the mother's womb, to that original state of pure, uncontaminated existence'.[13]

The introduction of nationalism into Iran in the nineteenth century, however, redefined the nostalgic Islamic and allegorical Sufi concept of 'vatan' in territorial and politically defined terms. While, prior to this, Iran considered itself part of an Islamic abode at large, after the encounter with nationalism it began to be defined in terms of nationalistic boundaries under the domain of the political and military rule of the Qajar Dynasty. In this new context, 'vatan' was no longer religiously defined or simply the place of one's birth, but articulated through a 'nationally imagined community'[14] as a political and physical geo-body with defined boundaries and threats from enemies. This 'vatan' was 'the bounded territory within which the collectivity of national brothers resided'.[15] Thus, in its vulnerability to foreign invasions, the homeland came to be 'envisaged as the outlines of a female body: a body to love and be devoted to, to possess and protect, to kill and die for',[16] the body of a beloved mother.

In short, the mother's symbolic existence gradually transformed into a source of belonging for male writers and characters on different levels. Early Islamic writings formulated the mother as the nostalgic symbol for the home, through which male travellers and writers could maintain their sense of belonging. Later, Sufi poetry transformed the mother into a spiritual symbol. Finally, with the articulation of nationalistic discourses, the mother was transformed into a nationalistic symbol, a physical geo-body, defining identity in relation to a nation of brothers[17] in which she became an 'icon of national values, or idealized custodian of tradition'.[18]

However, despite forming a major part of the literary discourse that had created and sustained a collective sense of male belonging, spiritual affinity, and a sense of national identity, the mother as an individual, as both a writer and a character, had always been absent in Iranian literature. Iranian mothers who were, like African and Caribbean mothers described by Susheila Nasta, defined as 'powerful symbolic forces, repositories of culture and creativity', and who formulated and defined male identity, 'were essentially silent and silenced by the structures surrounding them'.[19]

While the mother at least enjoyed this symbolic presence, the daughter, and women belonging to minority groups such as Jews, have been almost completely absent, not only from the Iranian literary scene, but also throughout the discourse of Iranian history. The traditions of the Jews living in the Middle East developed in the context of a Muslim society, and this influenced their outlook on the world. In Iran, strict gender segregation and lack of women's presence in public also impacted on the position of Jewish women as mothers, daughters and wives. However, Jewish Iranian mothers were doubly marginalised due to their social status. Already living on the fringes of Iranian society, their position was affected by the onset of nationalistic sentiments and religious devotion. As Eliz Sansarian observes, in Iran 'nationalism [...] turned into an intense anti-other diatribe and religious devotion [...] moved to bigotry'.[20] These women, to use Boehmer's words, were 'doubly or triply marginalized [...] [as] they were disadvantaged on the grounds not only of gender but also of race, social class [...] religion and caste'.[21] Needless to say, in this environment, Iranian Jewish women have had no presence in Iranian literary history. Their absence has left a deep gap in the Iranian literary tradition, as Farideh Goldin, a Jewish Iranian novelist explores in her essay 'The Ghost of Our Mothers'. When Goldin, as an avid reader, decides to compile a list of such women in Iranian literary history, her search leads her to a 'complete vacuum of literary tradition for Iranian Jewish women'.[22]

It is in response to this literary vacuum, silences and symbolic representations that many diasporic Iranian writers are engaging with the mother–daughter and homeland theme. In their various responses one can see a parallel between their work and post-colonial theories that go right back to the singularity of narrative and voice in a dominant tradition. Particularly relevant here is Homi Bhahba's definition of post-colonialism as the realm of the 'beyond', where the beyond 'is neither a new horizon, nor a leaving behind of the past', but rather it is a movement in 'transit where space and time cross to produce complex figures of difference and identity, past and present, inside and outside, inclusion and exclusion'.[23] In this movement there is 'a sense of disorientation, a disturbance of direction, in the "beyond": an exploratory, restless movement'.[24] As he puts it:

> it is the move away from the singularities of 'class' or 'gender' as primary conceptual and organizational categories, [that] has resulted

> in an awareness of the subject positions – of race, gender, generation, institutional location, geopolitical locale, sexual orientation – that inhabit any claim to identity in the modern world.[25]

But for Bhabha to move beyond these singularities, there is a need to think 'beyond narratives of originary and initial subjectivities and to focus on those moments or processes that are produced in the articulation of cultural differences'.[26] He writes 'these "in-between" spaces provide the terrain for elaborating strategies of selfhood – singular or communal – that initiate new signs of identity, and innovative sites of collaboration, and contestation, in the act of defining the idea of society itself.'[27]

Elleke Boehmer contextualises this particularly to post-colonial women's responses in literature. She puts forth some strategies that post-colonial women writers employ to write beyond dominant unifying modes of representation, which include an insistence on the representation of the 'diversity and layeredness of women's experiences, and on the validity of forms of self-expression'.[28] For these women 'social determinants of class, race, national affiliation, religion, and ethnicity, [. . .] necessarily cut across and made more problematic a politics of identity based on gender'.[29] Consequently, in their writing these women often 'demanded a different complexity', which reflected their unique experiences, encapsulating a 'mosaic or composite quality: the intermingling of forms derived from indigenous, nationalist, and European literary traditions'.[30] In this tradition there is great emphasis on 'the need for a lively heterogeneity of styles and speaking positions in their work'.[31]

Diasporic Iranian writers, particularly women writers, share this desire for transgression and the expression of the multiplicity of their untold experiences as mothers and daughters. One of the major ways through which they are breaking down limitations has been, like post-colonial writers, through transgression of dominant singular forms of narration and expression. For them this has translated itself into resistance to the dominant forms and narratives that had formulated their identities. Through this resistance, they also aim to 'bring to the fore the specific textures of their own experience' by 'work[ing] against the unifying viewpoint [. . .] typical of [. . .] nationalist male writers'.[32] In this process they are aware of 'the need for a lively heterogeneity of styles', which can accommodate and 'retrieve suppressed oral traditions, half-forgotten histories, unrecorded private languages, moments of understated or unrecognized women's resistance'.[33] However, frequently this expression is not solely about the experiences of mothers and daughters in Iran, it is also inclusive of the often untold experiences of diasporic Iranian women as mothers and daughters, and the damage that migration may entail to the mother–daughter relationship. In foregrounding the mother and daughter's voices and experiences, one of the strategies that they have employed has been a kind of polyphonic narrative form.

Polyphonic narration

If we look at a range of narratives by diasporic Iranian writers in English with a strong mother–daughter theme, we discover many stories that are told from multiple Iranian mothers' and/or daughters' perspectives. In Firoozeh Kashani-Sabet's *Martyrdom Street* (2010), for instance, we hear the voices of three women: Nasrin a young exilic woman in New York; Fatemeh, her mother who lives in Iran; and Yasaman, Nasrin's best friend, who also lives in New York. Told in a mosaic form, the narrative jumps from one woman's story to the next, giving all an equal chance to tell their stories. Similarly in Farnoosh Moshiri's *Against Gravity* (2005), we hear the touching story of a young exilic mother, Roya, and her young daughter, Tala, as they try to navigate their way in their new environment, working through exilic pressures that affect their relationship.

In these books each woman speaks, and tells of tales never before told, because the multiple narrative form gives them the ability to do so. Multiplicity of narratives, this 'cross-hatched, fragmented, and choric'[34] style of writing that enables each woman to speak, is one of the most significant techniques in post-colonial resistance against unifying modes of narration. For a marginalised group of people, such as Iranian mothers and daughters whose voices have been suppressed throughout Iranian literary history, a polyphonic form of narration can be very empowering.

Polyphonic narration allows for marginalised women's voices to be brought forth and heard, and their experiences recognised. This recognition has psychological impacts that can contribute to the ability of those who had been silenced to reconstitute their damaged sense of identity. Returning once again to Kelly Oliver's argument, 'subordination, oppression, and subjectification' damage and distort one's sense of identity and selfhood as they 'affect a person at the level of her subjectivity, her sense of herself as a subject and agent'.[35] Iranian women as mothers and daughters, particularly those from minority backgrounds, had been subordinated by years and layers of social and cultural oppression. This, as Oliver argues, has the ability to 'render individuals or groups of people as other by objectifying them, [and] objectification undermines subjectivity [since] objects are not subjects'.[36] It is this objectification that has historically led Iranian mothers and daughters to silence. To counter this process, Oliver believes subjectivity can be regained and identities reformed 'by taking up a position as speaking subjects'.[37] She defines a speaking subject 'by virtue of address-ability and response-ability', or their 'ability to respond to, and address others', in a dialogical manner, an action which she believes is 'the root of subjectivity which is damaged by the objectifying operations of oppression and subordination'.[38] A polyphonic narrative, which gives many a chance for self-expression, can allow speakers to become response-able and address-able subjects, a process through which they can regain their sense of damaged subjectivity.

However, while in most books by diasporic Iranian women, mothers and daughters begin their stories willingly and thus become response-able and address-able by virtue of sharing their stories, in some cases it is the structure of the novel that forces them into becoming speaking subjects. In *Moonlight on the Avenue of Faith* (2000) (from here on referred to as *Moonlight)*, for instance, Gina Nahai, a Jewish Iranian–American writer, forces the oppressed Jewish Iranian mothers and daughters into much needed response-ability and address-ability through the polyphonic form of the novel. Although the main plot revolves around Lili as she tries to find her mother, Roxanna, who had opened wings and flown away from their house in Tehran, *Moonlight* is a novel that spans generations of conflict between Jewish Iranian mothers and daughters as it follows them from the ghettos of Tehran into eventual exile. Throughout *Moonlight* we witness the unfolding of an historically damaged mother–daughter relationship, and its inherent reconstruction, for the mother and daughter as individuals and for their relationship, through the polyphonic narrative form.

The mother–daughter relationship in *Moonlight* begins as historically extremely negative, full of fear and paralysis. In explaining the nature of this relationship, Luce Irigaray's essay 'And the One doesn't Stir without the Other' is useful in that she describes this relationship as paralysing, as one in which the mother and daughter are bound together, their voices inseparable. Although beginning with the daughter's voice, the essay soon yields to a multivocality in which the mother and daughter's voices become indistinguishable, reflecting their inseparability. But this inseparability is limiting, for neither can ascertain their individuality. For the mother and daughter to establish themselves as individuals, they must break free from each other. But separation is not easy. Irigaray writes from an ambiguous position that could be the mother and/or the daughter: 'And if I leave, you lost the reflection of life, of your life. And if I remain, am I not the guarantor of your death?'[39] Here, the mother and daughter's roles are reciprocal. Neither has the power to change it yet both are its agents. But as the essay ends, there is a sense of hope, a kind of rebirth, that allows both to break free from the paralysis and reinvent themselves by breaking down barriers of silence. 'This breach of silence where we constantly reenvelope ourselves in order to be reborn. Where we come to relearn ourselves and each other, in order to become women, mothers, again and again.'[40]

The nightmarish paralysing repetition of the mother–daughter relationship, like Irigaray's, looms over *Moonlight* from its early pages. For mothers and daughters in *Moonlight* this paralysis is rooted in a patriarchal history. As the novel begins, Lili has just found her mother, Roxanna, after 13 years. But instead of being joyful, she holds bitter resentment towards her for abandoning her, and refuses to utter a word to her. Roxanna, too, does not have the physical ability or the desire to speak to her daughter. But what Lili does not know is that through this resentment and inability to speak she is unwittingly perpetuating the oppressive matrilineal cycle that is rooted back in their foremother's attempt to break free from the patriarchal Jewish society which had, as we learn, all begun with the rabbi's wife in the year 1800. To set an example for the community, the rabbi had forced his wife to stay covered at all times, even indoors. He had forbidden her to speak, even among her daughters lest strangers hear her voice. The community, who had only seen her completely veiled in black, had given her the nickname 'the Crow'. One day on Yom Kippur, the holiest day in the Jewish calendar, when everyone had been outside praying, the Crow appears naked from her house. With a white shining body and glistening hair she sings songs that only lower caste women would sing and circles among the participants. As everyone watches in awe, she walks out of the city gate, never to be seen or heard of again. It had been her sudden madness and very public and naked departure, which 'augured a series of escapes among the female members of the rabbi's offspring',[41] that had led to the destructive matrilineal cycle within the rabbi's family. As the result of their foremother's 'devastating act', within every generation of the rabbi's family, mothers feared their daughters for the shame they might cause by running away. Daughters, too, were paralysed, not only by the fear of being the one to fulfil the role of the runaway, but also of their mothers and motherhood. The need to prevent the shame of having a daughter run away had forced mothers into monstrous acts of torture and even attempted murder. Thus, motherhood – instead of the nurturing potential which would normally would have been the epitome of a woman's life in that culture, a definition of identity – had been transformed into a cursed cycle of madness, 'an invincible determinism' that had trapped 'each succeeding generation of mothers and daughters in a cycle of rejection, self-denial and cruelty as unbreakable as any hereditary curse'.[42] Similarly, the identity of every daughter was formed around this fear, as she was 'raised on stories of her wayward ancestors, many wandering naked and sorry through the deserts of central Iran, where scorpions perished, wanting to return home and beg forgiveness but not being allowed to'.[43] Every girl was suspected of having the potential of running away 'in her blood'. But this unfortunate and shameful lineage was a secret and never discussed openly. It had severely damaged the mother–daughter relationship, until the polyphonic form of the novel forces the mother and daughter to address it openly.

When we first encounter Lili, after she has found her mother, she is oblivious to the destructive cycle of the mother–daughter relationship. Her aunt, Miriam the Moon, knows about it, and is determined to break it. This is why, as soon as Lili expresses her resentment, Miriam interrupts her and begins to tell her Roxanna and their foremothers' stories. However, Miriam's narrative gives way to a myriad of tales and voices that eventually allows both the mother and daughter to become speaking subjects and to heal their conflicted relationship.

This process replicates the oral tradition of women's story telling in Iranian society. As Goldin argues, although Jewish women in Iran historically did not have the education to write about their experiences, they shared their stories orally with other women. She highlights how women's afternoon gatherings were the space where they shared their stories, where they could *dardedel* or have a heart-to-heart talk with each other. She believes that *dardedel* had many functions. One of these was that it provided a therapeutic space in which women could speak about their problems and eventually heal themselves through sharing. She writes, *dardedel* 'worked as a healing tool, as a source of empowerment, as a psychotherapy, and as a Middle Eastern version of a "support group"'.[44] These groups provided a safe space where women could have a voice and speak without fear of consequences.

In *Moonlight*, the polyphony of the narrative operates almost in the tradition of a *dardedel* session. Set in a time when women no longer shared their stories orally, and when dominant male narratives had led to their silence, *Moonlight* replicates this space for women to share their stories through the polyphonic narrative form. It is this form that eventually leads to both the mother and daughter's address-ability and response-ability. By cutting up and responding to Lili's short narrative in the first pages, and demanding that Lili listen to her in order to understand her mother's reasons for running away, Miriam immediately positions the daughter as an address-able character in relation to her mother and foremothers' untold stories. As Miriam begins, and Lili listens in silence, Lili eventually responds, becomes a speaking subject, and her voice becomes integrated with Miriam's narrative. As Miriam's narrative leads into Lili's birth, for the first time her story is interrupted, and we hear Lili's voice in response to Miriam's: 'Like my mother, I would be raised alone. Like Roxanna, I would be despised by my grandmother.'[45] Although Lili's voice is initially sparse, it gradually increases to the point that it becomes one of the dominant voices of the novel.

Similarly, it is the dynamics of this dialogical relationship between Miriam's third person narrative and Lili's dominant first person narrative that forces Roxanna, the mother, into an address-able and thus response-able position. When Miriam begins her tale, Roxanna lies in bed filled with a mysterious fluid that is choking her, unable and refusing to utter a single word, but close enough to hear her sister and daughter's conversation. It is Lili and Miriam's intentional proximity to Roxanna that makes her bear witness to all their foremothers' sorrows. It is this that forces Roxanna into an address-able and thus response-able position.

While throughout the novel Roxanna's story has been told in the third person, near the end of the book her voice comes to the foreground for the first time in response to her daughter and sister's stories:

> 'All the secrets,' Miriam promised Lili last night.
>
> They were talking in the living room, but I could hear them as clearly as if they were standing next to me. Miriam has a high-pitched voice, but she knows how to moderate it, how to be louder or more quiet depending on what she wants me to hear at any given time.
>
> 'I will tell you everything you want to know,' she said, hoping to coax Lili into her scheme, trying also to warn me, I think, that the time to speak is now.[46]

Although not until the very end does Roxanna's actual silence break when she eventually speaks to Lili, it is upon hearing those stories that she feels a sense of responsibility to speak to correct Lili's perceptions. She tells us:

> There is a sorrow within me so deep, I have not been able to give it a name, I want to tell Lili.
>
> It is my mother's sorrow, and her mother's – the tears that they shed in the tear jar, that they drank alone, inconsolable.
>
> I did not want my daughter to have this sorrow. I did not want to leave you those tears.
>
> That is why I left: to take the sorrow out of your eyes.
>
> It is not as if I sacrificed myself to save you. It was not your needs I was thinking of, but my own. More than anything else, more than the need to be with my child [...], more than the instinct simply to live, I wanted to end this sorrow.
>
> I came back and saw that I had lost.[47]

It is this forced address-ability and response-ability that helps both the mother and daughter regain their individual subjectivity. However, the effects of this resonate into the mother–daughter relationship as it establishes a new sense of recognition between mother and daughter, a recognition that breaks the destructive cycle. As Oliver reminds us, a significant part in the process of regaining subjectivity is recognition and being recognised, as 'subjectivity is dialogic because the subject is a response to an address from the other'.[48] Recognition, according to her, occurs only when a 'subject recognizes [. . .] something familiar in that other, for example, when he can see that the other is a person too'[49] through the process of address-ability and response-ability, and visibility. Oliver argues that, as well as speech, vision connects us to the world and other people, and allows people to recognise similarities in the other. It is by this process of recognition of similarities through speech and vision that the destructive and oppressive mother–daughter cycle is broken in *Moonlight.* By making the mother and daughter become response-able and address-able characters through multiplicity of narrative, they also gain the ability to recognise and see the similarities of their experiences in each other. For instance, it is through hearing Lili's perspective and her repetition of a sense of isolation and abandonment that Roxanna recognises her daughter's similarity to herself. Lili narrates her feelings after her mother's departure:

> I had become invisible to myself and to everyone else. I had vanished in the cloud of fear and anxiety that had surrounded me on the flight to America – or maybe before it, on the night Roxanna left, when I called her and she turned around, looked at me, and did not *see* me.[50]

It is the repetition of Lili's horrors of abandonment, together with Miriam's narratives, that remind Roxanna of her own forgotten past and of 'how [her] own mother tried to kill [her]'[51] that triggers a sense of recognition of herself in Lili, so that when she first sees her daughter after 13 years, she tells us:

> I saw her and felt I was looking at myself [. . .] she has the same air of isolation about her that I have always felt, the same sense of being removed and unreachable. With her frail, thin body, without the weight that I have gained, she still looks like an island alone in the infinite sea.[52]

As Roxanna recognises the similarities to herself in her daughter, she remembers how she had tried to break the predicted destructive mother–daughter relationship by rendering her daughter invisible, hoping that in this invisibility, in her lack of recognition of her daughter, the cycle would break. She confesses: 'I tried to make her vanish while I was with her – all those years when I told her I was going to leave and refused to see her, when I thought only of my own need to escape. I made her vanish then'.[53] However, as she recognises resonances of herself in Lili, she realises that instead of closing her eyes on her daughter, she needs to acknowledge her by looking at her. It is only then that she looks into her daughter's eyes, recognises her as an address-able subject, and breaks the bond, freeing her daughter from the impersonal cycle of oppression. She tells us, 'in her eyes I see it now: she has understood me [. . .] Lili has seen the *possibility* of another truth'.[54] Similarly, it is Lili's recognition of the similarity to her own anxious existence in her mother, and the realisation that her mother's departure 'had not been Roxanna's idea but the result of forces that had been in motion for centuries',[55] that allow her to forgive her mother. The novel's conclusion, like Irigaray's essay, is hopeful. It gives a chance for the mother to become a speaking subject; it celebrates the ability and possibility of breaking the cycle of oppression and silence, and offers a renewed mother and daughter relationship. As Roxanna finally tells her daughter when she breaks her silence, 'it is possible to know and, at last, feel at peace'.[56]

While in *Moonlight* we do eventually hear the mother's voice, in some novels the mother's voice is so deeply oppressed that we can only hear her through another character, usually the daughter. In 'Sexual Violence/ Textual Violence', Geetha Ramanathan proposes that in some cultures, such as in Iran, there is an elision between femininity and maternity. Because in this elision femininity or feminine expression is obfuscated by dominant male narratives and male interpretations of femininity, maternal voices and narratives have very low audibility. Ramanathan goes on to describe one strategy that writers employ to 'achieve an oblique articulation' of the mother, a process she names 'transpositioning'. Transpositioning, as she puts it:

> suggests that the power of the maternal in the text is so drastically abbreviated by the narrative structure, (which mimics the master narrative of society in silencing the mother), that the maternal voice, if it is to be heard at all, can only be 'spoken through' since the other does not have the status of a speaking subject.[57]

Ramanathan demonstrates how transpositioning operates by drawing on Manny Shirazi's *Javady Alley* (1984), a novel about the life of a young girl, Homa, in Tehran in the 1950s. Through Homa's first person narrative, we are taken on a journey into the everyday workings, gossips and difficulties of the domestic sphere. We hear stories of the domestic realm and her mother's stories only through Homa, because her mother, who is bound by both her husband and mother-in-law, does not have the ability or agency to speak herself. Ramanathan argues that in *Javady Alley* the mother's subjectivity is asserted through the daughter, but within the bounds of expected social norms that uphold the mother's position. As she puts it, the novel establishes 'the authority of the mother in non-traditional terms without sacrificing a stringent critique of Iranian society's positioning of the mother'.[58]

The weakness of Ramanathan's argument, however, is that although the mother's authority is asserted through the daughter's voice, the narrative is still bound within a patriarchal narrative form in which the mother is, and will remain silent. Indeed, the novel does not provide the mother or the daughter with any opportunity to break away from the silencing patriarchal tradition. It merely highlights the nature of this culture. The novel fails to break free, to offer us alternative perspectives, because of the young girl's narrative voice. Homa is simply too young and too inexperienced, bound too closely to her mother, and too afraid of her father, to be able to break free or offer us any alternatives for understanding the mother's subjectivity.

Gina Nahai replicates a similar troubled mother–daughter narrative in her novel *Caspian Rain* (2007). Told entirely from the perspective of the daughter, Yaas, we hear her mother, Bahar's, story of her troubled past in her marriage and motherhood. However, while Yaas does manage to offer us a perspective on her and her mother's life, her perspective is limited because she too, like Homa, is still too young and bound by the traditions in which she is narrating to break her and her mother's voice free.

Transpositioning really works as a method of reframing the mother's position only when the daughter, through whom the mother is speaking, has herself broken down the boundaries and has the ability to assertively offer us new perspectives. This is why transpositioning operates more effectively in diasporic Iranian daughters' narratives, the narratives of those who have already gone beyond the domestic restrictions of their home and country. If we look at a range of books by diasporic Iranian women writers, particularly the memoirs, we realise that in many there is a kind of transpositioning in which the diasporic daughter is speaking on behalf of her mother's repressed experiences. These mothers are silent, deceased, or simply do not have the ability to recount their own stories. For instance, in Jasmin Darznik's memoir *The Good Daughter* (2011), it is through Jasmin that we hear her mother's account of her first secret marriage because her mother chooses not to speak about it herself. Similarly, in *Things I've Been Silent About* (2010), Nafisi focuses on her relationship with her mother, who has now passed away and who, even if she were alive, would not have had the ability to coherently tell her own story, since in her old age she had lost sight of the boundary between actual and made-up events. In *Even After All This Time* (2005), too, Afschineh Latifi tells us of her mother's sacrifices to raise her and her siblings as a single mother in exile after her father's death. Similarly, in her memoir *Wedding Song* (2004), Farideh Goldin recounts her mother's marriage at a very young age to her father, and her journey as a Jewish Iranian woman in pre-revolutionary Iran.

In effect all these narratives bring forward the mother's silent voice through the daughter's gained ability to speak. Since these daughters themselves are outspoken members of their diasporic society (Darznik is an assistant professor in English literature at Washington and Lee University, Nafisi is a visiting fellow at Johns Hopkins University, and Latifi is a lawyer, while Goldin, too, was brought up in the United States) who have transgressed the social and cultural boundaries of their home country, they can now speak assertively on behalf of their mothers. This also operates in fiction, where only daughters who have separated themselves from their mothers and the home environment can speak on their mother's behalf. In *Moon Daughter* (2013), for example, Zohreh Ghahremani recounts the troubled relationship between mother and daughter, Rana and Yalda. While the first half of the book explores Yalda's birth from an omnipotent perspective, the second half is told from Yalda's perspective after she has lived and been educated in the United States and has returned with her mother to Iran, where she is, for the first time, trying to make sense of and understand her mother's story and her own relationship with her.

This is why the mother–daughter relationship is often explored in the context of a journey. Although polyphony, multiplicity of narrative voices, allows mothers and daughters to regain their subjectivity by becoming speaking subjects, for many this ability cannot be obtained unless they embark on a journey beyond the physical boundaries of spaces that had silenced them in various ways.

The journey

The journey can be understood as a form of transgression, and it is this transgressive journey that enables the mother and daughter to regain their subjectivity and heal the mother–daughter relationship. In explaining the reason why a journey is necessary, Martha Marotta's article 'MotherSpace' is a good starting point. Marotta believes that mothers' identities are framed in relation to the spaces that they inhabit. She argues 'built spaces and discursive spaces that [. . .] mothers inhabit constitute a powerful force that helps shape their subjectivities and their possibilities, define who mothers can be and what they can do at any given point in time'.[59] She believes that the male/female, public/private dichotomies that fix the mother within the domestic space, and which are usually instigated by male members of societies, are 'not only spatial control but also a social control on identity'.[60] One of the aims of this control, she claims, is 'to produce in mothers the desires and preferences, beliefs, and values that prompt them to keep themselves in [that space]'.[61] Any transgression beyond this space, for instance 'when [mothers] leave it or stay away for too long, [entails a risk] of being classified as "bad" mother'.[62] This risk of scrutiny limits the mothers' movement and 'the limits on their movement also limit their identity',[63] both in the way that the mother sees herself and in the way that she is seen by others. The mother cannot see herself, or her relationship with her children, in any other way than within what is defined in that space; her sense of subjectivity and identity, and her relation to others, cannot be asserted any differently as long as she remains inside the limitations of that space. This, Marotta believes, is 'one of the reasons many women have to leave home in order to form their own identities'.[64]

This is why in the works of many diasporic Iranian women writers, the mother and daughter's departure is of utmost importance for those who want to gain a sense of subjectivity and reconstruct the mother–daughter relationship. For mothers and daughters who journey, transgression begins with their very departure. The journey itself is important in this process since it is, as Pauline Dagninio puts it, 'often seen to symbolize the pursuit and achievement of a sense of personal identity'.[65] However, the journey in literature traditionally also 'seems to follow the paradigms of a masculine identity formation'.[66] In Iranian literary tradition in particular, the journey is almost always about a man who embarks on a trip but whose sense of identity is always defined by the mother's stable presence and her symbolism in terms of the homeland to which he belongs and to which he yearns to return.

Taking the particularly masculine form of the journey in Iranian literature, and the physical spaces that had bound the mother's sense of identity within Iranian society, the journey operates on two levels to redefine the mother's sense of identity and reconstruct damaged mother–daughter relationships. On one level it allows mothers and daughters to physically transgress the borders that had defined their sense of identity and relationship. On another level, by adapting the very formula that had hampered the mother's sense of identity, the journey becomes part of what Boehmer identifies as 'subversion by imitation [as] [. . .] an important mode of resistance'[67] in post-colonial discourse. This means that the mother and daughter's journey becomes a vehicle for the reconstruction of the identities of mothers and daughters and their relationship with each other, and carries with it wider connotations that reform traditional modes of expression and male-established ideas of identity and belonging, particularly in relation to the Iranian concept of homeland and nationalistic identity.

In many books by diasporic Iranian writers that deal with the mother–daughter and homeland theme, the mother and/or daughter embark on a physical journey; or by the time they are able to tell their stories, they have already travelled beyond the borders of their homeland. For most, however, departure is not an easy task and requires the breaking of numerous boundaries, including the fear instigated by society in mothers about moving. In *Moonlight*, for instance, while limitations of movement imposed upon women by ancient Jewish laws of virtue and segregation had already determined their sense of identity within the patriarchal domain of the ghetto, their foremother's defiance had highlighted this limitation in the form of a sense of fear of the consequences of movement beyond their defined space. Mothers and daughters had become paralysed with the fear of movement. For them, this fear had multiple roots. First, there was fear that departure or movement carried with it the stigma of being labelled as bad or even mad within the family and ghetto. Then, there was a fear of life outside the ghetto in a society that rejected them as Jews. Consequently, over centuries mothers themselves had defined this space for themselves, and had gradually gained the desire to remain in that state because of the fear and stigma attached to movement. Hence, they could only define their identities and the identities of their daughters within this limited space.

This is why the journey is such a significant step in Roxanna and Lili's story. Roxanna's journey, for instance, gradually breaks through the many layers of oppressions, definitions and fears that had formulated the mother's sense of identity. First, her move away from her mother's house rescues her from her mother's attempted murder and initiates a break in the destructive mother–daughter relationship. Then her departure from the ghetto marks a daring new beginning for a Jewish-Iranian woman outside the ghetto. However, although leaving the ghetto frees Roxanna from the limitations imposed within it, she finds herself trapped within the patriarchal and anti-Semitic systems of Iranian society at large. This new setting not only binds her within the social and traditional contracts of marriage and motherhood – the fear of which she had carried with her from the ghetto – but also rejects her as a Jewish woman. It is only by ultimately journeying beyond the physical boundaries of Iran that Roxanna finds a new space in the United States, in 'the land of choices and chances',[68] where she has the opportunity to start over and reconstruct her own sense of self free from the many layers of limitation.

While this journey offers hopeful possibilities for the mother's sense of identity, it also allows for the psychological reconstruction of the conflicted mother–daughter relationship. In her feminist approach to the stages of the mother–daughter relationship and the daughter's evolution as an individual, Vivien Nice argues that in traditional psychological and psychoanalytical theories of a daughter's development as an individual there is a process called 'separation-individuation' which follows 'on from the symbiotic mother–infant tie, the period of separation of mother and infant and of individual psychological growth for the infant'.[69] According to these theories, this process is essential for the daughter to gain a sense of individual identity. As Nice puts it:

> this process if successfully completed leads to the child's psychological separation from the mother and the beginnings of the autonomous self. The move, then, is from symbiosis to separation, from dependency to autonomy, from identifying with the mother to the establishment of the ego and the beginnings of a separate identity.[70]

If the daughter 'fails to separate' from her mother, she cannot gain a sense of independence, develop her own identity or move away from any traits or beliefs that her mother carries. Nice, however, goes on to argue that although separation of mother and daughter is a necessary step in the child's development, the implications of this theory have been 'distorted' since they have been 'interpreted via psychological theories of development which are steeped in male-defined concepts' wherein 'individuation, separation, independence – the language of the individualized, competitive, hierarchical male – are considered developmentally mature, whereas women's connectedness, mutuality, concern with relationships are seen as developmentally immature'.[71] What this means is that many theories that advocate mother and daughter's separation undermine the necessity of an intimate mother–daughter connection in maintaining a healthy relationship. In fact some feminist theorists of mother–daughter relationship psychology, such as Elaine Savory Fido, believe that 'there is a link between a woman's loss of mother and home and problems with [the daughter's] sense of identity'.[72] As she argues, 'let there be a break in nurturing support [of the mother] [...] and there is a danger of self-rejection or self-doubt which can cripple the confidence and dispose a young woman to risky ventures in order to escape'.[73] What this means is that in order to resolve any conflicted relationship, even the conflict aroused by separation, a reunion and reconnection, outside the boundaries of constrained definitions of the relationship, 'is all important and necessary if both mother and daughter are to feel free to pursue their own lives whilst still maintaining connection with each other'.[74]

Roxanna and Lili's journey, their separation and reunion, can be read from this perspective. In *Moonlight*, mothers and daughters are caught in an inability to separate from each other, preventing the next generation of the daughters to regain their sense of individual identity. But, it has been the socio-historical religious patriarchal authorities of the ghetto that had set up this relationship and instigated a fear of the mother and daughter's separation. Within a highly patriarchal society, what the rabbi's wife's departure had left mothers and daughters in the ghetto had been a sense of ambivalence, a fear of the previously harmonious mother–daughter relationship. It is only since then, when the similarities and connections between mothers and daughters carried with it a sense of negativity and hatred – that every mother and daughter had the potential to be a runaway passed down through the matrilineal link – that a stigma has been attached to the connection between mother and daughter. The irony in this situation lies not only in that the very basis of this desire for separation is the fear of separation, but also in the fact that the patriarchal ideologies that encourage this separation between mothers and daughters to prevent further instances of running away, limit, both physically and discursively, the possibility of separation. Thus, torn between the need to separate and the inability to break away, mothers and daughters of the ghetto were bound together in a cycle of fear and oppression.

This is why Roxanna's journey breaks the destructive male-instigated cycle of the mother–daughter relationship, as she separates herself from the society that had dictated that negative relationship. While Roxanna's initial departure, from her mother's house to her neighbour's, constitutes the first break in the cycle by distancing her from her mother, her final flight as a mother from her daughter completes the break. But while separation allows for the mother and daughter to construct their own separate and individual sense of identity, it does not necessarily resolve the conflicted relationship. In fact it leaves both mother and daughter more distraught. Lili, for instance, is traumatised by her mother's sudden departure, and sees it as the main source of the conflict she has with her. Roxanna, too, is guilt-ridden after her departure. In their separation, neither feels a sense of satisfaction or freedom. Rather, like Irigaray's daughter and mother, they yearn to reunite. But for them a healing reunion can only happen when they have both journeyed outside the physical boundaries of the limiting borders of the ghetto, Tehran, and Iran. In this way the novel not only reconstructs the mother–daughter relationship and their damaged identities but it also 'challenge[s] the various patriarchal practices that undermine the mother–daughter connection', and offers us a feminist perspective from which to understand the relationship, in which 'a strong mother–daughter connection [. . .] is what makes possible a strong female self'.[75]

Moonlight, however, operates beyond merely offering alternative perspectives for understanding the mother–daughter relationship. On an allegorical level, the reconstruction of the mother's identity and the renegotiation of the mother–daughter relationship, particularly as they happen outside the physical boundaries of Iran, rewrite the established notions of identity and belonging that the journey theme usually entailed in Iranian literature. As explained, the journey in Iranian literature was a common theme through which male writers would often emphasise a physical, spiritual and nationalistic sense of identity and belonging to the homeland, particularly by centralising the symbolic mother figure. However, the journey in *Moonlight* subverts those connotations, with their emphasis on belonging and identity, by rewriting certain parameters of the traditional journey theme.

In a study on the concept of the journey, Mohamed Hafizi examines 'some of the theoretical and philosophical conventional discourses of travel and displacement'.[76] He argues that 'voyage, in its traditional sense, implies that one leaves a familiar shore to confront the unknown and return back home.'[77] In this kind of journey, what he calls a 'restricted economy of travel', there is an 'apparent closed structure of departure (from home and origin) and arrival (at a destination)'.[78] It is circular, and guarantees or at least anticipates a return to the safety and security of the departed home. The restricted economy of travel, according to Hafizi, is usually teleological in its movement from origin to destination and 'more often than not, as an incarnation of knowledge and light, an unveiling of the secrets of the other'.[79] Adopting Hafizi's proposal, we can argue that early Islamic writers, Sufi poets and nationalist writers, applied this kind of restricted economy of travel in their writing, whereby the hero embarked upon a voluntary journey from a homeland he loved, and anticipated the return to it. Through his travels and encounters with the other, his sense of identity and of belonging to his homeland was strengthened. In this process the symbol of the mother as the home and homeland, as the 'warm bosom', formed a strong part of the shared sense of identity and anticipation of the return home.

However, Iranian writers are constantly challenging the implications of the journey theme by adapting its various elements. In *Moonlight*, for example, the journey as employed by Nahai offers a different set of meanings. While traditional writers were involved in the circular restricted economy of travel, mothers and daughters such as Roxanna and Lili in *Moonlight* are involved in what Hafizi calls the 'general economy of travel', in which the traveller 'departs from a non-origin, whose trajectory is not continuous, ordered or controlled, and whose destination is, what Derrida calls, a *destinerrance*, the being-destined-to-wander'.[80] Roxanna's journey stems from the idea of *destinerrance*. For her, departure is involuntary, a means of escape and survival with an unknown destination. It is through this general economy of travel that the novel questions established notions of identity and belonging that have been denoted traditionally through a restricted economy of travel.

By adapting a general economy of travel, the novel subverts the belief in the safety and security of the home and homeland, particularly one in which the mother's presence plays a significant part and contributes to one's sense of belonging and identity, an idea to which the restricted economy of travel writing adheres. In *Moonlight* the idea of home offers the opposite of this. For Roxanna, and other women in the ghetto, home does not offer any sense of security, safety or identity. On the contrary, it is the insecurity of home that instigates her departure. Her maternal home, with her mother's murderous rage, never provided her any safety or security. The ghetto imprisoned her with a set of rules. Her married home became her second prison, where she was physically locked up, and her country never accepted her, because she was a Jew. Considering that nothing in Roxanna's home or homeland provided her with a sense of safety, security or any sort of psychological or physical belonging, the journey for her does not involve the anticipation of a return as it did for the male hero in traditional narratives. On the contrary, this journey is about breaking repressive cycles by moving forward and away, surviving and not turning back. Unlike what is implied in narratives of the restricted economy of travel, in which return is necessary to strengthen one's sense of identity, here it is only by breaking away that a new sense of identity can be established.

Consequently, new utopian possibilities for notions of identity and belonging are offered. In *Moonlight* the mother and daughter's settlement and reunion in the United States subvert historically ingrained ideas that belonging and identity are necessarily associated with the homeland, and point towards alternative post-national implications of belonging and identity. As Roxanna herself expresses near the end of the novel 'you could love the old country all you want. Sometimes, exile is the best thing that can happen to a people.'[81]

While on a micro level this points to a new found space of belonging for individual oppressed Iranian mothers and daughters, on a macro level, the mother's embrace of these exilic possibilities allegorically offers a sense of hope for the large Jewish Iranian population in Iran and diaspora. To soothe the Jewish-Iranian population, who have endured years of oppression, the novel indicates that one's identity does not necessarily need to be attached to one's birthplace, nor does one have to return to the home country to find a sense of identity. As Tina Jackson, former arts editor of the *Big Issue* writes in the postscript of the novel, it offers the 'chance of a new beginning'[82] in which one can construct one's identity independent of the homeland. Nahai herself comments about the experience of exile that 'there was something about being cut loose [. . .] [which offered] possibilities I wouldn't have dared contemplate as a woman or a Jew back there, that gave me a sense of exhilaration and optimism'.[83]

Moonlight, and other texts that encourage a new beginning, offer readers, particularly those such as members of the Jewish Iranian community who may feel bound, opportunities to be part of imagined and hopeful communities in the future. As Phillip Wegner observes in *Imaginary Communities* with regard to diasporic communities and their literature, such texts are utopian in the way that they construct imagined communities, whereby, despite the fact that 'most of their members will never encounter one other, each believes they all share some deep, transhistorical bond'.[84] This is why such books can have 'political effects, shaping the ways people understand, and as a consequence, act in their worlds'.[85]

However, while writers such as Nahai point towards the necessity of transgression outwards from the physical boundaries of the homeland, and challenge the nationalistic ideas of belonging, particularly in relation to the mother's position, other writers challenge and reframe concepts of identity and belonging by transgressing back inwards to marginalised and forgotten centres of one's deep-seated sense of cultural identity. This is particularly true when a diasporic daughter who has been separated from her mother and who has marginalised her sense of Iranian identity, journeys back to her homeland. In many such cases, the narrative adopts the traditionally male-narrated journey, which symbolises the pursuit of achievement of a sense of personal identity for the male traveller, at the heart of which the symbolic figure of the mother emphasises the traveller's sense of nostalgia, spiritual and national identity. But instead of adhering to its conventions, these new narratives rewrite it from the neglected modern perspective of an Iranian diasporic daughter. These narratives usually subvert traditional male narratives of journey and use it to highlight the experiences of underrepresented daughters. Consequently, they become sites for the contestation of the identity crisis of diasporic Iranian daughters. At the same time, they can be seen as critiquing the situation that has led to the migration of millions of Iranians.

This kind of journey inwards to the forgotten aspects of oneself is best reflected in Nahid Rachlin's *Foreigner* (1979). As the novel begins, Feri, an Iranian–American woman, returns to Iran after 14 years. During her stay in the United States, she had worked hard to assimilate, consequently forgetting all aspects of her Iranian identity. When she returns to Iran, it is to reconnect to her forgotten roots. However, upon her return, her journey becomes more than a mere reconnection with her culture. Instead it transforms into a search for her missing mother, Banoo, who had suddenly abandoned her family when Feri was a child. Since Banoo had left Feri abruptly as a child, their relationship, like Lili and Roxanna's in *Moonlight*, is conflicted. It had been in response to this disrupted relationship that Feri had escaped and gone into self-imposed exile. As Fido reminds us, often when daughters are faced with the sudden departure of their mothers, they 'might be willing to perform that fundamental act of betrayal, that of loving someone, somewhere else',[86] as they try to seek a substitute for the disrupted connection and love of the mother. Fido argues that it is through the daughter's relationship with her mother, 'the first country that lies outside',[87] that the daughter first discovers her own sense of identity. This is why, she argues, an abandoned daughter may escape and seek

> not only substitute relationship with another woman, an adoptive mother, a substitute, but also an adoptive country, a place where [she] might hope to lose the sense of pain and inadequacy which stems from difficulties in [her] relation with [her] source of self-image.[88]

As Feri herself recalls after her mother had left, 'I ached with memories of my mother'.[89] The home, which had reminded her of her mother in every corner, had become a site of distress and unbelonging. Soon after her mother's departure, Feri, too, had begun to insist on leaving Iran and 'dreamed of escape into a different world'.[90] Her choice to leave had been based on a need to distance herself from the situation and to seek an adoptive substitute for her loss through which she could reconstruct her sense of belonging.

However, according to Fido, the adoptive country breeds what she calls a 'false self', in which the daughter's image of herself is constructed in the eye of the other. Abandoning her 'true' self, Feri had successfully assimilated into the United States, married a blue-eyed American in whose gaze she envisioned herself. But, after many years, when she suspects her husband is having an affair and no longer views her as before, her sense of identity starts to become undone, becoming 'empty of everything'.[91] It is this that ignites in her the desire to return to her homeland and seek her oppressed 'true self'. Upon her return to Iran, however, Feri is caught in what Helena Grice calls a juxtaposition of '*un*belonging alongside the desire for home'.[92] Although she had been filled with a sense of excitement 'in Iran, things had quickly reversed'[93] and instead of a sense of belonging Feri begins to feel anxious, particularly in the absence of her mother. She feels uncomfortable in a house where every object and room reminds her of her mother, and soon realises that she must search for and find her mother if she is to overcome her identity crisis and feel at peace. Thus, the journey of self-discovery transforms into a journey for the discovery of the missing mother.

The mother's physical absence, the daughter's discomfort in her absence and her eventual search for her, rewrites the traditional connotations of the symbolic mother and reconceptualises notions of identity and belonging. Recalling that in traditional Iranian literature the mother functioned as a symbolic figure of the homeland to whose warm bosom travellers returned safely, the absence of Feri's actual mother de-symbolises and de-mythologises the mother figure. Here, the mother is not simply a symbol or a myth who connotes belonging, but rather she has a name, an individuality and a physical presence which is greatly missed. Furthermore, the mother's absence and the daughter's search, contradicts and undermines traditional nationalistic notions of identity and belonging to the homeland. In the beginning of the novel it appears that Feri's sense of unease in the United States was due to her neglect of her Iranian identity combined with distance from her homeland. But upon her return to Iran, where she reconnects with aspects of her Iranian identity, she still feels dissatisfied. This dissatisfaction undermines nationalistic notions of identity, the belief that one's sense of identity is necessarily associated with an external sense of belonging to a politically defined physical nation. Rather, the novel offers an alternative possibility whereby one's sense of belonging and identity is connected to neglected aspects of one's self. For Feri, this lies in reconnection with her mother, who had been 'sealed inside [her] like an illusion too real to discard'.[94] This is why the mother and daughter's reunion, a return and reunion with forgotten aspects of herself, gives Feri a sense of complete belonging and peace. Feri's last words, after she had decided to stay in Iran indefinitely to be near her mother, point to this:

> I stood there for a while, listening, watching my mind filled at the same time with other similar scenes from the past. I suddenly thought of my body as an immense shell, emptying from one side and filling from the other. The stars, the pink flowers on my chador, the knobs on the singer's black hair, the dark eyes of a young man standing in the crowd and smiling at me just then – were all little grains being fed into me. I took them with each breath, slowly...
>
> I turned over and looked at my mother. Her face was so serene in her sleep. I knew soon I would have to make decisions beyond the day, but for the moment I lay there. Tranquil.[95]

There is, however, another way that this novel could be read. If we consider Banoo's role in the traditional sense, the mother as a symbol of the homeland, as Mother Iran, and Feri as her children, then the novel could be seen as a critique of Iranian society at large. Seen from this perspective, Banoo's sudden abandonment of her family could be seen as Iran's abandonment of its own people. As mentioned, there was a strong gendered nationalistic discourse in Iran, with great emphasis on envisioning Iran as 'a female body: a body to love and be devoted to, to possess and protect, to kill and die for'.[96] In this society its male members were strongly involved in the construction of this vision through poetry, prose, and even in the press, during the earlier part of the twentieth century.[97] However, while they were involved in envisioning this body, Mother Iran had abandoned the interests of its people, making alliances with other countries, the result of which was forced secularisation and modernisation, and a general sense of discontent among the population. While prior to the revolution this forceful ideological invasion had left many in a 'crisis of cultural identity and anomie',[98] the Islamic government brought with it new policies that further alienated its people and forced many, like Feri, into exile. Feri's return to Iran and reunion with her mother, consequently, points towards a new possibility of national identity in relation to the homeland: one in which there is separation between the government and certain aspects of one's homeland to which one will always feel a sense of belonging.

Other writers too explore this journey inward to the motherland as a means to come to terms with their disrupted relationships. In *Aria* (2007), Nassim Assefi explores this relationship through a journey that takes her character across the world and eventually to her homeland of Iran. *Aria* follows the story of Jasmin, an Iranian–American woman, who has lost her husband, Justin, when pregnant and then her daughter, Aria, in a tragic car accident in the United States. Told entirely through letters that she writers to her dead daughter, grandmother and husband, and through exchanges with her mother and friend Dot, Jasmin realises that in order for her to come to terms with the tragedy, she needs to travel. Initially she sets out and travels to Mexico and then Tibet, avoiding travelling to Iran where she has disrupted her relationship with her mother when she had, against her mother's will, married Justin. But eventually, like Feri, Jasmin realises that for her to truly come to terms with the tragedy of her daughter's death, she needs to reconnect to her own mother by travelling back to Iran. As the book ends, Jasmin has travelled to Iran, where she reconnects with her mother, and finds a sense of solace not only with her but in coming to terms with her own daughter's death.

Magic and dreams

Sometimes, however, when distance between mother and daughter is too great, due to migration, separation, the mother's sudden departure, or even socio-political restrictions, other kinds of intervention are needed in order for the relationship to heal. In such cases, it is only through other-worldly intervention, modes that offer a break in the realist conventions of expression, that the mother and daughter can journey or speak on each other's behalf. This is why, while in the works discussed above mothers and daughters traverse various formal and physical barriers, whether in gaining the ability to speak or to embark on a journey, in most cases the many thick layers that they have to traverse can only be penetrated with the aid of elements from other realms, such as magic realism and magical dreams. In fact, sometimes the mother and daughter's very survival and reunion depends on the interference of such forces.

In explaining the importance of other-worldly elements, such as magic and dreams, Wendy Faris' 'Scheherazade's Children: Magical Realism and Postmodern Fiction' is extremely informative. Faris defines magic realism as a genre that 'combines realism and the fantastic in such a way that magical elements grow organically out of the reality portrayed'.[99] She goes on to 'invoke Scheherazade's children as its standard bearers because they might be imagined as "replenished" post-modern narrators, born of the often death-charged atmosphere of high modernist fiction, but able some-how to pass beyond it'.[100] According to her, Scheherazade's children are all

> postmodern story tellers [who] may need magic to battle death, a death more depersonalized even than the one their mother faced from King Shariyar; they inherit the literary memory, if not the actual experience, of death camps and totalitarian regimes, as well as the proverbial death of fiction itself.[101]

But Faris argues that, while Scheherazade is 'concerned with epistemological questions, with figuring out how to extend her store of knowledge to stave off her death', her children need strategies for a different, narrative, kind of survival. She believes that although these children have 'come into being as epistemological objects', attached to Scheherazade, if they are to survive, they 'must go forward as subjects, crossing into the ontological domain'.[102] These children must find their own narrative voices; they have to 'contend with their own narrative existence [...] they must invent their fictional identities for themselves'.[103] But as Faris argues, these narrators need to invent ways to surpass the crushing forces of their past, things that realism and male-dominated realist modes of narrative would not let them surpass. This is why, she argues, these narrators need magic to secure their own survival. As she writes, 'the difficulty of that task is perhaps another reason why they need magic to perform it'.[104] Although Faris focuses on Latin American, Caribbean and Indian writing, her argument may be extended to include the new writings of diasporic Iranian writers in English. This is not only because Scheherazade's Persian background and Iranian women's responses today make this parallel relevant but also because many of these mothers and daughters also need magic and elements from other-worlds to help them cross over into the ontological domain as subjects of their own narratives.

In *Moonlight*, for instance, it is Roxanna's magical ability to fly that contributes to her epistemological and ontological survival. Had it not been for her ability to grow wings and fly she would have died as a child at the hands of her own mother who had thrown her off the roof to avoid the shame of having her daughter run away, in which case the destructive mother–daughter cycle would have continued in silence. It is also this ability that allows her to escape her marriage and her own doomed relationship with her daughter, and to transcend the boundaries of Iranian patriarchal society in which, as her husband claims, 'no woman can get beyond a city's borders without her husband's permission'.[105] In the United States, too, it is magic that leads to her eventual reunion with her daughter. As Roxanna settles in the United States her once frail body gradually fills up with over 300 pounds of mysterious liquid, and when doctors are tending to her, her family accidentally discover her and inform Lili. It is only after she is bedridden with this liquid that Roxanna is forced to silently listen and become an address-able and eventually a response-able character, which consequently leads to the reconstruction of the mother–daughter relationship. The liquid, Miriam tells Lili, is made of unreleased sorrow and guilt:

> She's dying of Guilt, you see. Over what she did to you, and to your father before you. She's dying of Sorrow, over the life that she wasted, that she could have fixed but didn't. So much pain bottles up in you, so many tears, and after a while it has nowhere to go, and it begins to kill you. There is a word for it in Farsi: *Degh,* 'to die of Sorrow.' I figure Roxanna never got the chance – gave herself the chance – to go back and ask forgiveness. I figure if she

> did that – with you, at least [. . .] she might release some of those tears and start to recuperate.[106]

After hearing all the stories, followed by a ritual performed by Lili to release the pain, Roxanna begins to shed bucketfuls of tears, releasing the guilt and gaining the ability to speak to her daughter and heal the damaged relationship.

In Rachlin's *Foreigner,* too, it is Feri's magical dreams that allow her to turn inwards to come to terms with her shattered sense of identity and enable transpositioning – the mother speaking through the daughter – to take place. This is not to collapse dreams and magic into one category. Rather, while magic allows characters to break out and away from externally imposed obstacles, such as the patriarchal society in which they live, dreams allow a turning inward from personally imposed limitations. Here, the role of dreams in fiction can be described as

> the gate to the unconscious mind, that unruly territory over which the ego claims something like a colonial jurisdiction, the peripheral, colonized side of the self, [. . .] [that] break into the daytime unitary narration of the self and bring forth other-worlds of hidden possibilities, usually kept under by the conscious mind.[107]

It is through this function of dreams that neglected aspects of the daughter's identity are manifested in *Foreigner*, leading not only to her eventual return to Iran and her reunion with her mother, but also to the foregrounding of the mother's silenced voice.

Although dreams in *Foreigner* appear only briefly, and their significance may even be overlooked within the dominant realistic first-person narration, their importance lies in driving the narrative forward and in helping the inward reflection of characters. The most significant dream in *Foreigner* occurs just after Feri has felt a sense of dissatisfaction with her life in the United States and begins contemplating a return to Iran:

> The plan had begun to form in my mind one late afternoon as I stood behind the picture window of our living room in Lexington, looking out at the grass-covered backyard, actually

> aware of a stillness all around me. The trees, a bird sitting on a branch, the backyards of neighbors, seemed to have gone to sleep or frozen to death. Color had bled out of them. How different this was from that other world, I had thought. Our sun-choked, dust-swept courtyard, the melancholy sunsets and hazy noons. The hum of prayers pouring out of mosques, a child climbing an ancient tree. Uncertainty, a mystery in the air.
>
> That night I had dreamt of Iran, something that I had not done since I married Tony. In the dream I was sitting in the hollowed-out stump of a tree in our courtyard. It was a very clear day and all the flowers and leaves were vividly outlined in the sun. Then the air suddenly changed; a harsh wind began to blow and it quickly turned into a hurricane. Someone was walking towards me in the darkened air, calling my name, asking for help. I jumped out of my enclosure and ran towards the figure whose voice became more and more desperate – a tiny, featureless figure with its hands stretched out, trying to move forward but not able to. As I came closer I could see that the figure was someone very much like me, only she was smaller and younger.
>
> 'Who are you?' I asked.
>
> 'Don't you know me?'
>
> I shook my head.
>
> She began to laugh, trembling all over, her features becoming distorted and frightening. It was as if I were looking at my image in a broken mirror.[108]

Considering dreams as agents that manifest suppressed sides of one's unitary sense of subjectivity, and applying Hermans-Janson and Hermans' distinction between subject and object levels of dream interpretation, this dream can be interpreted as subconsciously featuring the oppressed aspects of Feri's life. According to them, when a dream is interpreted on the level of the subject 'the other people refer to aspects of the dreamer's self [. . .] the coactors are to be interpreted as characteristics of the dreamer'.[109] At this level of interpretation the other figure in the dream can be seen as aspects of Feri herself. Thus the distressed figure who is crying for help could be seen as Feri, who is immobilised and calling out for help to herself. Her inability to recognise herself, coupled with the image of the broken mirror, points to her shattered sense of identity.

However, when interpreted on the object level, 'the other people in the dream refer to characteristics of other people in the dreamer's actual social situation'.[110] Although unrecognisable, the other figure in Feri's dream arguably refers to characteristics of Feri's mother, who, alongside her Iranian side, had also been reduced to 'a dark memory'.[111] Read on the object level, Feri's inability to distinguish herself from her mother reflects a close bond between mother and daughter. Although at this point the mother's 'function remains faceless',[112] the dream establishes a deep sense of connection between mother and daughter, and it this invisible and private connection that finalises the daughter's decision to return to Iran. Furthermore, if we are to believe that the other person in the dream is Feri's mother, then the cry for help can be interpreted as the mother's cry for help to her daughter. Feri's decision to return to Iran after this dream can be interpreted as her response to her mother's cry for help, and a desire for reconnection. It is this internal connection that is maintained throughout the novel with other dreams that leads to transpositioning, where we eventually hear the mother's voice in silence through the daughter. As Feri returns to Iran guided by the dreams, she becomes the mouthpiece for Banoo's experiences, the speaking subject, the missing daughter of Iranian literary tradition, who rescues the Iranian mother from her symbolic and mythical death.

But the use of magic and other-worldly elements such as dreams play another significant role in establishing the position of Iranian mothers and daughters, as well as the position of Iranian writers at large within the arena of world literatures in English. Magic realism, according to Stephen Slemon, 'carries a residuum of resistance towards the imperial centre and to its totalizing systems of generic classification'.[113] This resistance is formed as it focuses on what Theo D'Haen calls the 'ex-centric', by 'speaking from the margins, from a place "other" than "the" or "a" centre',[114] by 'a voluntary act of breaking away from the discourse perceived as central'.[115] In relation to traditional Iranian literature, magic realism, and dreams that operate in a similar manner, act as a kind of resistance towards the realism of the unitary and coherent narrative forms of patriarchal Iranian literature in which mothers and daughters had very little presence. Like Scheharzade's daughters, for these women to survive, they need magic and elements of dreams to breach the boundaries of realist Iranian literature. But more importantly, magic and dreams provide them with a unique discursive space in which diasporic

Iranian women writers can express themselves and their foremothers according to their own needs, as 'subjects, and protagonists of their own reality rather than objects and antagonists in the Father's drama'.[116]

Furthermore, magic realism and other worldly elements operate as a vehicle for foregrounding the Iranian experience within the larger discourse of Western and English literatures. As D'haen argues, magic realism can be a

> way of access to the main body of 'western' literature for authors not sharing in, or not writing from the perspective of, the privileged centers of this literature for reasons of language, class, race, or gender, and yet avoiding epigonism by avoiding the adoption of views of the hegemonic forces together with their discourse.[117]

While in this manner magic realism, according to Faris, 'seems to provide [. . .] a revitalizing force that comes often from the "peripheral" regions of the Western culture – Latin America and the Caribbean, India, [and] Eastern Europe'[118] these writers' appropriation of the magic realist discourse and use of other worldly elements, has not only contributed to a resistance, foregrounding, and recontextualising of the identities of Iranian mothers and daughters. It has also contributed to the centralisation, foregrounding and construction of a new discourse for Anglophone Iranian literature in the same manner that Gabriel Garcia Marquez contributed to Latin American literature and Salman Rushdie to Indian and Pakistani literature.

The engagement with the mother–daughter relationship, against a history of silences in Iranian literary tradition, has enabled the reconstruction of the image of the mother from a symbol to an actual speaking subject, in turn reconstructing the mother–daughter relationship itself. Just as diasporic Iranian writers tap into various elements of traditional Iranian literature to construct a new hopeful space of belonging for themselves, so too diasporic Iranian daughters are drawing on and challenging those literary elements to renegotiate certain deep-seated elements that traditionally defined Iranian nationalistic and diasporic sense of identity. The continuously increasing attention to this theme points to the fact that diasporic Iranian writers, especially second-generation daughters, are aware of the power they possess to reconstruct their mothers' subjectivities and negotiate their own.

CHAPTER 5

IRANIAN MASCULINITIES – 'HYPERVISIBILITY/INVISIBILITY'

In the early 1990s my father was given a post as the manager of a nearly inoperative representative branch of an Iranian bank in Tokyo. Since this post was authorised during the school season, my father decided to travel ahead and prepare everything for our arrival during the summer holidays. Because the bank for which he worked was a governmental bank, it was made clear to us even before our departure that we would be representatives of the Islamic Republic of Iran. This meant abiding by the rules of the republic. For my mother and I this meant wearing the headscarf in all public places, as if we were still in Iran. For my father, this translated into wearing a beard, an unspoken rule agreed by most men with some sort of government-related job. My mother and I followed the rules and continued to wear the scarf in Japan; but my father, who despite having studied at the seminaries of Qom and working for a governmental organisation had never worn a beard, was not about to start.

In Tokyo, our new home was a three-bedroom mansion of an apartment by Japanese standards, decorated with 1970s furniture, which had been in the lease of the bank for 30 years, during 20 years of which the bank had been inoperative and the apartment empty. The owners of this building were a Japanese–Chinese couple named Mr and Mrs Toba. As dedicated occupants of one of their 12 luxury apartments, the Tobas were very kind to us and often invited us for dinners and lunches. Mrs Toba became a good friend of my mother's, and took her places and taught her the ropes of living in Japan. She was very excited by the concept of Iran and often boasted about having Iranian tenants. As a frequent traveller to exotic locations, Mrs Toba was keen to visit Iran, and every time we extended an invitation, she complemented us on our kindness and hospitality. She particularly admired the tall, handsome bachelor-banker with 'romantic eyes' who had occupied the apartment years before us.

About a year and half after our arrival, however, this relationship was permanently damaged when the Japanese cable television showed the film *Not Without My Daughter* (1991). An adaptation of a memoir of the same name by Betty Mahmoody, starring Sally Field, the film tells the story of Betty, an American woman who had married an Iranian doctor in the United States. In 1985, following the revolution and at the height of the Iran–Iraq war, Dr Mahmoody, who had been faced with racial discrimination at work, decides to travel to Iran for two weeks with Betty and their daughter, Mahtob. After much inducement, Betty is persuaded to travel to Iran. It is not, however, what she had imagined. Iran is depicted as a dirty desert of a country, with basic facilities, and 'primitive' customs that she does not understand. Betty wants to return to the United States as soon as possible, but on the day of their return, her husband reveals that he has been fired from his job in the United States and that he has decided to stay in Iran indefinitely. It appears that he had known this all along, even before swearing on the Quran and promising a two-week return. As Betty protests, Mahmoody, led on by others in his family, becomes violent and abusive. When she attempts to run away to seek help at the US consulate, he separates her from Mahtob, imprisons her in an abandoned house and brings her only water and food; when she decides to 'behave' and is let into the family again, he has his family monitor her every move. But Betty manages to sneak out occasionally and meets some people who are willing to help her escape. After months of abuse and mistreatment, with help from those she met, Betty and Mahtob eventually escape through dangerous mountains into Turkey, where they seek refuge at the US consulate and find their way back to the United States.

The film, which we found a grotesque and culturally inaccurate representation of Iran and Iranian culture, offended and appalled us. Shown at the height of Western conflict with Iran, it also single-handedly changed the dynamics of our relationship with the Tobas. After the film, Mrs Toba, who had usually kept in touch with my father, calling him in the office to make sure that everything was well, did not contact him for several months. It was as if she chose not to see my father anymore. When she would bump into him in the elevator, it would be an awkward encounter, an uneasy and casual hello, the greeting of someone confused, fearful, and whose trust, like Betty's, had been betrayed. It felt as if somehow my father had become invisible as an individual but visible in relation to the type of man depicted in the film. During this time, however, Mrs Toba became more of an ally to my mother. She would take her to places more often, and soon the conversation would turn towards the situation in Iran. Although my mother had always felt Mrs Toba's discomfort with us wearing the scarf, after the film, she could sense her unease even more. She would tell my mother that no one would be in this restaurant, shopping centre, little spa town, that she took her to and that it would be okay for her to take off her scarf. And by 'no one' she meant my father. She felt that it was he who had been forcing us to wear the scarf, and once or twice she had even asked outright if that was the case. My mother was clearly offended every time, as she effusively narrated the conversation for us later in the day. In her broken English, however, she could not explain the complexity of Iranian society to Mrs Toba, but she always made sure that she realised that my father was not the one forcing us to wear the scarf. Despite all this, Mrs Toba did not recover from the shock of the film, was never again fully comfortable with my father, and never again during the three more years that we were her tenants did she express interest in travelling to Iran.

The way our relationship with the Tobas was affected as the result of this film is only a small but tangible example of the effect of this representation. I can argue with assurance that Mahmoody's representation, particularly in the book, has had a huge effect on the way Iranian culture, and particularly Iranian men, are perceived today in the West. Mahmoody's memoir (1987), nominated for a Pulitzer in the year of its publication, has been one of the most successful bestsellers of the genre. According to the website of Dr Mahmoody's literary agent, Andrew Lownie, up to 2010 the book had sold 11 million copies, and had been translated into numerous languages. Even to date, it is still listed as one of the top 100 books sold by major bookstores, alongside other classics such as *Catcher in the Rye* and *Sense and Sensibility.* Betty herself went on to become a spokeswoman on issues about women's situation in the Middle East, and was given an honorary doctorate from Alma College in Chicago.

I linger on Mahmoody's book and subsequent film because I witnessed first hand how it contributed to the transformation of Iranian masculinity. Looking back at the situation after 20 years, I cannot help but see how it Orientalised my father. My father, who was once a beloved friend of the Tobas, suddenly became hypervisible as a type, and invisible as an individual. His identity became synonymous with a kind of primitive masculinity, the kind of Orientalist generalisations that the film and the book constructed of Iranian men. The impression that *Not Without My Daughter* left on Mrs Toba, and her subsequent treatment of my father, was far from unique. In 'Displaced Masculinities', Shahram Khosravi blames this book for the way Iranian men have been perceived in the last 20 years. As he writes, 'the construction of Iranian men's "primitive masculinity" started in the late 1980s. The most conspicuous and influential mediawork operation has undoubtedly been *Not Without My Daughter* [...][which] has created a widespread stereotype of the Iranian man.'[1] But this portrayal of Iranian masculinity dates further back in history, to early encounters of the West with the Middle East. In fact, Iranian men in the West, both historically as subjects of the Western imagination and more recently as members of the Western populus, have been subjected to ambivalent representations. For years we had witnessed this ambivalence in Western representations, whether in films or books, in which the Middle Eastern man was either the main antagonist or a simplified one-dimensional character constructed to fulfil an expected role.

However, the ambivalence of Iranian masculinity has not only been constructed by Western representations. Ironically, many books by Iranian women writers in English replicate a stereotypical Orientalist depiction of Iranian men similar to that in *Not Without My Daughter.* In many, Iranian men are depicted hypervisibly, as negative, violent fanatics, sexually deviant, or, worse still, rendered almost invisible. This has extended to their presence as authors in English. A close look at the body of diasporic Iranian literature in English reveals the near invisibility of Iranian men's voices within the larger framework of diasporic Iranian writing in English and the recent scholarship that surrounds it. For example, Betty Mahmoody's husband, who had been so blatantly demonised by Betty, tried to defend himself in the form of a memoir entitled *Lost Without My Daughter.* But the memoir, which was to be published in 2010, was not listed anywhere except on the website of the Andrew Lownie Literary Agency, which was representing Dr Mahmoody. When I enquired about the book, there was a short reply, 'Not yet published'. But before the book could be published, Dr Mahmoody passed away in Tehran in August 2009 at the age of 70 due to a kidney problem, never having told his side of the story publicly.[2]

However, while Dr Mahmoody's silence is due to the fact that his account was never published before his death, those who have been published suffer an equally silent presence. While Iranian women's fiction and memoirs have received significant attention from publishers, readers and reviewers, Iranian men's narratives have been pushed into the background. Indeed, Iranian men's publications in English have been so low-profile that one would think that there have hardly been any such books in recent decades. It is surprising to discover that post-revolution to date, Iranian men have published over 65 memoirs and fiction in English. Yet, while many books by Iranian women have become part of the popular English literarily discourse, the same applies to very few of the men's accounts. Furthermore, while Iranian women's narratives have attracted much scholarly attention, only a small number of reviews and essays engage with works written by Iranian men.

In this context, this chapter highlights the representation of Iranian masculinities and Iranian men's writing in English within the broader context of diasporic Iranian writing in English. However, since until recently most of our perception about Iranian men and masculinity have been constructed primarily through the stream of narratives by diasporic Iranian women writers, it's necessary first to consider how Iranian masculinity has been represented within this framework in relation to feminist discourse. It has been Iranian women's narratives, usually filtered through a critique of patriarchy and/or Orientalist feminist discourses, coupled with Iranian women's tendency to self-Orientalise in their literature, that have contributed to Iranian men's hypervisibility/invisibility in diasporic Iranian literature in English. The increasing popularity of diasporic Iranian men's narratives, particularly after the events of 2009, could be read as a psychological response, as a means for the reconstruction of Iranian masculine subjectivities and individual identities.

Iranian men's hypervisibility/invisibility and Iranian women's self-Orientalisation

The current hypervisibility/invisibility of Iranian men is nothing new. It has a long history that can be traced back to the legacy of the Orientalist discourses that historically describe Middle Eastern Muslim men as autocrats who lock up women, 'oversexed degenerates', as Said puts it in *Orientalism*, 'capable of cleverly devious intrigues, but essentially sadistic, treacherous [and] low'.[3] In light of these representations, discourses around Middle Eastern masculinity have hardly touched upon other attributes. Instead, representations of the Middle Eastern man have become synonymous with fundamentalism, associated with terror, rage and savagery.

In Iran, the onset of modernisation, and Iran's encounter with the West, which produced 'civilised' Western educated men who encouraged the public presence of women in society in the earlier decades of the twentieth century, enabled certain stereotypical images to shift slightly. However, following the Islamic revolution and the US Embassy hostage crisis in the early 1980s, the negative connotations were renewed and reconfirmed for the Western gaze. As the Western world watched in horror, 'wild-eyed' Iranians[4] shook their fists in the air and sent death messages to the Untied States as they took the representatives of their country hostage, Iranian men regained their position as 'devilish savages of Islam'.[5] As Khosravi argues, this primitive image of Iranian masculinity was based on fundamental Islam and promoted through various media outlets.[6] It was this image, later heightened by the events of 9/11 and the ensuing 'war on terror', that has perpetuated the hypervisibility of Iranian masculinity in the West.

What makes the position of Iranian men even more complicated, however, is that until recently much of the understanding of Iranian masculinity in the West has been constructed through a feminist perspective. As Lahoucine Ouzgane observes, in the last three or four decades, scholarly attention to gender issues in the Middle East and North Africa has been focused almost exclusively on a quest to understand femininity: what is it and how it is made and regulated.'[7] Steeped in an Orientalist vision of the Middle East, which rendered Muslim women as 'victims of religious dogma',[8] oppressed by dominant patriarchal discourses, Middle Eastern women have become subjects of study and recognition in the West. This is why Middle Eastern women's narratives, particularly after 9/11, and in the wake of new conflicts between the Middle East and the West, have been greatly welcomed by readers. Consequently the publishing industry has realised the marketability of these books, and that is why over the last decade, hundreds of titles have been published by and about Middle Eastern women in the West, with a significant proportion of these by and about Iranian women.

The socio-political interest in these books, at a time of political unrest between Iran and the West, has also brought with it particular modes of reading. As we know, and as Elizabeth Fernea puts it, historically 'many articles and books even in this century have been written as though the female half of the Middle East did not exist or, if so, lived in a kind of semi-world of passivity and seclusion, removed from the actual life of their own society'.[9] This has, historically formed a certain belief system about the lives of these women. In *Rethinking Global Sisterhood*, Nima Naghibi outlines the intent of her book as an analysis of 'how particular kinds of (often contradictory) representations of the Persian woman as abject, as repressed, and, paradoxically, as licentious [has] become consolidated as unquestioned "truths" in dominant Western and Iranian feminist discourses'.[10] A seminal text that critiques and outlines the relationship between Western white feminism and 'third world', in this case Iranian, women, Naghibi provides an explanation of how the idea of 'global sisterhood' has functioned in the past and present to benefit Western women at the expense of the Other. Naghibi explores this relationship through an analysis of various texts by Western women about Iranian women, and comments on how these representations have also influenced Iranian feminism and Iranian women's representation of themselves. She positions her argument around the current political situation, and concludes that these texts have great influence on the recent Western declaration of war on the Middle East in the name of liberating its women.

The relationship Naghibi outlines has been influential not only in the way Iranian women are represented but also in how they represent themselves. What has been missing in current analyses of Iranian masculinities is the fact that the relationship between Western feminism and Iranian women has also influenced much of the recent representation of Iranian men both in Iran and abroad. Here I want to extend Naghibi's premise, that 'particular kinds of (often contradictory) representations of the Persian woman as abject, as repressed, and, paradoxically, as licentious become consolidated as unquestioned "truths" in dominant Western and Iranian feminist discourses',[11] and examine how these representations have in turn led to the construction of certain myths about Iranian masculinities.

Although many of these concerns have become visible in recent decades, particularly clearly in the works of diasporic Iranian women writers, the origins of these representations date back to the introduction of concepts of Western modernity, including feminism, to Iran. This can be understood by looking at the history that has led to its evolution. In *Refashioning Iran: Orientalism, Occidentalism and Historiography*, Mohammad Tavakoli-Targhi proposes that much of what forms the modern narrative of Iranian history is influenced by Western and Eurocentric notions of modernity and concepts of 'occidental rationality'. He believes that:

> The universalist claims of European enlightenment has blackmailed non-European modernity and debilitated its historiography by engendering a tradition of historical writing that used a dehistorized and decontextualized 'European rationality' as its scale and referent. Iranian historians and ideologues, like their Indian and Ottoman counterparts, developed a fractured conception of historical time that viewed their contemporary societies ahead of their own time. This conception of historical time parallels the time-distancing devices of European anthropologists who denied *coevalness* to their contemporary non-Western societies. Such a *schizochronic* conception of history informs the nationalist historiography of Iranian modernity, a historiography that assumes the non-contemporaneity of the contemporaneous Iranian and European societies.[12]

In this discourse 'whereas Europeans reconstituted the modern self in relation to their non-Western Others, Asians and Africans [and Middle Easterners] began to redefine their self in relation to Europe, their new significant Other'.[13] At the heart of this definition was a sort of 'binary opposition' influenced heavily by colonial and Orientalist language that defined what constituted modern (Western) and what was not. Although there were a few markers of socio-political differences that clearly distinguished Iranian society from the modernised West, one of the most prominent signs of difference was the condition of Iranian women, particularly their position, status and visibility in society. This difference was clearly marked in how Iranian women dressed, which immediately became a sign of Iran's backwardness not only in the eyes of the West but also from the perspective of certain groups of Western educated Iranian modernists. As Tavakoli-Targhi states, 'for Iranian modernists, viewing European women as educated and cultured, the veil became a symbol of backwardness. Its removal, in their view, was essential to the advancement of Iran and its dissociation from Arab-Islamic culture.'[14] Although these ideas were not entirely welcomed by traditionalist Iranians, they were influential enough to construct a specific class within Iranian society in which women were given new forms of freedom. With new models of modernisation Iranian women had the opportunity of being educated and, though in small numbers and for the first time, they became part of the public sphere. This not only exposed women to alternative concepts of gender relationships, particularly those driven by the newly imported concepts of Western feminism, but also gave them the ability to actively comment and challenge masculine and patriarchal social norms. Even as early as the 1920s, Iranian women began publishing their opinions and views on different aspects of Iranian society, including concepts of veiling and unveiling.[15]

As Nasrin Rahimieh argues 'this conceptualization [. . .] has informed [much of] Iran's understanding of its own history',[16] and one can argue that this is what also informs much of diasporic Iranian women's contemporary writing, especially their views of Iranian gender relations and Iranian masculinity. A glimpse at some diasporic women who have been published over the last three decades reveals a list of names that belong to modern Iranian elite families. Just to name a few, Azar Nafisi, the author of *Reading* Lolita *in Tehran*, is the daughter of one of Tehran's mayors during the Shah's regime; her mother was one of the first women representatives in parliament during the Shah's regime. Nafisi always finds pride in her mother's role, as well as in the fact that her grandmother attended university when other women barely left their homes. Sattareh Farman-Farmaian, the narrator of *Daughter of Persia*, is a Qajar princess with a father who insisted on her daughter's education, even letting her go to the United States as one of the first women to travel outside Iran by herself in the early 1900s, at a time when her friends were being plucked out of middle school to get married. Lily Monadjemi, who wrote *Blood and Carnations* (1993) and, more recently, *A Matter of Survival* (2010), is the descendent of Nasser-Al-Din Shah, one of the Iranian Shahs responsible for Iran's encounter with modernity. Marjan-Satrapi, creator of the *Persepolis* comic series, is a descendent of a Qajar monarch. Davar Ardalan, the author of *My Name is Iran* (2008), is the daughter of Laleh Bakhtiar, one of the most prominent Iranian/American women scholars, and one of the only women who has translated the Quran from a feminist perspective. She traces her family tree back to Fath-Ali-Shah Qajar. Similarly, Shusha Guppy, the author of many books, including *The Blindfold Horse* (1988), also a songwriter, singer and filmmaker, was the daughter of a famous Iranian theologian who sent her to Paris in 1952 to study oriental languages and philosophy when she was only 17.

Although the above list is not inclusive of all writers with similar background, and excludes women of equal calibre in other areas, such as in sciences, politics, humanitarian work and so forth, as contributors to Western (and Iranian) society, it is inclusive enough to demonstrate that most of what is being written about Iran outside Iran presently is informed by a specific class of Iranian society. This is not to deny or ignore the fact that women of non-aristocratic background, including Marina Nemat, Firoozeh Dumas, Gina Nahai and Susanne Pari, are also contributing to this discourse. However, they too, though not carrying royal blood, by the virtue of living outside Iran and writing in English can be considered to occupy a place within this privileged class of Iranian society, and their contribution will be considered in the same category.

This class difference is highlighted because the social situation, personal experiences, and education of many of these women who are now cultural leaders and representatives of Iranian experiences in diaspora, are very much Westernised or influenced by the Western concept of modernity that was introduced to Iran in the twentieth century and formed a great part of subsequent Iranian history. This influence, however, as Nasrin Rahimieh and Tavakoli-Targhi both argue, is very much steeped in Orientalist notions and dichotomies that were carried across with Western notions of modernity. As Rahimieh argues 'these Orientalist discourses [. . .] underwrite the history of modern Iran'.[17] However, the Islamic revolution, which re-emphasised the

East/West and gender dichotomies, created unresolved contradictions, not only between Iran and the West but also between Iranians themselves. As Said tells us, 'if all told there is an intellectual acquiescence in the images and doctrines of Orientalism, there is also a very powerful reinforcement of this in economic, political, and social exchange: the modern Orient, in short, participates in its own Orientalizing'.[18] This means that Iranians themselves, whether, as government supporters from Iran emphasising the difference between Iran and the West, or as educated diasporic writers writing about the perils of life for Iranians under the Islamic regime, or even defending women's rights, are involved in the politics of what Rahimieh calls 'self-Orientalisation'.

While diasporic writers, particularly women writers, are involved in this process of self-Orientalisation, the impact of this on their representation of Iranian men and forms of masculinity is more subtle. As Naghibi puts it:

> in representing Persian women, [many] draw on what Foucault has called the 'already-said,' or rather the repressed 'never-said' of manifest discourse. The truth of Iranian women's representation as abject, veiled subjects is thus further entrenched by the self-referentiality of the already-said of colonial discourse.[19]

Many Iranian women writers, coming from that privileged and educated class of Iranian society, to some degree identify with this discourse. As Naghibi reminds us:

> the Western woman, modeled on an Enlightenment figure of autonomous subjecthood, contrasts herself in each instance to the Persian woman, represented as the devalued Other against which Western woman consolidates herself. Privileged Iranian women in the nineteenth centuries also participated in the discursive subjugation of their working-class Persian counterparts. By positioning the Persian woman as the embodiment of oppressed womanhood, Western and elite Iranian women represented themselves as epitomical of modernity and progress.[20]

I believe that this still applies today, particularly among diasporic Western-educated women, and this self-Orientalising tendency has a direct influence on how Iranian masculinity is perceived and represented in the West. A survey of both memoirs and fictions by diasporic Iranian women writers reveals that in most cases women are depicted as oppressed and lacking freedom, mostly at the hands of various male members of their society or by patriarchal society at large. Women's dystopia, it seems, has been created by the men in their lives. In these books hardly ever do we come across likeable and rounded male characters or even a loving male/female relationship. More often than not when men are present they are representative of a specific type of masculinity: patriarchs, abusive, sexually deviant or religiously fundamental.

For instance, the controlling patriarchal father figure who can get abusive if pushed to the limit and against whose word no other member of the family dares to speak, keeps reappearing across a range of books. In Nahid Rachlin's memoir *Persian Girls* (2006), for example, Rachlin's father is represented as the all-controlling patriarch who always has the last word. Although Nahid, with her brothers' persuasion, manages to leave for the United States to study, it is her father's decision that leads to her sister Pari's unsuccessful marriage to an abusive man and subsequent divorce. It is also his insistence that leads to Pari's second marriage to a mentally unstable man who puts her in mental institutions because he feels she is the one who is sick. This marriage finally leads her into depression and an eventual mysterious death. Similarly, in Zohreh Ghahremani *Sky of Red Poppies* (2010), Roya's father, a powerful landowner but a secret opium addict, is a fearsome figure who makes sure his children, especially his girls, do as they are told. When Roya's sister disobeys his orders and becomes involved in politics he quickly ships her off to the United States without giving her much choice. In Manny Shirazi's *Javady Alley* (1984) too, we are taken into the lives of Homa and her mother, who live under the constant fear of a verbally and sometime physically abusive father who demands his every need be met instantly.

In Azar Nafisi's *Reading* Lolita *in Tehran* (2004) similar figures keep appearing in different forms in the lives of the seven girls in the book club. All seven girls are living in some sort of fear of their domineering brothers, fathers or other male family members. Nafisi, in fact, introduces each girl in relation to the difficulties she has had with her male family members to get herself to the very first session of the book club. For instance, Sanaz is seen running into Nafisi's house for the first session looking 'harassed, as if she had been running from a stalker or a thief', after her younger brother 'the darling of their parents', who had 'taken to proving his masculinity by spying on her, listening to her phone conversations, driving her car around and monitoring her actions',[21] had dropped her off with disapproval. Another girl, Nassrin, reveals in a conversation with Nafisi how she could finally make it to the book club:

> I mentioned the idea [of attending this book club] very casually to my father, just to test his reaction, and he vehemently disapproved. How did you convince him to let you come? I asked. I lied, she said. You lied? What else can one do with a person who's so dictatorial who won't let his daughter at *this age,* go to an all-female literature class?[22]

Other typical male figures who appear across various books are religious fanatics, sexually deviant or a combination of both. For instance, one of the few male students who Nafisi introduces is a devout religious man named Mr Bahri. In describing him, however, Nafisi paints a very childlike and one-dimensional picture:

> Mr. Bahri, who was at first reluctant to talk in class, began after our meeting to make insightful remarks. He spoke slowly, as if forming his ideas in the process of expressing them, pausing between words and sentences. Sometimes he seemed to me like a child just beginning to walk, testing the ground and discovering unknown potentials within himself. He was also becoming increasingly immersed in politics. He became an active member of the student group supported by the government – the Muslim Students' Association – and more and more often I would find him in the hallways immersed in arguments.[23]

Other religious men who make their appearance in *Reading* Lolita *in Tehran* are sexually abusive. Nassrin, for instance, reveals how her youngest uncle, a devout and pious man, had sexually abused her when she was barely 11. She recounts

> how he used to say that he wanted to keep himself chaste and pure for his future wife and refused friendships with women on that

> count [...]. He used to tutor Nassrin [...] three times a week for over a year. He helped her with Arabic and sometimes with mathematics. During those sessions as they sat side by side at her desk, his hands had wandered over her legs, her whole body, as she repeated the Arabic tenses.[24]

Similarly in *Javady Alley*, young Homa is abused on the shoulders of a trusted clergyman who volunteers to carry her through crowded demonstrations. As they walk through the crowd, he fondles her through her skirt, pretending to keep her steady on his shoulders.

The repression that many of these women face from male family members extends to society at large and into the public domain, particularly after the revolution. In *Reading* Lolita *in Tehran*, for example, Iranian society is depicted as highly oppressive. It is controlled by fanatically religious men and allows women to have little freedom of movement or expression. As Nafisi puts it, 'a stern Ayatollah, a self-proclaimed philosopher-king, had come to rule our land', and under his rule '[women] were never free of the regime's definition of them as Muslim women'.[25] Although this is constantly a theme of discussion during the book club, in one particular situation, Nafisi portrays this condition and how it affects Iranian women in public by drawing on one of the girls' typical walks from her book club back home:

> Let's imagine one of the girls, say Sanaz, leaving my house [...] She puts on her black robe and scarf over her orange shirt and jeans [...] We follow Sanaz down the stairs, out the door and into the street. You might notice that her gait and her gestures have changed. It is in her best interest not to be seen, not be heard or noticed. She doesn't walk upright, but bends her head towards the ground and doesn't look at passersby. She walks quickly and with a sense of determination. The streets of Tehran and other Iranian cities are patrolled by militia, who ride in white Toyota patrols, four gun-carrying men and women [...] They patrol the streets to make sure that women like Sanaz wear their veils properly, do not wear make up, do not walk in public with men who are not their fathers, brothers or husbands [...] If she gets on a bus, the seating is segregated. She must enter through the rear door and sit in the

> back seats, allocated to women. Yet in taxis, which accept as many as five passengers, men and women are squeezed together, like sardines [. . .] where so many of my students complain of being harassed by bearded and God-fearing men [. . .].[26]

Although there is no denying that such descriptions may be representative of some women's experiences in Iran, it is these representations of oppressed Iranian women, narrated from a position of privilege by Western-educated women, that signal a hypervisible stereotype of Iranian men and masculinity. But while these representations often stem from personal experiences and reflect upon Iranian society and our understanding of Iranian masculinity at large, they can also operate and be read on a symbolic level with connotations that can reach beyond Iranian borders. This is best demonstrated in a statement that Nafisi makes about the reappearing Mr Bahri. After the description of Mr Bahri cited above, she writes, 'I was not unfond of Mr Bahri, and yet I developed a habit of blaming him and holding him responsible for everything that went wrong.'[27] Read symbolically this sentence indicates that blame does not rest on Mr Bahri's shoulders alone. Iran's nationalistic discourse, ever since its introduction, has been clearly gendered. Najmabadi points out that the concept of nationalism in Iran was described through masculine terms such as 'a territory with clear borders, within which the collectivity of national brothers (baradaran-i vatani) resided'. In describing and defending this territory, 'the boundedness of this geobody was [. . .] envisaged as the outlines of a female body: one to love and be devoted to, to possess and protect, to kill and die for'.[28]

However, for many Iranians who were affected by the events leading up to and after the revolution, which led to the exile and imprisonment of many, the Iranian band of brothers who were supposed to protect, kill and die for this female geobody had turned against what they were meant to protect. Consequently many, particularly those of influential background such as Nafisi, whose family had contributed greatly to the progress of the nation, felt betrayed by the outcome of events. In this context, the typical pro-government Iranian man, like Mr Bahri, could be seen a representative of that collective band of brothers who failed to protect its own people and that is to be blamed for everything that they feel went wrong with the revolution.

This type of hypervisible representation, especially when it does not allow for the men to speak for themselves as individuals, can be seen to be oppressive. As Kelly Oliver reminds us, both hypervisibility and invisibility are 'bad visibility', as neither allow for those represented to be seen or recognised as individuals. This is an oppressive force, according to Oliver, since 'the seeing/being-seen dichotomy mirrors the subject/object dualism that is symptomatic of oppression. The seer is the active subject while the seen is the passive object.'[29] As she argues:

> oppression makes people into faceless objects or lesser subjects. The lack of visage in objects renders them invisible in any ethical or political sense. In turn, subjectivity becomes the domain of domination. Subjectivity is conferred by those in power and empowered on those they deem powerless and disempowered.[30]

By representing Iranian men, in general terms, and without giving them the opportunity to express themselves, these writers are replicating the kind of oppressive force that many are writing to escape. In doing so, they are rendering Iranian men, and alternative aspects of Iranian masculinity, invisible.

Furthermore, considering that the majority of such texts are circulated within a Western context, where there are already 'anti-Iranian attitudes [. . .] and anti-Iranian propaganda that began during the hostage crisis',[31] coupled with an 'ignorance and refusal to distinguish pro- and anti-Khomeini Iranians living [outside Iran]'[32] these books can be seen as further emphasising the hypervisibility of a highly limited version of Iranian masculinity. These operate in the same way that Derek Stanovsky believes representations of post-colonial masculinity often operate, whereby the 'essentializing and homogenizing of masculinity serves to obscure the actual diversity and plurality of lived masculinities'.[33]

This is not to say that all Iranian women writers are oblivious to this type of representation of Iranian men and masculinities. Indeed over the last several years there have been some writers who have been deliberately breaking down these stereotypes by offering a different kind of perspective of Iranian men and masculinities by presenting narratives that inject humanity into the male characters. Porochista Khakpour, an upcoming and very successful writer, for instance, focuses entirely on a conflicted father–son relationship between Darius and his son Xerxes in her *Sons and Other Flammable Objects* (2007). As the migrant father and son engage with each other, we begin to see a new kind of narrative of Iranian diasporic identity revolving around the exploration of this under-represented relationship. In fact Khakpour admits to this deliberate exploration in an interview where she tells the viewers that she did not want to write another novel about 'Iranian women weeping in the corner of the kitchen. Not another Orientalist not *Not Without My Daughter* type'.[34] She goes on to say that 'there are all these memoirs about Iranian women. But what about stories about Middle Eastern men?'[35]

To explore and highlight Iranian masculinity in a new way Fatemeh Keshavarz demonstrates her engagement with her uncle and father in her memoir *Jasmine and Stars*. Her uncle a faithful man and a painter, and her father a feisty man with whom Keshavarz continuously engages in heated debates about various issues, including poetry, form strong pillars in her own personal life. Her father and uncle are round characters who, far from the flat characters demonstrated in other books by Iranian women, defy stereotypes associated with Iranian men. Dedicating an entire chapter to her uncle, Keshavarz makes a deliberate attempt to overcome stereotypical representations, particularly drawing on the representation of men in *Reading* Lolita *in Tehran*. She tells:

> In New Orientalist narration of the Middle East, men like my uncle are almost entirely absent. [...]
>
> In the New Orientalist reading of Iran, however, most men have forgotten to smile. In fact, there are few close-ups, candle lights, to let us see their individual faces. What is in sharp relief is the coldness and cruelty of their acts. They seem to do very few ordinary human things like read a funny book, walk in a park, hold a woman's hand, or sit down with her to a cup of tea. Instead they aspire to be a walking harassment with one mission: degrading women.[36]

Through her representation of her uncle and her father, Keshavarz deliberately sets out to counter the stereotypical representations of Iranian masculinity.

Although narratives like Keshavarz and Khakpour's do exit, they, however, make but a small contribution to shifting the perspectives of Iranian men and masculinity because their perspective is outnumbered by stereotypical and generally accepted representations. On a larger scale, however, the stereotypical representations of Iranian men and masculinity can be seen as feeding into the post 9/11 discourse of the war on terror. As Gargi Bhattacharyya reminds us in *Dangerous Brown Men*, one of the justifications given for the Western declaration of war on terror has been to liberate women from the oppressive forces of their patriarchal societies. As she tells us, in the last ten years especially, 'the abuse of women and the denial of their public rights has been used as a marker of barbarism and as indication of societal sickness, a sickness requiring intervention'.[37] When Nafisi, for instance, constantly emphasises that the lives of Iranian women are 'doomed', claiming that 'the [Western] novels were an escape from the reality in the sense that we could marvel at their beauty and perfection, and leave aside our stories about the deans and the morality squads on the streets',[38] her words can be read as feeding into the discourse that appeals to what Spivak famously describes as 'white men saving brown women from brown men'. These assumptions can consequently be read as advocating the war on terror and attack on the Middle East on the basis of liberating Muslim women from religiously fanatic Iranian men. It is in response to this hypervisible oversimplification of Iranian men and masculinity that diasporic Iranian male writers have begun to respond.

Iranian men writing Iranian men

Khosravi sums up two significant elements that have affected the representation and sense of identity of diasporic Iranian men. As he puts it, 'Iranian man's masculine identity has been challenged and renegotiated on the one hand by the Iranian women's struggle for emancipation and on the other hand by the [western] mediaworks.'[39] In response to this, it is only recently that Iranian men have begun making themselves publicly visible in various ways, including through literature. Over the years, diasporic Iranian men have been aware of their hypervisible/invisible position, and have lived everyday trying to negotiate their identity in the West. Siamack Baniameri begins his humorous anecdotal book *The Iranican Dream* (2005), about an average Iranian–American man trying to raise his two teenagers by himself, with a chapter entitled 'It Sucks Being Me': 'being a Middle Eastern-American man nowadays is as hard as a stash of beef jerky sitting on top of a pick up truck's dashboard in the Arizona summer heat. You sure grow thick skin.'[40] However, despite the awareness of this position, until very recently two factors had made it almost impossible for Iranian men to be recognised beyond stereotypes through a body of literary work.

The first and most important factor has been, as already described, the high level of interest in Middle Eastern women's narratives, which have flooded the market and media, leaving little room or interest for other accounts. This does not mean that Iranian men were not writing or participating in the literary scene in English. In fact, Iranian men have been writing in English ever since the 1960s, one of the pioneers in the United States being Fereydun Esfandiari, who published several novels in that decade, including *The Day of Sacrifice*, *Identity Card* and *Beggar*. In each decade since then a few male Iranian writers, mostly writing in the United States, have published works in English. The 1970s saw Masud Farzan's *Airplane Ticket* (1970) and Donne Raffat's *Caspian Circle* (1979), while the 1980s and 1990s, a period of increased interest in Iran after the hostage crisis and the revolution, saw several books by Iranian men including *The Feet of a Snake* (1984) by Barry Chubin, *The Mantle of the Prophet* (1982) by Roy Mottahedeh, *The Night's Journey* (1984) and *Dead Reckoning* (1992) by Bahman Sholevar. During this time Majid Amini also authored several books in English including *Dreams of a Native Son* (1987), *The Howling Leopard* (1989) and *The Sunset Drifters* (1995). Similarly Manoucher Parvin has been writing for over three decades, with his first book *Cry for My Revolution* (1987) followed by *Avicenna and I* (1996) and two more novels, *Dardel* (2003), *Alethophobia* (2007), and add after (2007), and Out of the Gray: A Concerto for Neurons and Synapses (2011). The 2000s saw a slight surge in publications by Iranian men, with the two works of Parvin, Simack Baniameri's *The Iranican Dream* (2005), Morteza Baharloo's *The Quince Seed Potion* (2004), Massoud Alemi's *Interruptions* (2008), Salar Abdoh's *The Poet Game* (2004) and Farsheed Ferdowsi's *Mushroom in the Sand* (2009) as well as Mahbod Seraji's *Rooftops of Tehran* (2009), and Said Sayrafiezadeh's *When Skateboards Will Be Free* (2009). Additionally, recently, following the controversial 2009 presidential elections in Iran, a number of narratives by Iranian men have emerged, including Houshang Assadi's *Letters to My Torturer* (2010), Reza Kahlili's *A Time to Betray* (2010) and Arash Hejazi's *Gaze of the Gazelle* (2011).

Despite the range of books published by Iranian men over the last few decades, however, they have not received nearly as much interest or exposure as Iranian women writers. As we know, in the publishing business youth, talent, and potential for further literary endeavours attracts publishers to invest in an author.

This leads to the second issue that has hampered Iranian men's acknowledged presence in the literary scene: the practicality of their social position. The majority of Iranian migrants needed to establish themselves, and it has usually been the men who have been burdened by this responsibility. This had left very little time for creative self-expression. Indeed a glimpse at the profiles of some male authors reveals an entirely different demographic than women writers. While Iranian women writers range in age and profession, many purely dedicated to writing and cultural work, male authors, with the exception of a few, are older with primary professions entirely different from their literary endeavours. In fact many have become writers only after becoming successful at their primary professions and securing themselves and their families. Mahbod Seraji, for instance, the author of *Rooftops of Tehran*, one of the most successful recent books by an Iranian man, migrated to America as a poor student in the early 1970s, and had to work over 20 hours a week on campus while studying full time to afford his college tuition. After graduation, he worked for 20 years at Motorola as a senior manager until he was 'let go' in 2000. It was only then that he started working on *Rooftops of Tehran*, an idea he claims in interviews he had had ever since the hostage crisis. Siamack Baniameri, the author of *The Iranican Dream*, is a middle-aged established computer engineer who writes part time. Similarly, Morteza Baharloo, who wrote *The Quince Seed Potion*, states on his website that his primary study interests, like Seraji's, were arts and literature. But his parents refused to send him money to study arts when he was a young man in the United States. It would be years before he could fulfil his dream of writing. As he writes on his website, 'After Mort finished pharmacy training, he determined that a sound financial base was a necessary precursor to pursuing his literary and artistic passions.'[41] Since then it took him 15 years and a company of 600 employees before he could publish his debut novel. Farsheed Ferdowsi, the author of *Mushroom in the Sand*, is an equally successful businessman and engineer turned writer. Manoucher Parvin, the author of four novels including *Alethophobia*, is an academic turned novelist.

Out of a handful of Iranian men who have written fictional books, there are only a few devoted and self-declared full-time writers. In America, one can name Salar Abdoh, the author of *The Poet Game* (2004), *Opium* (2009), and more recently *Tehran at Twilight* (2014). who studied and teaches creative writing at USC, the brother of Reza Abdoh, a budding theatre director and a bravely self-confessed homosexual who died of AIDS at the age of 32 in the United States in 1992. In Australia, Ali Alizadeh, who is lecturer in creative writing at Monash University and the author of several poetry collections and *The New Angel* (2008) *Iran: My Grandfather* (2010) and *Transactions* (2013), is also one of the few men who could be considered a writer by profession.

So the position of Iranian diasporic men, which usually carried with it the weight of financial responsibility, coupled with current socio-political interest in the West that favours women's narratives, has made it difficult for diasporic Iranian men to be recognised by publishers as contributors to the literary scene. A glimpse at the availability of these books today is a telling indictment of the status of this body of work. The majority of these books, with the exception of only a few, have been published by small publishers and in small numbers, or been self-published online. Without prestigious publishers and their professional marketing strategies, diasporic Iranian male writers are not getting the attention they deserve. Additionally, in contrast to the majority of books by Iranian women, many of which are reprinted, most books by Iranian men are out of print and hard to obtain, even from major booksellers and libraries. Thus, many remain obscure or are sometimes lost and forgotten. For instance, while most books by Iranian women surface through a simple search on Amazon.com, and the majority are carried by libraries and major bookshops across the world, my search for books by Iranian men was a journey through numerous articles and obscure websites. Obtaining copies of these books, which were either out of print, not in any major library, or sold at random by no-name online sites, was an even greater task than proving their presence. In fact, in order to identify a body of literary work by Iranian men worth further analysis, it is necessary to undertake an intensive, time-consuming search.

This is why, given their near invisibility both as individuals and as writers, many of these books can be read as responses to the hypervisibility of Iranian men and masculinity as constructed by historical Orientalist narratives and Iranian women's self-Orientalisation. Taking this as the point of departure, these books can be seen as a medium to reconstruct Iranian men's sense of individual identity against the limiting hypervisibility that had constructed their identities as stereotypes. Many of the books that counter the negative stereotypes that made Iranian men invisible can be read as post-colonial responses to the marginalising and oppressive forces that limited the representation of Iranian masculinity.

These responses often target two specific aspects of stereotyping that contributed greatly to the hypervisibility of Iranian masculinity: the representation of Iranian men as religiously violent fanatics and terrorists, and as sexually deviant. Many of these writers, using various strategies, are challenging stereotypes and enabling the recognition of similarities between Iranian men and their Western readers, which can reconstruct Iranian masculinity, shifting it from hypervisibility/invisibility to visibility/individuality based on similarity within a Western context.

Terrorism and the hostage crisis

The hostage crisis and the more recent events of 9/11 have greatly affected the social position and sense of identity of many diasporic Iranian men. These events have created tension both in the way Iranian masculinity is perceived and in how Iranian men see themselves. While 9/11 affected the general Middle Eastern population in the West, it was the hostage crisis, a 'miniwar'[42] between Iran and the United States, that directly influenced representations of Iranian men and masculinity in the West. As Mohsen Mobasher argues, the discourse surrounding the hostage crisis operated on the legacy of Orientalist discourses, and constructed a new kind of binary opposition between Iran and the United States. As he puts it, it 'created the first xenophobic anti-Iranian and anti-Islamic reaction with new images of Iran, Islam, and Iranian and other Muslim immigrants as barbaric, uncivilized terrorists – a reaction that continues today.'[43] Consequently many diasporic Iranians, particularly men, were exposed to open discrimination of various kinds, and lived with the stigma and shame of being Iranian.[44] For many, particularly those who wanted to excel in their new environment, discrimination and the stigma of being Iranian 'motivated [them] to cover up their Iranian national origin'.[45] As Ali Behdad, an Iranian–American professor of comparative literature, confesses:

> For so long I did not have a sense of national identity. [T]he Iranians of my generation who came to the United States have a particular kind of shame [. . .] to be Iranian was marked for people of my generation in this country by the hostage crisis, the way we were ashamed of our Iranianness. I did not cook anything Iranian until about four or five years ago. I didn't have any Iranian things as I now do in my apartment [. . .] Those were elements of culture that were being repressed. When I wanted to go out and socialize with people during the hostage crisis I would say I was Afghani, I was Italian–anything so as not to say I was Iranian, I was ashamed of my own Iranianness.[46]

Othered and pushed into the margins like colonised subjects, as a survival mechanism, as Behdad also acknowledges, it has only been recently that Iranian men have decided to openly deal with the trauma of the hostage crisis and the label of terrorist associated with Middle Eastern men. Among the many strategies that Iranian men have employed to recontextualise this image, one of the most popular approaches has been through humour and comedy. In fact, in the last decade, humour has become one of the key modes through which Middle Eastern men have obtained international recognition. When pioneering stand-up comedian, Iranian–American Maz Jobrani, teamed up with Egyptians Ahmed Ahmed and Aron Kader, Palestinian Dean Obeidallah, and Korean-Jordanian Won Ho Chung in 2005, they formed the 'Axis of Evil Comedy Tour'. Touring internationally at booked-out events, the comedians pick up on stereotypes of Middle Eastern characteristics, and have joked themselves to world fame. Although there are a number of Iranian stand-up comedians, the majority of whose acts revolve around stereotypes of Middle Easterners, comedy has also seeped into literature, and is one of the most effective methods of subverting socio-historical patterns that have established society's central and marginal power dynamics. In *On Humour: Its Nature and Its Place in Modern Society*, Michael Mulkay contextualises the importance of humour in addressing a serious social matter. He writes:

> humour can be used effectively to perform serious work within reasonably well defined social contexts. [. . .] Humour can be used to challenge existing patterns [. . .] but only when it is given

> meaning in a relation to criticism and confrontation that is already under way within a serious realm.[47]

In a post-colonial context, or in any situation where there is a serious imbalance of power between margin and centre, as Mark Stein and Susanne Reichel argue, 'laughter and humour can release some of the tension and relieve some of the potential aggression'.[48] More importantly, humour can be an apparatus for destabilising power relationships between centre and margin by 'challenging and subverting the established orthodoxies, authorities and hierarchies'.[49]

For Iranian men, who have been marginally present in the West, invisible as individuals in the shadow of the concept of terrorism and the hostage crisis, humour can be a means through which they can reconstruct their sense of identity and inject humanity into the literary representations of Iranian men. Both as comedians and as writers, many Iranian men have used humour to address issues of terrorism, and through it they have attempted to reconstruct Iranian masculinity and subvert the established authorities and hierarchies that have marginalised them. Among them, Siamack Baniameri's *The Iranican Dream* is one of the most memorably humorous books. An anecdotal book that delves into the mind of an unconventional Iranian–American man, as the back cover tells us, it

> is a humorous account of a paranoid Iranian–American man in post-9/11 America who is raising two rambunctious teenagers by himself while dealing with a hormonally imbalanced ex-wife, a conspiracy buff father, a ninety-year-old sexually zealous grandfather, outrageously traditional Middle Eastern relatives, and a transsexual best friend who goes to the heart of a war zone for his sex change operation.

Although at times 'outlandish' and bizarre, nonetheless, the smile that each episode brings to the reader reframes certain stereotypical characteristics of Iranian men and masculinity from a fresh perspective.

Sculpting a human and witty character out of the stereotypes that surround diasporic Iranian men, terrorism is one of the many issues that Baniameri deals with in *The Iranican Dream.* In one of the episodes, the narrator's cousin has asked him to pick up his five-tiered wedding cake, made of exotic spices and ingredients and worth $7000 from the cake maker's house. Arriving at the house, the narrator waits as the cake maker disassembles the cake and puts it in boxes, ready for him to transfer to the wedding reception, when suddenly 'the door to the apartment blew to pieces, and a group of armed men in commando outfits stormed the apartments'.[50] With their guns ready to shoot, the commandos fill the house with tear gas, push him down on the floor, put a bag over his head and transfer him elsewhere. Once the police commandos take off the bag from his head, he is terrified:

> 'What the hell is going on here?' I screamed.
> 'Shut up, you goddamn terrorist.'
> 'What?'
> 'Who are your contacts? Where were you taking the bomb?' the agent said.
> 'The bomb? What bomb?' I asked.
> 'Don't play games. We know everything. Where were you taking it?
> 'Taking what?'
> 'The bomb.'
> 'What bomb?' I asked.
> 'Listen you asshole, I'll have you shipped to Guantanamo before you know it. I'll have your ass in there till you turn seventy.'
> 'I want my lawyer.'
> 'Lawyer? You don't get no freakin' lawyer. Al-Qaeda gets no lawyers, you scumbag.'
> 'Al-Qaeda? What the hell are you talking about?' I asked.
> 'You know what I am talking about. You were supposed to pick up the bomb and deliver it to your Al-Qaeda contacts. Who are they? I want names.'
> 'What bomb? I was picking up a cake.' I said.
> 'There were dirty bombs in those boxes. Where were you takin' 'em?'
> 'It's a cake. I was picking up a cake for my cousin's wedding.'
> 'Shut up. We know it's a dirty bomb; we know everything about you. Who are your contacts? What were you going to blow up? Where is Osama?'

> 'What the hell are you talking about?'
> 'Give me some names and make things easier for yourself. Who are your Al-Qaeda buddies? Where are your safe houses?'
> 'It was a cake. I swear. It was a wedding cake. I was sent by my cousin to pick up his wedding cake,' I said.
> 'So your cousin is an operative. Who is he? Did he meet with Osama before coming here?'
> 'My cousin can't even tie his own shoes. Are you people crazy?'
> 'Well, we sent the boxes to the crime lab. We'll have the results back in a few minutes, and when they tell me it's a bomb, your ass is mine.'
> 'It's a cake,' I said.
> 'Shut up.'
> 'Wait, I know, my ex-wife put you up to this. This is a joke, right?'
> 'It's as real as it can get, you stupid towel-head.'
> 'What are you gonna do to me?' I asked.
> The agent gave me the universal symbol for 'I'll-slash-your-throat' and smiled. I couldn't believe this was happening to me.[51]

Suddenly, the narrator's tone changes as he continues:

> Like millions of Middle Eastern–American folks, my life was turned upside down on September 11th. I couldn't comprehend how a group of Middle Eastern men could commit such horrendous crimes. Why would you want to kill innocent people like that? It just didn't make any sense to me.
>
> I've lived most of my life in the United States and I love this country. And like the majority of the Middle Eastern folks in the U.S., I believe in what this country stands for. I believe in freedom, democracy and human rights. I love America because unlike where I came from, I press forward in life based on what I know, not who I know. I love America because no body tells me and my children what to do, what to wear, how to look, how to think, what to eat, what music to listen to, what book to read, what politics to believe in and what religion to practice. I love America because I'm not above the law and neither is the chap sitting next to me. And most

> of all, I love America because she lets me be. It's true that the system is not perfect, but it's better than what I'm used to.
>
> I like to form my own opinion about subject matter, and I don't give a crap what Osama or the ayatollah says about America; I know what I know and I don't allow others to think for me. It doesn't matter who you are. The moment you entitle yourself to present your stupid ideology on my behalf, you automatically appear on my shit list.
>
> [. . .]
>
> Having said that, I couldn't believe I was being accused of being a terrorist. What happened to my rights? How can this happen in America?[52]

After a while, the matter is resolved when the officers come back and sheepishly confess that the cake was indeed a cake, and that they had raided the wrong apartment, and after finding out that the bomb was a cake, had eaten it all because it was so good.

In this episode, using 'humour as a form of rebellion against unbearable social conditions',[53] Baniameri is subverting the serious stereotype of the Arab-looking man as terrorist. In *Rebellious Laughter*, Joseph Boskin argues 'just as it has been utilized as a weapon of insult and persecution, so, too, has humour been implemented as a device of subversion and protest'.[54] In Baniameri's book, too, humour operates in the same manner by recontextualising and inverting the relationship between Iranian men/ terrorists and the non-Iranian, presumably white, men/commandos.

By the time this episode takes place, as readers we have already entered into the life of our narrator and realised that, although very frank, unconventional and at times brash, he is a typical Iranian man without any strong political and religious views living a normal life. Although this is a serious encounter, it appears funny because of the contextual circumstances: our ordinary man arrested on charges of being a terrorist while he is trying to transport a $7000 cake. But what makes it even funnier, however, is the absurdity of the encounter with the police, who have mistaken a cake for a bomb but who insist on their accusations. The police's insistence and their eventual apology, coupled with the fact that they end up eating the entire cake, turns the table, and releases the tension by creating a scene that challenges and undermines the authority and seriousness of such accusations. The joke, here, however, is on the ineptitude of the seemingly powerful police commandos who cannot distinguish between a cake and a bomb.

Added to this, the sudden change of tone in the narrator's account further undermines the police's sense of authority and reverses the power dynamics. Considering the ordeal he has just been through, there is a double meaning in his statement: 'It doesn't matter who you are. The moment you entitle yourself to present your stupid ideology on my behalf, you automatically appear on my shit list.' Although on the one hand he could be referring to Muslim leaders who are pressing their ideas onto others, on the other hand his statement refers to all others, including those like the commandos, who see all Middle Eastern men as a type, and thereby reduce his identity to a terrorist. Moreover, the sudden shift of tone realistically presents readers with a perspective from the viewpoint of someone affected by stereotypical images of Middle Easterners. The frankness of his statements, in contrast to the absurd interrogation, suddenly allows him to be seen as an individual. As readers, we feel a sense of sympathy with our Middle Eastern man, who, along with many others, has come to the United States with the hope of trying to make a better life for himself, but who has to live with these labels everyday.

Other writers, such as Said Sayrafiezadeh in his memoir *When Skateboards Will Be Free* (2009), appeal to a similar sense of human sympathy to make Iranian men recognisable as individuals through a more serious and emotional account. The memoir recounts Sayrafiezadeh's life as the child of socialist parents, an Iranian father – who left to go to Iran to run for president on behalf of the Socialist Party – and a Jewish-American mother. It recalls not only the difficulties of growing up with a mother who chose to live in self-inflicted poverty and who moved often from place to place, but also the pain of carrying an Iranian name as a middle school student during the hostage crisis. One of the most emotionally touching memories recalled by Sayrafiezadeh is of when his mother finally decides to settle in one place. After they have settled, Sayrafiezadeh enters a predominantly black middle school with clear racial segregation, where white students, after a simple examination, were filtered into more advanced classes as 'scholars' while everyone else stayed with the school's normal curriculum. Soon Sayrafiezadeh finds himself in the scholar classes, where for the first time he befriends a few of his classmates, Daniel and Tab. Daniel is a confident, 'handsome' white boy, who soon takes an idealised shape in

Sayrafiezadeh's mind, whose own physical appearance, with dark bushy eyebrows, clearly marks him as different from others in his class. As they become close friends, Sayrafiezadeh, in seeing his own difference, dreams of looking like Daniel: 'I fantasized about being Daniel, literally, his body taking the place of mine. I was sure the girls liked him, or loved him.'[55] But Daniel 'had one flaw, only one, and that was his blatant and unconcealed racism'.[56] As their friendship grows, and the two boys become closer, the hostage crisis takes place. When Iran is mentioned for the first time in school, and as the crisis escalates, Sayrafiezadeh finds himself caught between his unease with his friends' blatant comments about Iranians in Iran and his desire to hide his Iranian identity. However, having been brought up with an opinionated socialist mother, he makes an unruly comment that brings him to the spotlight. When one afternoon Daniel asks him 'what do you think about the hostage crisis, Said?' unable to control himself he blurts out 'I believe the hostages are spies and should be tried for their crimes against the Iranian people. [. . .] They deserve what they get.'[57] This episode brings him to the attention of his classmates. It marks the end of his friendship with Daniel, and the beginning of a difficult school life where he is constantly beaten up, bullied, and eventually transferred from the scholar class to the class with the black students. Consequently, Sayrafiezadeh becomes hypervisible as a type of person associated with the hostage crisis. This hypervisibility leads to his invisibility as an individual in school. His friends, who once used to play with him, begin to run away from him. Gradually, he starts to suffer an internal struggle about how he sees himself, becoming invisible even to himself. As he writes:

> Daniel continued to remain handsome in my eyes. In fact, he became more handsome, while I, in turn became more ugly. This was the unhappy side effect of having first perceived him as my flawless opposite. I grew skinnier, frailer, as he grew more strapping. My features became loud and prominent while his became refined and elegant. I was sure that he would be a movie star when he grew up. It was as if my face was cannibalising the flesh from my body, absorbing it into itself, so that my nose and eyes and eyebrows intensified with each day, growing darker, larger, hairier. It was a hideous face, I was sure, loudly calling attention to itself. Now I avoided mirrors at all costs.[58]

This statement is telling of the psychological operations of hypervisibility/invisibility that affected the Iranian sense of masculinity as the result of the hostage crisis. Theorists of subjectivity and identity, such as Oliver, place great emphasis on the way our subjectivities are constructed intersubjectively, particularly by the way others perceive us and we perceive ourselves. As she puts it, 'a positive sense of self is dependent on positive recognition from others, while a negative sense of self is the result of negative recognition or lack of recognition from others'.[59] She goes on to argue that 'when others respect us as capable of judgment and action, only then can we respect ourselves as autonomous agents'.[60] According to Oliver this operates on a social level, where positive recognition from a dominant culture is an important part of the way we perceive ourselves. As she puts it, 'recognition from the dominant culture is necessary to develop a strong sense of one's own personal and group identity'.[61] Stereotypes and misrecognition based on differences construct an antagonistic relationship and create a kind of 'inferiority complex' which is the result of the 'internalization of stereotypes of inferiority'.[62] This inferiority complex, however, operates not only on a psychological level but can also affect the way we are perceived and perceive ourselves physically. As Oliver puts it:

> values of dominant culture are not so much internalized psychologically but forced onto the bodies of the oppressed. The oppressed are chained to the body, represented as unable to think, to reason, to act properly. They are reduced to an egoless, passive body that is at the same time in need of control and discipline.[63]

What this means is that those who are oppressed also begin to see themselves as physically inferior to the one who is dominating. Sayrafiezadeh's statement about the body bears witness to the way this kind of oppression by the dominant culture leads to internalisation of inferiority. For Sayrafiezadeh, Daniel is the representative of the superiority and power of the dominant culture. When Sayrafiezadeh is bullied and his friends stop associating with him, he is objectified and oppressed. This lack of intersubjective relationship and recognition affects his sense of subjectivity, and he begins to internalize this inferiority. This, in turn, influences how he sees himself physically. That in his eyes Daniel grows into a stunning man while he appears thinner and frail points to the internalisation of this kind of inferiority on the physical level. When he stops looking in the mirror, he becomes invisible even to himself, losing all sense of identity and subjectivity. This consequently affects his entire life in the United States. Growing up he turns into a solitary and almost invisible adult with little self-confidence about his appearance, with occasional self-confessed kleptomaniac tendencies, working in a low-level job for Martha Stewart's company, hoping everyday to be recognised by her for his genius.

This touching and emotionally disturbing account of Sayrafiezadeh's childhood, leading to an unimpressive and difficult adult life as a man with Iranian heritage, brings to our attention the evolution of the oppression of Iranian men in diaspora from an overexposed hypervisibility as a type, to a contrasting invisibility as an individual, both of which, as Oliver points out, are oppressive forces that turn people into 'faceless objects, or lesser subjects'.[64] However, Sayrafiezadeh's narrative of this oppression operates on a level that breaks the oppressive cycle and offers him the ability to reconstruct and regain his sense of subjectivity by making his own reality. As Oliver reminds us:

> it is not merely being seen, or being recognized between spectacle and oblivion, that makes for an ethical or just relation. Rather [. . .] the oscillation between invisibility and hypervisibility [is] a matter not so much of being seen but of making one's world.[65]

At the end of the memoir, Sayrafiezadeh points to this possibility when he writes, 'It was up to each of us to bear our private miseries alone, until that glorious day in the future when it would all be resolved once and for all, and a perfect world would emerge.'[66] This statement, coupled with an earlier sentence, 'the truth must not only be truth, it must also be told',[67] points to the possibility and necessity for other Iranian men to construct their own world in their own image in order to bring themselves to visibility.

Sexuality and romance

One of the recurring elements in diasporic Iranian men's literature in recent years has been the theme of sexuality. Until recently, Iranian masculinity in the West has been framed as a kind of uncontrollable, deviant and violent sexuality. This type of representation stems historically from Orientalist harem narratives and is confirmed by modern Iranian and Middle Eastern women's narratives that contribute to its continuation, affecting the way Iranian men are perceived in the West today. In demonstrating the significance of these types of portrayal and their consequence, Mahbod Seraji, the author of *Rooftops of Tehran* recalls an episode in a blog post which shows the extent to which Iranian and Middle Eastern men are affected by these representations. After a long separation, Seraji reunites with a friend, Hesam, in Dubai. Hesam is a family man who cares greatly for his wife and children. Over dinner, Seraji reveals that he has recently published a book. As his friend's children show great interest in this book, his kind host suddenly becomes uneasy and changes the topic. Later, when the two men are walking by the ocean, Hesam brings up the subject again, abruptly:

> 'Is your story going to become an international bestseller by making the Middle Eastern men look wicked and evil, like so many others have?' Hesam asked me with a pleasant smile.
>
> The confused look on my face made him chuckle. Then his tone turned soft. "My father, whom you met tonight," he said as he pointed toward the house behind us, 'is almost eighty years old. My mother is seventy five, may they both live to be one hundred-twenty, Inshallah – God willing. Did you know that he can't read or write, but that he has most of the Holy Koran memorized?'
>
> 'Wow,' I whispered still anxious to know where the conversation was leading, suspecting a link to the delayed reaction to my book announcement.
>
> 'My grandparents lived in a tent,' he continued. 'So did my father, until he was ten years old. But you know, my father has never beaten my mother. I have never beaten my wife...'
>
> I remained silent as we trudged our way forward through the sandy beach.
>
> 'They portray us like animals,' he complained. 'Ugly, heartless, family hating, wife beating misogynists. Why do they do that? Why do they paint us all in one stroke? All in one color? Made of the same cloth? Why?'
>
> I shook my head.

> 'Does every Middle Eastern man have to be a wife beater in their stories? Don't they know that there are men here who would give their lives for their families? In some ways I am glad that my father can't read. They have marred and tarnished the reputation of real men like him, like my decent in-laws, whose warmth and pleasant temperaments make them great proud fathers, compassionate considered brothers, lovable husbands and partners for life.'
>
> He stopped momentarily. I could see under the moonlight that his face had turned red.
>
> 'I don't deny that such men exist in our culture but that's not how all of us are. Do you think people understand that?'[68]

This episode effectively demonstrates some of the concerns of diasporic Iranian men about the way they have been represented. One can see this concern reflected in their literature as they introduce alternative types of gender relationships that counter the dominant perception of Iranian masculine sexuality. One of the ways through which many writers have worked against dismantling this stereotype has been by introducing the missing element of romance and spiritual love in Iranian male–female relationships. Among the many novels that focus on this, the most successful so far has been Seraji's own *Rooftops of Tehran.* In fact, so successful has this novel been in breaking down stereotypes that when Seraji sends a copy of the book to his friend in Dubai, he receives a single line letter, saying 'thank you'.

Rooftops is an emotional *bildungsroman* that follows Pasha, a 17-year-old boy who practically lives on the rooftop of their middle class family home in Tehran during the summer of 1973, as he falls in love with the girl next door, Zari. But Zari is engaged to another young man known as Doctor. Set back by his sense of loyalty to Doctor, who is a man of values and a good friend, Pasha tries to hide his love for Zari. However, Doctor, who is involved in anti-governmental activities, is taken by the Shah's secret police and eventually killed, and Pasha is left behind to console Zari, who also has feelings for Pasha. However, in an act of protest at what has happened to her fiancé, Zari sets herself on fire in front of the Shah's entourage and is badly burned and thought to be dead. But Zari has not died. To protect her and those associated with her from the government's wrath, her family acts as if she is dead, while all along she still lives with the family, wearing a full chador, even covering her face, posing as a distant cousin who has moved in with the family to console them after her death. Though living next to each other for months, the lovers never reunite. As the novel ends, Pasha eventually migrates to the United States to study, while Zari's family moves away to a distant city.

Everything about this book, from the red rose on the cover, to Pasha and his friends' jokes and games, to the lovers' near kiss on the rooftop, and Pasha's temporary insanity at the thought of losing his love, counters the image of the Iranian man as sexually deviant and violent. By depicting an Iranian man who shares emotions, actions and feelings with everyone else in the world, it breaks the stereotypes and allows him to be recognised as an individual human being. As Oliver argues, this sort of recognition can break the cycle of oppression and marginality, because oppression and domination operate on difference and invisibility while 'recognition requires the assimilation of difference into something familiar'.[69] This means that 'the subject recognizes the other only when he can see something familiar in that other, for example, when he can see that the other is a person too'.[70]

Rooftops has been praised for breaking stereotypes and injecting a kind of familiar human quality into the Iranian male character, as it has gone on to win numerous awards and listed as favourite reads on various websites. Almost every review and statement in praise of the book picks up on its human appeal, making it a work that many across cultural and social divides identify with. The author's site[71] shares some of the reviews: Kirkus, for instance, reviews the book as 'Refreshingly filled with love rather than sex, this coming-of-age novel examines the human cost of political repression', while *The Milwaukee Sentinel* writes 'Seraji's wonderfully appealing characters, living universal teenage emotional lives of dreams and minor worries, lose their innocence in the brutalities that foreshadow the Iranian revolution.' According to another review, from *TruthOut*, '"Rooftops of Tehran" calls on America to open its eyes and ears to Iran: its people, its pain, its beauty, its love. Hopefully America will listen.' Similarly, Reese Erlich, the author of *The Iran Agenda*, writes, 'You learn a lot about Iranian culture while coming to understand characters with universal appeal.' William Kent Kruegar, the author of *Red Knife* also writes, 'Thank God for authors like Seraji who show us that no matter how distant apart our worlds may be, in the humanness of our hearts we are all united.'

Individual readers, too, have picked up on the universal appeal of this book. *Rooftop's* page on Amazon.com is filled with reviews and comments that emphasise how readers came to recognise the similarities between themselves and Iranians through this book. One effusive reviewer in particular demonstrates this point well when she writes:

> 'Rooftops of Tehran' is much more than a love story. It is an affirmation of shared human experiences. We all dream, love, laugh and cry. We have fears and want good things for our children. Mr. Seraji has given us a glimpse into the unknown and it is up to us to recognize that regardless of religion or culture we are more alike than some would like us to believe.

Such positive responses to this book not only indicate its success in breaking down stereotypes that exist about Iranian men and masculinity, but also how it helps to break down the national and political barriers that emphasize an us/them dichotomy. This recognition of the similarity of human experiences can assist faster integration and acceptance of diasporic Iranians in their new setting. On a global level, at a time of tension and possible war with Iran, these narratives can operate to diffuse the tension by emphasising the shared human experience.

In breaking down this barrier, however, Seraji is not alone. Another book, which also represents a more romantic notion of Iranian masculinity, is Manoucher Parvin's *Avicenna and I* (1996). The book tells the story of Professor Pirooz, a diasporic Iranian academic who is caught between his home and host cultures, and is disenchanted by the social ills of consumerism, random violence and conflict that surround him in New York. When he meets a neighbour, Sitareh Poonia, an Indian woman well educated in spiritual philosophy, they instantly fall in love through a spiritual connection and their mutual love for the ninth-century Iranian mathematician and physician, Avicenna. But soon Sitareh is murdered in the basement of their apartment block. Distraught at the death of his love, but guided in his dreams by Avicenna's spirit, Pirooz sets out on a soul-searching journey to Iran, to the city of Hamedan where Avicenna is buried. At Avicenna's mausoleum, however, he meets Sitareh Bastan, who greatly resembles

Sitareh Poonia. The two also bind as a result of their love for Avicenna and begin a life together.

Avicenna and I operates on several levels to challenge the kind of gender relations taken in the West to be the norm between Iranian men and women. In her review of the book, Marta Simidchieva argues that *Avicenna and I* is reminiscent of a Persian 'court romance'. In particular, she suggests that the novel 'evokes a faint echo' of Nezami's *Haft Peykar* (*Seven Beauties*), a narrative poem from the twelfth century. In *Haft Peykar*, the Persian King Bahram Gur gains knowledge and spiritual awareness from his seven brides from far corners of the world. As she compares the two, Simidchieva writes, 'in Nezami's romance, as in Parvin's novel, the protagonist's journey of spiritual enlightenment starts in the abode of an Indian beauty and is brought to a close in his union with an Iranian one'.[72]

The book's resemblance to Persian court romance suggests the possibility of a reconstructed representation of Iranian gender relations. In traditional Persian court poetry, this kind of romantic gender relationship is common, and it is reflective of the romantic tradition in Iranian society. However, in the Western representation of Iranian gender relations, this romantic aspect has been nearly completely invisible. *Avicenna and I* taps into that tradition and brings forth the romantic gender relationships so prevalent in it. Thus it challenges normalised Western perceptions of Iranian masculinity. Pirooz's spiritual romanticism and his soft-spoken nature offer alternative visions of Iranian masculinity, rewriting Orientalist perceptions of Iranian men as violent and sexually aggressive.

Furthermore, Pirooz's close spiritual relationship with both Sitarehs, who act as guides in his spiritual journey, reframes our understanding of gender hierarchy and agency, both in traditional Iranian literature, and in the way the West normally perceives Iranian gender relations. As Simidchieva argues, the novel presents 'romantic love as a means of spiritual maturation of the male protagonist and the role of the woman as a guide on his journey'.[73] But in traditional Persian poetry, even court poetry, although women played a significant role in guiding the male protagonists, they were often passive in their roles. Even Simidchieva observes this, commenting that in Parvin's narrative, 'the female characters [. . .] are more assertive than their medieval counterparts'.[74] In Parvin's account, women are not only powerful, active spiritual leaders who guide the male character, but they are also the ones who are sexually more assertive than their male partner. When it comes to initiating a relationship, it is Sitareh Poonia who invites Professor Pirooz to her house for dinner first and, in Iran, it is Sitareh Bastan who, after housing Professor Pirooz for a few days, suddenly appears in his bedroom in the middle of the night 'like a gentle flame [. . .] in a golden negligee',[75] catching him by complete surprise, to initiate passionate, spiritual and sensual lovemaking. However, Pirooz's reserve, politeness and initial remoteness to a possible sexual relationship with Sitareh, reframes our understanding of expected sexual dominance and gender hierarchy. This reconstructs the image of Iranian men as sexually aggressive, while Sitareh's assertiveness reverses the expected sexual norms of Iranian women as passive and sexually dominated.

Homosexuality

In Iran homosexuality is officially taboo and often socially unacceptable. This attitude is rooted in history, as Afsaneh Najmabadi points out in her book *Women with Moustaches and Men without Beards*, 'in the nineteenth century, homoeroticism and same-sex practices came to mark Iran as backward; heteronormalization of eros and sex became a condition of "achieving modernity," a project that called for heterosocialization of public space and a reconfiguration of family life.'[76] Additionally, viewed through an Islamic lens, and based on a selected few verses in the Quran, homosexuality is deemed sinful and punishable by death. Ironically, more recently, homosexuality, once a 'Persian vice', has come to be known as a 'Western disease', and as Brian Whitaker points out in *Unspeakable Love*:

> although it is generally accepted in many parts of the world that sexual orientation is neither a conscious choice nor anything that can be changed voluntarily, this idea has not yet taken hold in Arab [and other Muslim] countries – with the result that homosexuality tends to be viewed either as wilfully perverse behaviour or a symptom of mental illness and dealt with accordingly.[77]

In Iran, particularly since the Islamic revolution, and despite the fact that transgendered are legally accepted, homosexuals are frequently discriminated against and forced into secrecy. Various sources indicate that an estimated 4,000 homosexuals have been prosecuted and executed in Iran since 1979. This discrimination was confirmed by President Ahmadinejad's speech at the UN in 2007, when he publicly announced that 'in Iran we don't have homosexuals like you do in your country. [. . .] In Iran we do not have this phenomenon, I don't know who has told you that we have it.'[78] As Whitaker observes, homosexuals in Arab countries, and similarly in Iran, 'are condemned to a life of secrecy, fearing exposure and sometimes blackmail; many are forced into unwanted marriages for the sake of their family's reputation.'[79] Needless to say, rendered invisible, homosexuals in Iran have never had the chance to openly deal with their sexuality.

This is ironic in a country in which, until the introduction of modernisation in the nineteenth century, the display of homoerotic love had been blatantly present and accepted. In fact there is no doubt among scholars of Iranian literature that the concept of the beloved and the loved in Persian Sufi poetry, which with the advent of nationalism was translated into a heterosexual allegory of the beloved as the mother and the loved as the band of brothers who are to protect her, originally connoted a male homoerotic relationship. A glimpse at classical Persian literature reveals homoerotic love as a recurrent theme in the poems of Attar (d.1220), Rumi (d.1273), Sa'adi (d.1291), Hafez (d.1389), Jami (d.1492), and even in those of twentieth century Iraj Mirza (d.1926). As scholars such as Janet Afary have acknowledged over the years, the works of these poets are 'replete with homoerotic allusions, as well as explicit references to beautiful young boys and to the practice of pederasty'.[80] Indeed, so manifest and explicit had been this theme that scholars such as Cyrus Shamista claim that, with more than 90 per cent of references to love relationships in classical Persian literature being associated with homoeroticism, 'Persian literature is essentially a homosexual literature.'[81] But while over the years, with the advent of modernism and the emergence of the social taboo on homoeroticism, this allegory came instead to be seen in terms of a heteroerotic male/female relationship, after the Islamic revolution there was more emphasis on the spiritual symbolism of man and the divine. The Islamic government censored and suppressed homoerotic readings of classical Persian literature, and more importantly it suppressed and marginalised all homosexual activity, to the point of punishment by death.

In diaspora, although experiencing more opportunity for expression of their neglected sexualities, many Iranian homosexuals still live with the stigma that their families and cultures have carried with them abroad. Consequently, many continue to live double lives. While some have started dealing with homosexuality in diaspora through fiction, as Abdi Nazemian does in his quirky novel, *Walk in Closet* (2014), as far as my research indicates, no Iranian homosexual man or woman has so far written a memoir in which they make their sexuality public and openly deal with the issue. However, in recent years some Iranian men have brought the subject of homosexuality in Iran into public light through fiction, and recently poetry.

In his 2004 historical novel, *The Quince Seed Potion* (2004), for instance, Morteza Baharloo recounts 60 years of recent Iranian history, from 1921 to 1981, from the perspective of a devoted homosexual servant, Sarveali Jokar, who is deeply disturbed by his own sexual tendencies. Raped as a child by his uncle, Sarveali is sold as a servant to the Shirlu family dynasty. As he grows older he gradually but secretly falls in love with, and is aroused by, his master. But, living in a society in which homosexuality is seen as a disease and abnormal, he hides his tendencies. When the mistress of the household, a woman interested in alternative and natural medicine, announces that quince seed potion can cure all sorts of ailment, it becomes Sarveali's mission to ask her for some of the potion, hoping it will cure his 'disease'. But he never works up the courage to ask for the potion; instead, to preserve appearances, when the very same uncle who had raped him forces him to marry his promiscuous daughter, he accepts. But the marriage does not succeed, because after repeated attempts he is unable to perform sexually. His wife, not feeling the slightest attraction to him either, instead turns elsewhere and ends up sleeping with their master. Sarveali, knowing his own incompetence, chooses to ignore this until he realises his wife is with more men than their master. In a drunken rage, stemming from his own inability to perform and his wife's disloyalty, he hammers her to death. Consequently he is imprisoned, during which time he becomes highly addicted to opium. Although freed from prison by his master's influence, he continues to hide his sexual tendencies until the end of his life. After everyone in the Shirlu family that he had been devoted to has either passed away or gone abroad, he commits suicide by jumping into an abandoned well, never having expressed or explored his true sexuality during his 60 years of life.

As one of the first narratives to deal with a homosexual man's position in Iran, particularly from a servant's perspective, the novel operates on several levels. On one level, it foregrounds the neglected voice of a homosexual man in Iran who, conditioned by his society, feels uneasy about his sexuality. On another level, told from the perspective of a servant and his sincere devotion to his master, it also highlights the neglected voice of the servant in a master–servant relationship. Although throughout the novel Sarveali is constantly silent and silenced by his masters and his social position, the novel itself acts as his only voice, and it is through this that we come to see the many layers of patriarchy and hierarchy that exist in the Iranian social system. The ending of the novel, which has Sarveali commit suicide, points to the realities of life for this group of people: abandoned and used by everyone around him, there is no hope for a better future for him or others such as him.

On another level, the novel can be read as a critical reflection of Iranian society. Sarveali's relationship with the Shirlus is a reflection of class and hierarchies in Iranian society more broadly. The ruling elite, like the Shirlus, use, abuse, and even betray the working class by taking their wives and by using their services, but when it comes to accepting them for who they are, or providing them safety and security, they abandon them in times of need. Sarveali's death is not only the death of a servant who had worked 50 years for a family and at the end went unnoticed and entirely neglected, but it is the ontological death of the working class who die everyday, neglected under the patriarchal and heterosexual class systems that rule Iranian society. The fact that Sarveali commits suicide soon after the Islamic revolution indicates that while people such as him, sexually repressed and at the margins of society, might have had a chance during that era, there was no chance for them following the revolution.

While Baharloo's novel ends at the beginning of the revolution in 1981, Massud Alemi's *Interruptions* (2008) picks up where Baharloo leaves off. Set in the summer of 1981, *Interruptions* tells the story of a young gay man, Farzin, a school teacher who, on his way to rendezvous with his lover, Bijan, is accidentally caught up in a protest, and is picked up by the newly established revolutionary guards and accused of being a ring leader for an anti-governmental group. Unable to confess to where he was headed, and, having been caught in the middle of the protests, unable to deny his involvement in the activities, he is taken into Evin prison and interrogated. His interrogator, who insists on getting a confession out of him one way or another, gives him a piece of paper and a pen and tells him to write down all that he can about himself. Having had no involvement in the activities, and hoping to linger until proven innocent without having to confess to where he was headed, Farzin begins to write down his family history. Starting with his great-great grandfather's magical spiritual abilities and bravery, and working his way through his family's background, he gradually feeds his interrogator with this information. His interrogator, waiting for the important information to be revealed, keeps sparing him day after day, until one day, just before Farzin has a chance to hand him the last report, in which he confesses that he was headed to see his lover the day he was caught, he realises that this man is truly innocent. He tries to convince his superior interrogator, not of Farzin's innocence but that he has converted from his anti-governmental ways. To test this, the superior interrogator hands Farzin a gun and asks him to shoot a man who had just been tortured. Instead of shooting him, however, Farzin puts the gun into his own mouth and pulls the trigger. But the gun had been emptied of bullets and Farzin survives, after which he is released.

Like *The Quince Seed Potion*, Alemi's *Interruptions* tells of the hardship of being homosexual in Iran. But what makes his account different is that, unlike Sarveali, who did not have the means to express himself and went along passively and silently until there was no choice for him but death, Farzin actively participates in telling his story and in trying to avoid imminent death. While Sarveali belongs to the illiterate lower class caste of Iranian society, and has little ability to revolt against this position, Farzin is the representative of middle class Iranians who have the ability to free themselves from oppression to some degree. But while their class difference provides them with this ability, their sexual difference does not. Here, Farzin is like Scheherazade, in that his life, like hers, depends on his sexuality and storytelling abilities. But while Scheherazade's narrative complements her sexuality and keeps the king interested to save her life, Farzin has to narrate tales around his sexuality and weave fantastical historical tales to avoid getting to the point, which will ensure his death. Although he manages to successfully do that, the many levels of oppressions and hierarchy of Iranian society do not let him off easily. Being freed comes at the expense of living under the oppression of another force. If it is not his sexuality, then it is the government. Just like Sarveali, there is no escape for him but death. In being released, he knows that he is still not freed from the forces of the Iranian government who continue to rule people's lives.

These narratives that focus on male sexuality, however, do more than foreground the oppressed voices of Iranian homosexuals, or even offer us alternatives to the way Iranian masculinity is perceived. Rather, in a bold move, by focusing on homosexuality, they are tapping back into, resurfacing and rewriting the neglected and repressed tradition of homoerotic Persian poetry. Instead of sugar coating these narratives with allegories of male/female or divine love, these men in diaspora have found the courage to tell it as it is, and they can claim that in doing this they are making a direct contribution to the field of homoerotic Persian literature. *Modern Gay Persian Poetry About Love* (2011), by a poet who calls himself Dr Ali, is one such book, following the traditions of the masters by openly expressing homoerotic sexuality. In its foreword, Payam Ghassemlou acknowledges this as he writes 'one can find validation of gay love by reading love poems by Sadi, Hafiz, and Rumi', and Dr Ali's poems 'reflect the homoerotic Eros that has always been part of Persian literature'.[82] He believes that the new wave of poetry 'in this vein [. . .] is contributing to Persian poetry'.[83] Such contributions play an important role not only in bringing 'same gender love out of the closet', as Ghassemlou puts it, but also in providing a space in which writers and poets can stay true to, and be reminded of the true values of, Persian literature, which have been forcefully transformed through centuries.

Although there have a variety of ways in which diasporic Iranian men have reconstructed themselves against stereotypes, in the years following the controversial 2009 elections, a shift has occurred in the kind of narratives that represent the Iranian experience. This has provided a new framework and mode of reading, offering alternative ways in which both Iranian men and women's narratives can be received.

CONCLUSION

THE 'NOT-YET' FUTURE OF IRANIAN WRITING

When I embarked on the study of diasporic Iranian literature in English in the early 2000s, I had no idea that this body of work was going to grow so quickly and expand to provide such a rich contribution to the already vast oeuvre of world literatures in English. When I started out, there were only a handful of books and even less scholarly study on the topic. Now, that number almost exceeds well over 200, with new titles emerging every day, accompanied by a considerably growing body of scholarly work that addresses various aspects of this literature.

As one of the first studies to cover such a large number of texts by diasporic Iranian writers, this book has revealed the existence of these works as a substantial category in world literatures in English. It has examined the significance of various aspects of this literature for diasporic Iranian communities, as a means through which they are maintaining, constructing and negotiating their sense and understanding of diasporic Iranian identities.

This book covers narratives that have emerged through two different historical waves. The first, and relatively small, wave which appeared immediately after the 1979 Islamic revolution, at the onset of the ensuing mass migration from Iran, and the second wave that emerged nearly two decades later in the wake of the events of 9/11, when interest in the Middle East was once again renewed at the dawn of America's declaration of war on terror, and when there was particular interest in women's issues in the Middle East. Recently, however, we have been seeing the beginning of a third wave of writing by Iranian writers in diaspora. Following the controversial 2009 presidential elections, in which the population suspected the government of vote rigging, leading to deadly riots with international coverage, a shift occurred in the way Iran and Iranians were viewed in the West. While prior to 2009 Iranians were generally viewed as uniformly fanatical Muslims, an image still resonating with the bitterness of the American hostage crisis, after the 2009 elections the world began to distinguish Iranians from their Islamic government. The literature that has followed also reflects this shift in perspective.

A huge contributing factor to this distinction has undoubtedly been the digital platforms of communication. Although the Iranian government has a very strict censorship policy on internet access, Iranians have been extremely active bloggers, and Persian is one of the most frequent languages in which blogs are written.[1] However, as Niki Akhavan observes, after 2007 'the sheen of blogs and blogging was beginning to dull on the Iranian internet, and social networking sites were showing signs of becoming more popular among resident and Diaspora Iranians'.[2] This social networking played a significant part in the distribution and dissemination of information after the 2009 elections. As Akhavan observes, 'protestors' much-touted uses of social media in the aftermath of the disputed election remain a hallmark example of how these platforms can successfully attract transnational attention and support.'[3] Social media, including Facebook pages and updates, YouTube clips that were uploaded from mobile phones, and tweets, played a significant role in bringing what was going on in Iran to the attention of the world, immediately and directly from those were affected by it. With the rapid circulation of clips from protests, a different Iran came into view.[4] Here, women were no longer silent, passive and domestic. Rather, they could be seen and heard shouting and screaming alongside men in opposition to the government. As the world witnessed through these clips, women such as Neda Agha Soltan, who was shot in the street and died on camera, suffered alongside men the violation of their rights as humans at the hands of the Islamic government.

Out of the ashes of these protests, a new interest was born in narratives emerging from Iran. The world was no longer interested in delayed stories by silenced and oppressed diasporic women.

Rather, people wanted to hear stories about what was happening now in contemporary Iran. There was now interest in a generation of men and women who had lived silently under the Islamic regime for the last several decades. Soon after these events, books began appearing that dealt with current issues. For instance, someone with the pseudonym Afsaneh Mogadam published a small book in early 2010 by the name *Death to the Dictator!: A Young Man Casts a Vote in Iran's 2009 Elections and Pays a Devastating Price*, which daringly takes us inside the events, and tells of the horrors, the rapes and the threats that were endured by young protestors. Similarly Saideh Pakravan wrote *Azadi: Protests in the Streets of Tehran* (2011), which follows the stories of several young people and their families as they become involved in the protests. In a more intriguing account, Neda Soltani tells us of her case of mistaken identity and ensuing life of tragedy leading to eventual exile, when her photo was confused with Neda Agha Soltan, the young woman who was shot and dies on camera, in her book *My Stolen Face* (2012). Similarly in his latest novel *Tehran at Twilight* (2014) Salar Abdoh takes us into 2008 Tehran with returning journalist Reza as finds his loyalties challenged in a city on the edge of revolution.

Since this period, there has also been an increase in the number of accounts of alternative religious groups and their presence in Iran. For example, for the first time we are seeing many narratives by the Christian minority in Iran. Daniel Shayesteh, for instance, writes about his experience of converting to Christianity from Islam in his memoir *The House I left Behind: A Journey from Islam to Christ* (2014), and Maryam Rostampour and Marziyeh Amirizadeh recount their captivity narrative in Iran as Christian women in *Captive in Iran* (2013).

Interestingly enough this period has also seen a rise in narratives by Iranian men, particularly those who were, in one way or another, involved with the political situation of the time. For example, in 2010 a double agent for the CIA and Iran, using the pseudonym Reza Kahlili, published an almost fictive memoir of his double life, *A Time to Betray: The Astonishing Life of a CIA Double Agent Inside Iran's Revolutionary Guard.* The book, a one of a kind narrative, takes us inside both the Iranian and US political systems and offers an intriguing account of the behind the scenes politics that rule the two societies. The book was so popular that it was reprinted in a paperback edition in 2013, with a new subtitle: *A Gripping True Spy Story of Betrayal, Fear, and Courage.*

Additionally, new platforms have been offering alternative possibilities for publication, which, without the many layers of censors, gatekeepers, allow for easier ways to share stories with the reading public. Over the last few years there has been an increase in self-publishing and digital or e-publications. While small, online self-publishing companies such as Lulu.com had already established systems through which anyone could publish their work, more recently, bigger and more mainstream companies have also been offering self and digital publishing options for anyone across the globe. For example, Amazon.com has set up new self and e-publishing possibilities through their digital Kindle Editions, as well as through Create Space Publishing.[5] These options offer accessible tools for publication whereby being a published author, and accessing audiences of millions worldwide, is as easy as uploading a cover image and the manuscript onto one of the digital platforms. The downside to this is that, without the professional gatekeepers to control the quality of the work, there is a definite and visible decrease in the literary merit and presentation of some of the books. However, on the upside, it means that those with a story but without the literary merit, or those whose topic might not interest large publishing houses, have an accessible platform for communication.

Particularly since 2011, a period in which digital publishing has become progressively more popular and accessible, these media have provided a new platform on which the Iranian diaspora can publish their work. In the last several years, one can see an increase in the number of self-published and digital books by Iranian writers in English. Since 2011 there have been at least 11 self-published books by the Iranian diaspora in English, including Simon Sion Ebrahimi's *Veiled Romance* (2011), Hossein Tirgan *Goodbye Iran* (2012), Hassan Tabib's *Under Pressure from the Pasdaran and the CIA* (2012) and *Mission in Tehran* (2012), Naser Shahrivar's *The Man Who Could Not Say Love* (2012), Jalil Mortazavi's *From Iran to America: Changes, Choices, Challenges* (2013), Ferdows Kazami's *Unwanted Son* (2013), Mary Noor's *The Secret Bond with my Jewish Friend* (2013), A. Mir's *My Hidden Past* (2013), Mehrdad Goudarzi's *A Letter from Iran* (2013), and Siavosh Khonsari's *Out of Iran: My Journey through Revolutions and Life* (2013) and Mahmoud Fotouhi's *The Visionary Memoirs of a Mirza-turned-Banker* (2014). While in many of the cases above, the lack of professional expertise makes itself clear even from the very cover of the book, this does not lessen their value in offering new and unheard perspectives to the existing body of diasporic Iranian literature in English. In fact one can argue that without the professional editors and gatekeepers, there is a greater possibility of hearing rawer and truer accounts, unscathed and unfiltered by the economical, political and marketing agendas of the big publishing industries.

In sum, the events of 2009 coupled with the new platforms of expression have provided diasporic Iranian writers with a new direction and space for writing, forming what we can identify as a third wave of writing in diasporic Iranian literature in English. Concurrently, we have to acknowledge that this third wave is not limited to a North American context. While much of this study has focused on the body of work by diasporic Iranian writers in English in North America, in the last few years there has been an emerging body of work in English by Iranians in other countries. For example in Australia, where in recent years there has been an increased Iranian, particularly refugee and asylum seeker, population, there has been an accompanying emergence of a body of diasporic Iranian literature. Although, because of the relative youth of the Iranian diaspora in Australia compared to North America and Europe, so that the first generation migrants are still grappling with issues of language and resettlement, the literature is still prominently in Persian,[6] one can see the blooming stages of a new body of work emerging in English. For instance, Ali Alizadeh is a young poet, novelist and playwright who teaches creative writing at the University of Monash in Melbourne. He is one of the few who writes fiction, and has published a number of books in English, including *Iran: My Grandfather* and *The New Angel* and more recently *Transactions*. Similarly, Mammad Aidani, who is also a lecturer at the University of Melbourne, has published some fiction in English, including a novella, *A Picture out of Frame* (1997). Aside from a few professional fiction writers, there have been a number of memoirs published by the Iranian diaspora in Australia by Australian publishers. Among them, for instance, Zarah Ghahramani published her prison experiences in her memoir *My Life as a Traitor.* Banafsheh Serov, who fled Iran with her family through the mountains to escape to Australia, recounts her journey in *Under Starless Sky.* In a self-published memoir, *Mirror from Stone* (2009), Koroush Keshavarz, too, recounts his migration experiences to Australia. More recently, Kooshyar Karimi recounts his experiences as a Jewish doctor in Iran in his memoir *I Confess: Revelations in Exile* (2012).

More broadly, there is a substantial increase in the number of Iranian creative writers in English, based in Australia, as well as an increase in scholarly work that examines various aspects of their work. For example, Nasrin Mahoutchi, who is a PhD candidate, and who came to Australia as a refugee, is working on a creative writing thesis at the University of Western Sydney. Similarly, Kaveh Akbari, a political advocate and poet who writes in English, has been in the process of establishing a poetry slam dedicated to the poetry of the Iranian diaspora in English.

There is also scholarly work being done on diasporic Iranian literature in English from Australia. The study that led to the publication of this book, for example, was conceived and carried out in Australia through the University of New South Wales and the Australian National University. Similarly, Laetitia Nanquette, working from the University of New South Wales, is conducting research as part of her post-doctorate programme on diasporic Iranian writing in Australia in both English and Persian. Mammad Aidani, Ali Alizadeh and Azadeh Davachi, who are creative writers themselves, are all active in researching various aspects of diasporic Iranian literature in English, in Australia and within the wider context.

The gradual expansion of creative expression in English by the diasporic Iranian communities, as well as an increase in the scholarly attention to this field worldwide, particularly after the events of 2009 coupled with the new mediums of digital expression, points to new possibilities of creation and understanding. This wave, unlike the previous ones when both expression and analysis were generally limited and controlled by gatekeepers in a North American context, has allowed for new voices and analysis to be heard. This means that Iranians now have more freedom to tell their stories in their own voices. This is an important step in the way Iranian narratives are received in the West.

As Arash Hejazi, the man who filmed Neda Agha Soltan's death and circulated the video on the internet, and who soon after the events escaped the country, writes in his memoir, *The Gaze of the Gazelle: The Story of a Generation*:

> We are part of a generation that was later called the Burnt Generation – the generation known in the US as 'Generation X'. We were between seven and 15 at the time of the Islamic Revolution. We were the generation that witnessed the murders of

> its uncles during the Revolution and the execution and imprisonment of its parents afterwards. A generation doomed to spend the best years of its life amid the horrors of the Iran–Iraq war, either on the front, running on landmines to open up a path for the troops, or at home, dreading the return of a friend from the front in a coffin and then walking in the funeral procession that set out from the schoolyard. A generation that entered puberty while being trained how to use AK-47 assault rifles, a generation not permitted to have any contact with the opposite sex and not allowed to dance or make merry. A generation that was taught not to trust anyone. A generation that dreaded its own shadow and saw too much, far more than anyone should be forced to witness in a lifetime.
>
> [. . .] We survived to bear witness to what we had endured for the next generation: Neda's generation.[7]

The accounts that are emerging as part of this new wave are not only telling the stories of a generation of Iranians who have, after many years, gained the opportunity to express themselves. Rather, this is the beginning of an exciting new body of work that will expand and broaden the way both Iran and Iranians are perceived in the world. It is also the beginning of a new discursive space with its own specific techniques that will contribute to this growing field, the study of which will have to be the subject of further work in the future.

APPENDIX

BOOKS PUBLISHED BY IRANIAN WRITERS IN ENGLISH AS OF MID-2014

1. Abdoh, S. (2000), *The Poet Game*, Picador, New York.
2. ——— (2004), *Opium*, Faber and Faber, London.
3. ——— (2014), *Tehran at Twilight*, Akashic Books, Brooklyn.
4. Abramian, J. (2006), *My Iranian Matriarchs*, PublishAmerica, MD.*
5. Agah, A. (2007), *We Lived to Tell*, McGilligan Books, Toronto.*
6. Aghdashloo, S. (2013), *The Alley of Love and Yellow Jasmines*, Harper Collins, New York.*
7. Aidani, M. (1997), *A Picture Out of Frame*, Black Pepper Publications, Melbourne.
8. Alam, A. (1991), *The Shah and I: the Confidential Diary of Iran's Royal Court 1968–1977*, I.B. Tauris, New York.*
9. Alemi, M. (2008), *Interruptions: A Novel*, Ibex, Bethesda MD.
10. Alizadeh, A. (2009), *The New Angel*, Transit Lounge, Yarraville VIC.
11. ——— (2010), *Iran: My Grandfather*, Transit Lounge, Yarraville VIC.*
12. ——— (2013), *Transactions*, University of Queensland Press, Brisbane.
13. Amini, M. (1985), *The Sunset Drifters*, Afsaneh Consulting Company, Canoga Park CA.

* Indicates autobiography.

14. ——— (1987), *Dreams of a Native Son*, Afsaneh Consulting Company, Canoga Park CA.
15. ——— (1989), *The Howling Leopard*, Afsaneh Consulting Company, Canoga Park CA.
16. ——— (2004), *Escape from Paradise*, Afsaneh Consulting Company, Canoga Park CA.
17. Amirrezvani, A. (2007), *Blood of Flowers*, Little, Brown and Company, New York.
18. ——— (2012), *Equal of the Sun*, Scribner, New York.
19. ——— and P. Karim (ed) (2013), *Tremors: New Fiction by Iranian American Writers*, Arkansas University Press, AR.
20. Andalibian, R. (2012), *The Rose Hotel*, Nightingale Press, CA.
21. Ansari, A. (2010), *My Dream of Stars: from Daughter of Iran to Space*, Palgrave Macmillan, Basingstoke.*
22. Aram, A. (2013), *Escape from Iran*, CreateSpace Publishing, online.
23. Ardalan, D. (2008), *My Name is Iran*, Holt Paperbacks, New York.*
24. Aryanpour, A. (2000), *Behind the Tall Walls*, 1st Book Library, Bloomington IN.
25. ——— (2004), *Simurgh: a Journey in Search of Truth*, AuthorHouse, Bloomington IN.
26. Asadi, H. (2010), *Letters to my Torturer: Love, Revolution and Imprisonment in Iran*, Oneworld Publications, Oxford.*
27. Asayesh, G. (1999), *Saffron Sky: a Life between Iran and America*, Beacon Press: Boston MA.*
28. Assefi, N. (2006), *Aria*, Harcourt Books, Orlando FL.
29. Azadi, A. (2009), *For the Life of a Butterfly*, Infinity Publishing, Philadelphia PA.
30. Azadi, S. (1987), *Out of Iran: One Woman's Escape from the Ayatollahs*, Macdonald, London.*
31. Azimi, S. (2007), *Crows in the Nightingale's Tree*, IUniverse, Lincoln NE.
32. Bahari, M. (2011), *Then They Came for Me: a Family's Story of Love, Captivity and Survival*, Random House, New York.*
33. Baharloo, M. (2004), *The Quince Seed Potion*, Bridgeworks, New York.
34. Bahrampour, T. (1999), *To See and See Again: a Life in Iran and America*, Farrar, Straus and Giroux, New York.*

35. Balali, M. (2009), *Houri: A Nymph of Paradise*, Permanent Press, Sag Harbour NY.
36. Baniameri, S. (2005), *The Iranican dream*, Virtualbookworm.com.*
37. Banisadr, M. (2004), *Masoud: Memoirs of an Iranian Rebel*. Al Saqi Books, London.*
38. Bashi, P. (2009), *Nylon Road: A Graphic Memoir of Coming of Age in Iran*, St Martin's Griffin, New York.*
39. Bidgoli, F. (2005), *Cracked Pomegranate*, Regent Press, Oakland CA.
40. ——— (2010), *The Twisted Path Home*, Dog Ear Publishing, New York.
41. Bijan, D. (2011), *Maman's Homesick Pie: A Persian Heart in an American Kitchen*, Algonquin, Chapel Hill NC.
42. Chubin, B. (1984), *The Feet of the Snake*, Arbour House, New York.
43. ——— (1989), *The 13th Directorate*, Ivy Books.
44. Consolver, M. (2009), *The Darkest Days of My Life in the U.S. and Iran*, Dorrance Publishing Co., Pittsburgh PA.*
45. Courtauld, P. (1990), *A Persian Childhood*, Pelican, London.*
46. Crowther, Y. (2006), *Saffron Kitchen*, Viking, New York.*
47. Daniealypour, N. (2007), *Oriental Beach*, BookSurge Publishing, Charleston SC.
48. Darabi, P. (1999), *Rage Against the Veil: the Courageous Life and Death of an Islamic Dissident*, Prometheus Books, New York.
49. Darznik, J. (2011), *The Good Daughter*, Grand Central Publishing, New York.*
50. Dayton, E. (2011), *The House that War Minister Built*, Octavio Publications, Washington DC.
51. Delijani, S. (2013), *Children of the Jacaranda Tree*, Atria Books, New York.
52. Dumas, F. (2003), *Funny in Farsi*, Random House, New York.*
53. ——— (2009), *Laughing without an Accent*, Random House, New York.
54. Ebadi, S. (2006), *Iran Awakening: from Prison to Peace Prize: One Woman's Struggle at the Crossroads of History*, Random House, Toronto ON.*
55. ——— (2011), *The Golden Cage*, Kales Press, New York.
56. Ebrahimi, S. (2011), *Veiled Romances*, Simon-Writes.com.
57. Ebtekar, M. (2000), *Takeover in Tehran: the Inside Story of the 1979 U.S Embassy Capture*, Talonbooks, Vancouver BC.*

58. Emtiaz, A.V. (2004), *Eve East and West of Eden: the Journey of Working Mother between Mideast and America*, AuthorHouse, Bloomington IN.*
59. ——— (2013), *Eve East and West of Eden: the Journey of Working Mother between Mideast and America: Two,* AuthorHouse, Bloomington IN.*
60. Entekhabifard, C. (2007), *Camelia: Save Yourself by Telling the Truth*, Seven Stories Publications, New York.*
61. Esfandiari, F. (1955), *Identity Card*, New York.
62. ——— (1959), *Day of Sacrifice*, New York.
63. ——— (1965), *The Beggar*, New York.
64. Esfandiari, H. (2009), *My Prison, My Home*, Harper Collins, New York.*
65. Eslami, E. (2010), *Bone Worship*, Pegasus Books, New York.
66. Fallahi, N. (2002), *The Nidus: Cradle of Terror*, Bonneville Books, Springville UT.
67. Faramaz, H. (2011), *Bi Parchamaan: the Flagless Ones*, A-Argus Better Books Publication, Kernersville NC.*
68. Farman-Farmaian, M. (1997), *Blood and Oil*, Random House, New York.*
69. Farman-Farmaian, M. (2007), *A Mirror Garden*, Random House, New York.*
70. Farman-Farmaian, S. (1996), *Daughter of Persia: a Woman's Journey from her Father's Harem through the Islamic Revolution*, Corgi Press, Auckland.*
71. Farzan, M. (1969), *The Airplane Ticket*, New York.
72. Fathi, N. (2014), *The Lonely War: One Woman's Account for the Struggle of Modern Iran*, Basic Books, New York.
73. Feghi, R. (2000), *Camelia's Ring*, IUniverse, Lincoln NE.
74. Ferdowsi, F. (2009), *Mushrooms in the Sand*, WingSpan Press, Livermore CA.
75. Firouz, A. (2003), *In the Walled Garden*, Little, Brown and Company, New York.
76. Fotouhi, M. (2014) *The Visionary Memoirs of a Mirza-turned-Banker.* Create space publishing, online.
77. Ghaffari, R. (2011), *A State of Fear: My 10 Years Inside Iran's Torture Jails*, John Blake, London.*

78. Ghahramani, Z. (2008), *My Life as a Traitor*, Farrar, Straus, and Giroux, New York.*
79. Ghahremani, Z. (2010), *Sky of Red Poppies*, Turquoise Books, New York.
80. ——— (2013), *Moon Daughter*, Turquoise Books, New York.
81. Ghasemzadeh, N. (2013), *Desert Mojito*, Museberry Press, San Diego CA.
82. Ghodstinat, S. (2003), *Journey to Starland*, Vanguard Press, New York.
83. Goldin, F. (2004), *Wedding Song: Memoirs of a Jewish Iranian Woman*, Brandeis University Press, London.*
84. Golmakani, A. (2011), *Solacers*, Red Corn Poppy Books, Traverse City, MI.
85. Golrang, A. (2004), *Parpin Flowers*, PublishAmerica, MD.
86. Goudarzi, M. (2012), *A Letter from Iran*, Smashwords.
87. Guppy, S. (1988), *The Blindfold Horse: Memories of a Persian Childhood*, Heinemann, London.*
88. ——— (1991), *A Girl in Paris: a Persian Encounter with the West*, William Heinemann, New York.*
89. ——— (2008), *The Secret of Laughter: Magical Tales from Classical Persia*, Tauris Parke Paperbacks, New York.
90. Hachtroudi, F. (2011), *The Twelfth Imam's A Woman?*, Key Publishing House, Toronto ON.
91. Hafezi, Y. Y. (2012), *Memoir: a Family's Life in Iran, 1850–1950*, CreateSpace.
92. Hakakian, R. (2004), *Journey From the Land of No*, Bantam, Auckland.*
93. Hamekas, H. (2009), *Omid's Shadow*, MM Books, Watertown MN.
94. Hejazi, A. (2011), *The Gaze of the Gazelle*, Seagull Books, London.*
95. Hojabri, A. (2013), *A Sip, a Bite, a Mouthful: A Memoir of Food and Growing up in Shiraz*, Fleur Publications, online.
96. Homa, A. (2010), *Echoes from the Other Land*, Tsar Publications, Toronto ON.
97. Hosseini, A. (2012), *The Lemon Grove*, Curbstone Books 2, San Diego CA.
98. Hovanessian, E. (2003), *Under the Blue Dome*, Xlibris, Bloomington IN.
99. ——— (2011), *One Life, Three Cultures: An Iranian Armenian Odyssey*, Gomidas Institute, London.*
100. Ilyaie, B. (2012), *Journey Back from Ixtlan: a Non-Ordinary Transformation Account of a Persian Enchanted Soul*, WestBow Press, Bloomington IN.*

101. Kahlili, R. (2010), *A Time to Betray: the Astonishing Life of a CIA Double Agent Inside Iran's Revolutionary Guard*, Threshold Edition, New York.*
102. Kamali, M. (2013), *Together Tea*, Eco, New York.
103. Kambin, S. and P. Kambin (2007), *Finding Refuge: My Journey from the Middle East to Michigan*, IUniverse, Bloomington IN.*
104. Karim, P. (ed.) (1999), *A World in Between: Poems, Stories and Essays by Iranian–Americans*, George Braziller, New York.
105. ——— (ed.) (2006), *Let Me Tell You Where I've Been: New Writing by Women of the Iranian Diaspora*, Arkansas University Press, Fayetteville AR.
106. Karimi, K. (2012) *I Confess: Revelations in Exile*, Wild Dingo Press, Melbourne.*
107. Kashani, F. (2007), *Poetry Lesson*, Booklocker.com.
108. ——— (2010), *Hero Pizza*, Booklocker.com.
109. Kashani-Sabet, F. (2010), *Martyrdom Street*, Syracuse University Press, Syracuse NY.
110. Kasirri, K. and R. Safarnejad (2006), *Veiled Souls*, Publish America, MD.
111. Kazerooni, A. (2005), *Little Man*, Tate Publishing and Enterprise, Mustang OK.
112. Keshavarz, F. (2007), *Jasmine and Stars: Reading More than* Lolita *in Tehran*, Caravan Books, NC.
113. Keshavarz, K. (2009), *Mirror from Stone*, CreateSpace.*
114. Keshavarz, T. (2010), *Between Cups of Coffee*, Matador, Leicester.
115. Khadivi, L. (2010), *The Age of Orphans*, Bloomsbury, New York.
116. ——— (2012), *The Walking*, Bloomsbury, New York.
117. Khakpour, P. (2006), *Sons and Other Flammable Objects*, Grove Press, New York.
118. ——— (2014), *The Last Illusion*, Bloomsbury, New York.
119. Khalili, N. (1994), *Sidewalks on the Moon: The Journey of a Mystic Architect through Tradition, Technology and Transformation*, Cal-Earth Press, CA.
120. Kherad, N. (2008), *In the House of My Bibi: Growing Up in Revolutionary Iran*, Academic Chicago Publishers, IL.*
121. Khonsari, S. (2013), *Out of Iran: My Journey through Revolution and Life*, CreateSpace.

122. Khorrami, M.M. and S. Vatanabadi (2000), *A Feast in the Mirror: Stories by Contemporary Iranian Women*, Lynn Reinner, Boulder CO.
123. Khorsandi, S. (2009), *A Beginner's Guide to Acting English*, CPI Cox and Wyman, Reading.
124. Kordi, G. (1991), *An Iranian Odyssey*, Serpent's Tail, London.*
125. Latifi, A. (2005), *Even After all this Time: a Story of Love, Revolution, and Leaving Iran*, Regan Books, New York.*
126. Mahmoody, S. (2013), *Lost Without My Daughter*, Thistle Publishing, London.
127. Mahvi, P. (2011), *Deadly Secrets of Iranian Princes: Audacity to Act*, Friesen Press, New York.
128. Majd, H. (2009), *The Ayatollah Begs to Differ*, Penguin, London.
129. ——— (2013), *The Ministry of Guidance Invites You to Not Stay: an American Family in Iran*, Doubleday, New York.
130. Manteghi, M. (2014), *The Street of Good Fortune*, Forefrtong Media Group, Johannesburg.*
131. Mashayekhi, R. (2013), *From Iran to America: Mahnaz and Shirin – A Love Story*, East to West Publications, San Diego CA.
132. Mehran, M. (2005), *Pomegranate Soup*, Fourth Estate, Harper Collins, Sydney.
133. ——— (2008), *Rose Water and Soda Bread*, Random House, New York.
134. Milani, A. (1996), *Tales of Two Cities: A Persian Memoir*, Mage, New York.*
135. Mir, A. (2013), *My Hidden Past*, Amazon Digital.
136. Moaveni, A. (2005), *Lipstick Jihad*, Perseus Books, New York.*
137. ——— (2009), *Honeymoon in Tehran: Two Years of Love and Danger*, Random House, New York.*
138. Moezzi, M. (2013), *Haldol and Hyacinths: A Bipolar Life*, Avery, New York.*
139. Mogadam, A. (2010), *Death to the Dictator*, Farrar, Straus and Giroux, New York.
140. Mohammadi, K. (2010), *Cypress Tree: A Love Letter to Iran*, Bloomsbury, London.*
141. Molavi, A. (1990), *Persian Pilgrimages: Journeys Across Iran*, W.W. Norton, New York.
142. ——— (2005), *The Soul of Iran*, W.W. Norton, New York.

143. Monadjemi, L. I. (1993), *Blood and Carnations*, Eldorado, Kirribilli NSW.
144. ——— (2010), *A Matter of Survival*, Austin and Macauley Publishers, London.
145. Morad, A. (2010), *A Surgeon's Incredible Life Journey: A Memoir*, ArtHouse, Bloomington IN.*
146. Mortazavi, J. (2013), *From Iran to America: Changes, Choices and Challenges*, David Dvorkin Self-Publication, Kindle.*
147. Moshiri, F. (2000), *At the Wall of the Almighty*, Interlink Books, New York.
148. ——— (2001), *The Bathhouse*, Black Heron Press, Washington DC.
149. ——— (2004), *The Crazy Dervish and the Pomegranate Tree*, Black Heron Press, Washington DC.
150. ——— (2005), *Against Gravity*, Penguin Books, London.
151. ——— (2014), *The Drum Tower*, Sandstone Press, London.
152. Mosteshar, C. (1995), *Unveiled: Love and Death Among the Ayatollahs*, Hodder and Stoughton, London.
153. Mostofi, S. (2011), *Cemetery of Dreams*, Emerald Book Company, Austin TX.
154. Mottahedeh, R. (1987), *The Mantle of the Prophet: Religion and Politics in Iran*, Penguin, Middlesex.
155. Nafisi, A. (2004), *Reading* Lolita *in Tehran*, Fourth Estate, New York.*
156. ——— (2010), *Things I've Been Silent About*, Random House, New York.*
157. ——— (2014), *The Republic of Imagination: America in Three Books*, Viking Adults New York.
158. Nahai, G. (2000), *Moonlight on the Avenue of Faith*, Scribner, Sydney.
159. ——— (2001), *Cry of the Peacock*, Scribner, Sydney.
160. ——— (2002), *Sunday's Silence*, Scribner, Sydney.
161. ——— (2008), *Caspian Rain*, MacAdam/Cage, San Francisco CA.
162. ——— (2014), *The Luminous Heart of Jonah S*, Akashic Books, Brooklyn.
163. Najafi, N. (1953), *Persia is My Heart*, Harper and Row Publishers, New York.*
164. ——— (1958), *Reveille for a Persian Village*, Harper and Brothers, New York.

165. Nakhjavani, B. (1983), *Four on an Island*, George Ronald, Oxford.
166. ——— (2000), *The Saddlebag*, Beacon Press, Boston MA.
167. ——— (2004), *Paper: Dreams of a Scribe*, Bloomsbury Publishing, London.
168. Naraghi, A. (1998), *The Big Green House*, Editions CEDAH.
169. Nasser, D. (2009), *Jumping through Fires: a Gripping Story of One Man's Escape from Revolution to Redemption*, Baker Books, Grand Rapids MI.*
170. Nayeri, D. (2013), *A Teaspoon of Earth and Sea*, Riverhead Books, London.
171. Nazarian, A. (2009), *Life as a Visitor*, Assouline, New York.*
172. Nazemian A (2014), *The Walk in Closet*, Curtis Brown Digital, Online.
173. Negarestani, R. (2008) *Cyclonopedia: Complicity with Anonymous Materials* (*Anamoly*) re.press, Prahan VIC.
174. Nemat, M. (2008), *Prisoner of Tehran*, Free Press, New York.*
175. ——— (2010), *Life After Tehran: A Life Reclaimed*, McNallyRobinson, Vancouver BC.*
176. Noori, N. (2003), *Dakhme*, Toby Press, Israel.
177. ——— (2013), *The Secret Bond with My Jewish Friend*, Amazon Digital.
178. Nowia-Pahlavi, C. (2009), *The Hidden One*, BookSurge, Charleston SC.*
179. Ohanian, A. (2010), *Dreaming of America: A Daring Escape*, AHO Publishing, Westhampton NY.*
180. ——— (2012), *The Apple Tree Blossoms in the Fall*, LazyDay Publishing.
181. Omid, G. (2004), *Living in Hell*, Park Avenue Publishing, Oklahama City OK.*
182. Pahlavi, A. (1980), *Faces in a Mirror: Memoirs from Exile*, Prentice-Hall, NJ.*
183. ——— (1995), *Time for Truth*, In Print, Auburn IN.*
184. Pahlavi, F. (2004), *An Enduring Love: My Life with the Shah, A Memoir*, Miramax, New York.*
185. Pakravan, S. (1988), *The Arrest of Hoveyda: Stories of the Iranian Revolution*, Blind Owl Press, CA.
186. ——— (2011), *Azadi: a Novel of Protest on the Streets of Tehran*, Parallel Books.
187. Pari, S. (1997), *The Fortune Catcher*, Warner Books, New York.

188. Parsipour, A. (2004), *Ali, an Iranian American View*, BookSurge, Charleston SC.*
189. Parvin, M. (1987), *Cry for My Revolution, Iran*, Mazda, Costa Mesa CA.
190. ——— (1996), *Avicenna and I: the Journey of Spirits*, Mazda, Costa Mesa CA.
191. ——— (2003), *Dardedel: Rumi, Hafez, and Love in New York*, The Permanent Press, New York.
192. ——— (2007), *Alethophobia*, IBEX, Bethesda MD.
193. ——— (2011), *Out of the Gray: a Concerto for Neurons and Synapses*, IBEX, Bethesda MD.
194. Pazouki, R. (2010), *Watch Me*, Lulu.com.*
195. Pedram, H. (2006), *Bazaar Stories*, Lulu.com.
196. Quaramby, K. (2013), *Blood and Water: an Anglo-Iranian Love Story*, Thistle Publishing, London.*
197. Rabiipour, S. (2009), *Farewell to Islam*, Xulon Press, Maitland FL.
198. ——— (2010), *Trapped in Iran: the Land of the Ayatollah*, Thomas Nelson, Edinburgh.*
199. Rachlin, N. (1979), *Foreigner*, W.W. Norton and Company, New York.
200. ——— (1983), *Married to a Stranger*, E, P, Dutton, Inc, New York.
201. ——— (1995), *The Heart's Desire*, City Lights Books, San Francisco CA.
202. ——— (2006), *Jumping Over Fire*, City Lights Books, San Francisco CA.
203. ——— (2007), *Persian Girls*, Tarcher, New York.
204. Raffat, D. (1978), *The Caspian Circle*, Houghton Mifflin, New York.
205. ——— (2000), *Folly of Speaking*, Blind Owl Press, CA.
206. ——— (2010), *Temporary Wife*, Xlibris, Bloomington IN.
207. ——— (2011), *Maya Blue*, Xlibris, Bloomington IN.
208. ——— (2012), *Solitaire*, Xlibris, Bloomington IN.
209. Radjavi, H. (2011), *French Hats in Iran*, Mage, New York.*
210. Razmara, N. (2002), *The Dance of the Rose and the Nightingale*, Syracuse University Press, Syracuse NY.*
211. ——— (2007), *Ups and Downs: a Memoir*, AthourHouse, Bloomington IN.*
212. Redjali, S. (2013) *A Symphony of Love: Triumph of Education over Adversity*, Xlibris LLC, Bloomington IN.*
213. Reid, M. and T. Reid (1995), *Snake's Marble: A Persian Memoir*, Vintage, New York.

214. Rostampour, M. and M. Amirizadeh (2013), *Captive in Iran: A Remarkable True Story of Hope and Triumph amid the Horror of Tehran's Brutal Evin Prison*, Tyndale, Atlanta GA.
215. Saadati, S. (2003), *Persian Weddings: a Personal Journey into Iran's Culture*, Xlibris, Bloomington IN.*
216. Saberi, R. (1982), *The Labyrinth*, Exposition Printers of Florida, FL.*
217. Sabri-Tabrizi, G.R. (1989), *Iran: a Child's Story, a Man's Experience*, International Publishers, New York
218. Saberi, R. (2010), *Between Two Worlds: My Life and Captivity in Iran*, Harper Collins, New York.*
219. Sahebjam, F. (1994), *The Stoning of Soraya M*, Arcade Publishing, New York.
220. Sametipour, A. (2014) *Tehran Moonlight: A Novel*, CreateSpace Publishing, online.
221. Sanati, P. (2009), *Under a Papery Roof*, VDM Verlag Dr. Müller, Saarbrücken.*
222. Sandler, J.M. (2013), *Caspian Diary*, Amazon.com
223. Sarfeh, I.J. (2013), *Beyond the Third Garden*, Musa Publications, Lancaster OH.
224. ——— (2014), *From the Ashes of Strife*, Musa Publishing, Colorado Springs, CO.
225. Sarram, M. (2008), *Transplanted: a Memoir of Faith and Vision for American Muslims*, Amana Publications, Beltsville MD.*
226. Satrapi, M. (2003), *Persepolis*, Jonathan Cape, London.*
227. ——— (2004), *Persepolis 2*, Jonathan Cape, London.*
228. ——— (2006), *Embroideries*, Jonathan Cape, London.
229. ——— (2009), *Chicken with Plums*, Jonathan Cape, London.
230. Sayrafiezadeh, S. (2009), *When Skateboards Will be Free*, The Dial Press, New York.*
231. Seraji, M. (2009), *Rooftops of Tehran*, New American Library, London.
232. Serov, B. (2008), *Under a Starless Sky: A Family's Escape from Tehran*, Hachette Livre, Sydney.*
233. Servati, A. (2006), *In Search of Heaven*, Senna Pictures.
234. Sewell, N. (2010), *The Ruby Tear Catcher*, SummerHill Press, Canada.
235. Shafii, R. (1997), *Scent of Saffron: Three Generations of an Iranian Family*, Scarlet Press, London.*
236. Shahrivar, M. (2012), *The Man Who Could Not Say Love*, Weston Kincade, New York.

237. Shahzadi, B. (2006), *Goldoon and Professor: Memoirs of a Bi-Cultural Marriage*, Trafford, Victoria BC.*
238. Shayesteh, D. (2013), *The House I Left Behind: a Journey From Islam to Christ*, Talesh Books, Sydney.
239. Shirazi, M. (1984), *Javady Alley*, Women's Press, London.
240. ——— (1992), *Seige of Azadi Square*, Women's Press, London.
241. Shirazi, R. (2010), *The Last Living Slut: Born in Iran, Bred Backstage*, Igniter, New York.*
242. Sholevar, B. (1992), *Dead Reckoning*, Concourse Press, Philadelphia PA.
243. Siletz, A. (2005), *Mullah with No Legs and Other Stories*, Nicholas Brealey Publishing, New York.
244. Sofer, D. (2008), *Septembers of Shiraz*, Harper Perennial, New York.
245. Soltani, N. (2012), *My Stolen Face: the Story of a Dramatic Mistake*, Random House, Munich.*
246. Sullivan, Z. (2001), *Exiled Memories*, Temple University Press, Philadelphia PA.
247. Tabib, M.M. (2012), *Mission in Tehran*, CreateSpace.
248. ——— (2012), *Under Pressure from the Pasdaran and the CIA*, Books on Demand.
249. Tabibzadeh, M. (2007), *Persian Dreams*, Dreambooks.
250. Taheri, K. (2011), *Broken Silence: a True Story of a Sixteen Year Old's Captivity in Evin...Iran's most Feared Prison!*, iUniverse, Lincoln NE.*
251. Tajadod, N. (2008), *Rumi: the Fire of Love: a Novel*, Overlook Hardcover, New York.
252. ——— (2010), *Tehran, Lipstick, and Loopholes*, Virago Press, London.
253. Talebi, S. (2011), *Ghosts of Revolution*, Stanford University Press, Stanford CA.*
254. Tirgan, M.H. (2012), *Goodbye Iran*, Amazon Digital Services.*
255. Yaghmaian, B. (2002), *Social Changes in Iran: an Eyewitness Account of Dissent, Defiance, and New Movements of Rights*, State University of New York Press, New York.*
256. Yaghoobi, J. (2011), *Let Us Water the Flowers: the Memoir of a Political Prisoner in Iran*, Prometheus Books, Amherst NY.*
257. Yalfani, M. (2000), *Two Sisters*, Tsar Publications, Toronto ON.
258. ——— (2002), *Afsaneh's Moon*, MacGilligan, Toronto ON.
259. Yazdanfar, F. (1993), *A Walnut Sapling on Masih's Grave and Other Stories by Iranian Women*, Heinemann, Portsmouth.

NOTES

Introduction – Essence of Desire for a Better World

1. Pari 1997, p. 421.
2. Pakravan's granddaughter, Saeideh Pakravan, is also a writer. She has published a semi-autobiography, *Hoveyda's Arrest: Stories of the Iranian Revolution* (1988), and more recently a novel about the protests in Iran entitled *Azadi: A Novel of Protest in the Streets of Tehran* (2011). She has been translating this novel into Persian and distributing it chapter by chapter on her very active blog and email list. http://azadipakravan.wordpress.com.
3. See for instance Mahmood Karimi-Hakkak's 'Exiled Freedom' in *TDR* (2003). Negar Mottahedeh's 'Off the Grid: Reading Iranian Memoirs in Our Time of Total War' in *Middle East Report* 2006. Also see Farideh Goldin's 'Iranian Women and Contemporary Memoirs' on Iranian Chamber, 13 June 2006; Azita Osanloo's 'Imperative: The Pressure to be Exotic' in *Poets and Writers*; Babak Elahi's 'Translating the Self: Language and Identity in Iranian–American Women's Memoirs' in *Iranian Studies* 39/4 (2006), pp. 461–80; Amy Malek's 'Memoir as Iranian Cultural Production' in *Iranian Studies* 39/3 (2006), pp. 353–80.
4. See the last chapter of the book 'The Pangs of Exile: Memoir out of Iran', pp. 167–86.
5. The thesis was entitled 'Writing outside the Veil: Literature by Women of Iranian Diaspora', and was produced at Princeton University.
6. See *MELUS* 33/2 (Summer 2008). Refer to the introductory essay by Karim and Rahimieh, 'Introduction: Writing Iranian Americans into the American Literature Canon' for an overview of the condition of Iranian–American writing as it stood then, and also an overview of the special edition.

7. This statement was originally posted on the organisation's website. However, since 2013 the group has ceased to exist, and the organisers wrote an open letter explaining to the members that because of their other obligations it was no longer viable to run the group. The website containing the above citation has been inaccessible since it was taken offline in April 2013.
8. See the special section in 32/ 2.
9. See his book *Iranian and Diasporic Literature in the 21st Century: A Critical Study*, McFarland and Company Inc., London.
10. Mirsepassi 2000, p. 73.
11. See Mahloujian's essay 'Phoenix from the ashes: a tale for the book in Iran' on Iranian Chamber website <http://www.iranchamber.com/literature/articles/tale_of_book_iran.php>.
12. Ibid.
13. Hoveyda 2003, p. 91.
14. Hiro 1985, p. 262.
15. Ibid., p. 258.
16. Hoveyda 2003, p. 1.
17. Hiro 1985, p. 61.
18. Ibid., p. 262.
19. Ibid.
20. Mahloujian 'Phoenix from the ashes: a tale for the book in Iran.'
21. Zanganeh 2006, p. xi.
22. Said 1978, p. 1.
23. Amory 1928, p. 15.
24. Benjamin 1887, p. 49.
25. Malcolm 1861, p. 66.
26. Mabro 1991, p. 3.
27. Mobasher 2006, p. 110.
28. Mostofi 2003, p. 685.
29. Ashcroft 2007, p. 411.
30. Bloch 1986, p. 4.
31. Ibid., p. 3.
32. Ibid., p. 5.
33. Ibid., p. 4.
34. Ashcroft 2009c, p. 704.
35. Boehmer 1995, p. 159.
36. Bhabha 1994, p. 1.
37. Ibid., p. 3.
38. Rahimieh 1992, p. 40.
39. For instance, in French there are numerous writers such as Sorous Kasmaii and Chahdorett Djavanne who are popular in France. There is also a body of scholarly work about French-Iranian literature. Laetitia Nanquette, for instance, has pioneered the field with her book *Orientalism versus Occidentalism: Literary Cultural Imaging Between France and Iran since the Islamic Revolution.* Kader

Abdolah is a well-known Iranian-Dutch author who has single-handedly transformed the relationship between Dutch and Persian literature through his numerous popular novels.

40. For discussion of diasporic Iranian literature and its classification see Mehrdad Darvishpour's blog entry 'The New Nest and Horizons of Exile' (2009). Maliheh Tiregol has also dedicated her entire site, http://www.mtiregol.com (in Farsi), to an analyses and discussion of what she calls 'thirty years of literature in exile'.

Chapter 1 History – 'Remembering and Narrating the Past'

1. Mostofi 2003, p. 685.
2. Bhabha 1994, p. 13.
3. Mostofi 2003, p. 682.
4. Hall 1996, p. 2.
5. Ibid., p. 4.
6. Mostofi 2003, p. 682.
7. Ibid., p. 685.
8. Ibid., p. 688.
9. See Ghahremani's blog entry 'Writing: on wings of memory' <http://www.zoeghahremani.com/blog1/?p=299>.
10. Check out the reviews on Mahbod Seraji's Amazon site for reviews: <http://www.amazon.com/Mahbod-Seraji/e/B001JSJP58/ref=ntt_dp_epwbk_0>.
11. Ibid.
12. Sabri-Tabrizi 1989, p. 7.
13. Ibid.
14. Mostofi 2003, p. 688.
15. Farman-Farmaian 1992, p. 11.
16. Sabri-Tabrizi 1989, p. 13.
17. Tirgan 2013, p. ii.
18. Ibid.
19. Fathi 2014, p. x.
20. Hall 1996, p. 2.
21. Netton and Salhi 2006, p. 3.
22. Mostofi 2003, p. 687.
23. Ashcroft 2009a, p. 8.
24. Mostofi 2003, p. 689.
25. Ibid., p. 689.
26. Naficy 2001, p. 152.
27. Whitlock 2007, p. 163.
28. Ibid., p. 165.
29. Ibid., p. 165.
30. See Ben Madadi's blog entry entitled 'Glorious Loneliness' on Iranian.com <http://iranian.com/Opinion/2004/November/Ben/index.html>.

31. Rahimieh 2002, p. 238.
32. Hall 1996, p. 4.
33. Ashcroft 2001b, p. 83.
34. Ibid., p. 92.
35. Ashcroft 2009c, p. 708.
36. Ibid., p. 709.
37. Ibid., p. 709.
38. Ashcroft 2009b, p. 3.
39. Ibid., p. 3.
40. Ibid.
41. Ibid., p. 4.
42. Hakakian, p. 13.
43. Ibid.
44. Ibid., p. 15.
45. Ibid., p. 11.
46. See Wanner's review 'Journey from the Land of No': Memoir paints child's life in shifting 1970s Iran', in *The Seattle Times*, 22 August <http://community.seattletimes.nwsource.com/archive/?date=20040822andslug=landofno22>.
47. Ashcroft 2001b, p. 92.
48. Amirrezvani 2007, p. 437.
49. Ibid., p. 448.
50. Ibid., p.450.
51. Amirrezvani 2013, p. 1.
52. See Sadegh's blog entry 'The Trial of Khosro Golsorkhi: Victim of the Shah's Firing Squad' on Iranian.com <http://iranian.com/main/blog/sadegh/trial-khosro-golsorkhi-victim-shahs-firing-squad.html>.
53. Seraji 2009, p. 143.
54. Ibid., p. 146.
55. Firouz 2003, p. 288.
56. See Anahita Firouz's website <http://www.anahitafirouz.com>.
57. Mottahede 1987, p. 10.
58. Ibid., p. 8.
59. See Willford's review 'The Mantle of the Prophet' <http://www.wrmea.com/component/content/article/126/1304-the-mantle-of-the-prophet.html>.
60. Ashcroft 2001b, p. 88.
61. Nahai 2001, p. 182.
62. Ibid., p. 223.
63. Ashcroft 2001, p. 89.
64. Ibid., p. 98.
65. Ibid., p. 92.
66. Ibid., p. 15.
67. Ashcroft 2009c, p. 706.
68. Hall 1996, p. 4.

69. Ibid.
70. Nietzsche qtd. Rabinow 1984, p. 81.
71. Hall 1996, p. 4.
72. Ashcroft 2009c, p. 705.
73. Ibid., p. 706.
74. Ibid.
75. Ibid.
76. Asayesh 1999, p. 3.
77. For a sociological perspective on the situation of diasporic Iranian identities see Diane Hoffman's 'Self and Culture Revisited'. With specific regard to the second generation sense of Iranian identity, see Ali Akbar Mahdi's 'The Second Generation Iranians: Questions and Concerns'.
78. Moaveni 2005, p. vii.
79. Ibid., pp. 24–5.
80. For various analyses of how Iranian–Americans have been coping with the stigma of the hostage crisis, see Mobasher's (2006) 'Cultural Trauma and Ethnic Identity Formation Among Iranian Immigrants in the United States'. Based on social research in California, Mobasher deals at length with some of the effects of the hostage crisis on the Iranian diaspora and the various measures that many Iranians have taken to overcome this association. Similarly see Mazyar Lotfalian's (1996) 'Working Through Psychological Understanding of the Diasporic Condition' and Nilou Mostofi's (2003) 'Who We Are: The Perplexity of Iran–American Identity?' For interesting data on how Iranian–Americans have worked in order to assimilate into their respective societies, see the fact sheet on the Iranian–American Community by Ali Motashari for the Iranian Studies Group Research Series of February 2004. According to this, the 2000 Census reports that Iranians have six times as many doctoral degrees as Americans on average. The 2000 Census also shows Iranian–Americans as having a 45 per cent higher per capita income and a median family income 38 per cent higher than the national average.
81. Ashcroft 2009c, p. 706.
82. Moaveni 2005, p. 26
83. Ibid., pp. 27–8.
84. Ashcroft 2007, p. 418.
85. Rahimieh 2002, p. 241.
86. Fathi 2014, p xiv.

Chapter 2 Sufi Poetry – 'Universal and Profound'

1. Dabashi in *The World is My Home: A Hamid Dabashi Reader*, ed. Davison and Muppidi 2011, p. 122.
2. Ibid., p. 122.

3. Keshavarz 2007, p. 30.
4. Karimi-Hakkak 1995, p. 1.
5. Nasr, 1991, p. 328.
6. Ibid.
7. Ibid., p. 329.
8. Ibid.
9. Zarrinkoub 1970, p. 139.
10. Trimingham 1971, p. 1.
11. Burckhardt 2008, p. 3.
12. Lewisohn 1992, p. 21.
13. Zarrinkoub 1970, p. 139.
14. Nasr 1991, p. 140.
15. Ibid., p. 331.
16. Zarrinkoub 1970, p. 140.
17. There is, however, some debate over some of the poets and their relationship with Sufism. For example, some believe that some poets, including Sa'adi, were indeed somewhat sceptical of Sufism as a practice. The debate has never clarified the truth about the poets' beliefs or whether their poetry should always be read in the light of Sufi philosophy and thought. See for instance Mohammad Ali Homa Katouzian's argument on his blog, <http://homakatouzian.com/?p=377>.

    For this reason, I am cautious to claim direct correlation between all Persian classical poetry and Sufism throughout this study.
18. For a complete list of Nasr's arguments on Sufi poetry, see his 'Persian Sufi Literature'.
19. Nasr 1999, p. 3.
20. Ibid.
21. Ibid., p. 8.
22. Ghazzali qtd. in McCarron's 'Baha'i, Sufi and Gnostic Shi'a spiritual cosmology', *Symbol Language and Cosmology* <https://sites.google.com/site/causeofgod/home/papers/cosmos-as-meditation/symbolic-language-cosmology>.
23. Nasr 1999, p. 5.
24. For an extended interpretation of the symbolism of wine see Saeidi and Unwin's 'Persian wine tradition and symbolism: evidence from the medieval poetry of Hafiz', *Journal of Wine Research*, 15/ 2, pp. 97–114.
25. Nasr 1999, p. 5.
26. Dutton 2010, p. 237.
27. Ibid., p. 236.
28. Nasr 1999, p. 5.
29. See Rashidian's blog entry 'Our Iranian Identity' <http://jahanshahrashidian-rashidian-blog.blogspot.com/2010/10/our-iranian-identity.html>.
30. Qtd in Ron Synovitz, 'Iran: clashes highlight "demonization" of Sufi Muslims' <http://www.unhcr.org/cgi-bin/texis/vtx/refworld/rwmain?docid=4742edf92d>.
31. Martin 2007, p. 33.
32. Ibid.

33. For a detailed analysis of this relationship refer to Matthijs Van Den Bos, *Mystic Regime: Sufism in Iran, from the Late Qajar Era to the Islamic Republic* (2002).
34. See Abdul Kasem's discussion in his blog 'Islam and poetry' <http://www.faithfreedom.org/Articles/abulkazem/Islam_and_poverty.htm>.
35. Nasr 1999, p. 6.
36. Rashidian 'Our Iranian Identity' <http://jahanshahrashidian-rashidian-blog.blogspot.com/2010/10/our-iranian-identity.html>.
37. Nafisi 'Azar Nafisi: Vladimir Nabokov', *Big Think* <http://bigthink.com/ideas/1966>.
38. Ghahremani 2010, p. 304.
39. Nasr 1999, p. 1.
40. Hall 1996, p. 223.
41. Davidson and Khun Eng 2007, p. 3.
42. Ibid., p. 3.
43. Hall 2003, p. 224.
44. Sullivan 2001, p. 17.
45. Although Latifi uses this line and quotes it from Hafiz, there is great debate among scholars and Hafez readers on the origins of the line. Some scholars argue that these verses are not actually Hafiz's lines and are not to be found in the Persian version of Hafiz. Rather, scholars believe that the lines were inserted into the English translation by American Sufi Poet Daniel Ladinsky. For more information on this debate see Arash Azizi's article 'Supposed Hafiz Poem recited by McGuinty turns out to be fake' <http://www.payvand.com/news/09/apr/1266.html>.
46. Sabri-Tabrizi 1989, p. 7.
47. Mostofi 2003, p. 688.
48. Meskoob 1992, p. 10.
49. Mostofi 2003, p. 688.
50. Ibid.
51. Refer to Nasr's 1999 essay 'Persian Sufi literature: its spiritual and cultural significance', for more detail.
52. de Bruijn 1997, p. 51.
53. There are various translations of these verses. This version is by Jonathan Star, qtd in Reza Rumi's blog <http://www.razarumi.com/2007/09/29/the-song-of-the-reed-on-rumis-birth-anniversary>.
54. Papan-Matin 2003, p. 246.
55. Mostofi 2003, p. 688.
56. Scott Meisami 1985, p. 245.
57. Ibid., p. 230.
58. Ibid., p. 231.
59. Moaveni 2005, p. 272.
60. Bahrampour 1999, p. 14.
61. Unfortunately Marsha Mehran was found dead in her apartment in a village in Ireland on 2 May 2014 at the age of 36.

62. Mehran 2005, p. 258.
63. Kho'i 2008, p. 49.
64. Mostofi 2003, p. 682.
65. Ibid., p. 345.
66. Ibid., p. 225.
67. Ibid.
68. Boehmer 1995, p. 227.
69. Rachlin 1995, p. 5.
70. Dutton 2010, p. 237.
71. Ibid.
72. King 1988, p. 222.
73. Ibid., p. 227.
74. Rachlin 1995, p. 165.
75. King 1988, p. 232.
76. Parvin 2003, p. 5.
77. Ibid., pp. 15–16.
78. Ibid., p. 19.
79. Ibid., p. 7.
80. Ibid., p. 10.
81. Ibid., p. 39.
82. Keshavarz 2007, p. 1.
83. Ibid., p. 7.
84. Ibid., p. 2.
85. Ibid., p. 7.
86. Ibid., p. 111.
87. Ibid., p. 110.
88. Nafisi qtd in Keshavarz 2007, p. 19.
89. Ibid., p. 70.
90. Ibid.
91. Ashcroft 2001, p. 5.
92. Ibid.
93. Ibid.

Chapter 3 The Memoir – 'Double-Edged' Narratives

1. See Nahai's article 'So what's with all the Iranian memoirs?' on *Publishers Weekly* <http://www.publishersweekly.com/pw/by-topic/columns-and-blogs/soapbox/article/4048-so-what-s-with-all-the-iranian-memoirs-.html>.
2. Ibid.
3. Whitlock 2007, p. 7.
4. Milani 1992, p. 209.
5. Ibid., p. 210.
6. Ibid., p. 213.
7. Ibid., p. 202.

8. Ibid., p. 46.
9. For an interesting analysis of the historical reasons for this kind of private/public dichotomy in the Muslim world, refer to Elizabeth Thompson's 'Public and Private in Middle Eastern Women's History'.
10. Milani 1992, p. 46.
11. Ibid.
12. Ibid., p. 201.
13. Her memoir was first published in Farsi, in 1982, under the title *Khatirat.* It was translated by Ana Vanzan and Amin Neshati and published in English under the title *Taj Al-Satlana Crowning Anguish: Memoirs of a Persian Princess from Harem to Modernity 1884–1914* (1994).
14. Milani further emphasizes Forough's controversy in her article 'Conflict Between Traditional Roles and Poetry in the Works of Forough Farrokhzad'.
15. Milani 1992, p. 46.
16. Esfandiari 1997, p. 1.
17. Nafisi 2010, p. xxi.
18. Henke 2000, p. xvi.
19. Ibid., p. xii.
20. Ashcroft 2007, p. 418.
21. Oliver 2001, p. 7.
22. Ibid.
23. Whitlock 2007, p. 10.
24. Ibid., p. 16.
25. Ibid., p. 11.
26. Whitlock 2000, p. 5.
27. Milani 1992, p. 212.
28. Ibid.
29. Nafisi 2010, p. xxi.
30. Whitlock 2008, p. 80.
31. Nafisi 2004, p. 76.
32. Ibid., p. 77.
33. Whitlock 2008, p. 80.
34. Azadi 1987, p. 1.
35. Mosteshar, 1995, p. 6.
36. Henke 2000, p. xvi.
37. See Eve Zibart's 'The power of the word: an Iranian writer recalls her youth in "the Land of No"', *Book Page* <http://bookpage.com/review/journey-from-the-land-of-no/the-power-of-the-word>.
38. Ibid.
39. Nemat 2007, p. 1.
40. Ibid., pp. 1–2.
41. See Sheehan's 'The unattainable feminist dream', *Sydney Morning Herald* <http://www.smh.com.au/news/opinion/the-unattainable-feminist-dream/2007/05/27/1180205070029.html>.

42. Nemat 2007, p. 2.
43. Oliver 2001, p. 8.
44. See her interview with Keira Butler, 'Thirty days in Iran's worst prison', *Mother Jones* <http://motherjones.com/politics/2008/01/thirty-days-irans-worst-prison>.
45. Nemat 2007, p. 250.
46. Ibid., p. 3.
47. Ibid., p. 4.
48. Ibid.
49. Ibid., p. 301.
50. Whitlock 2008, p. 81.
51. Bahrampour 1999, p. 357.
52. Moaveni 2005, p. 28.
53. Henke 2000, p. xii.
54. Bahrampour 1999, p. 203.
55. Hall 2003, p. 236.
56. Moaveni 2005, pp. vii–viii.
57. Motlagh 2008, p. 29.
58. Bahrampour 1999, p. 355.
59. Moaveni 2005, p. 26.
60. Oliver 2000, p. 4.
61. Ibid., p. 9.
62. Ibid., p. xvii.
63. Bahramitash 2005, p. 221.
64. Ibid., p. 223.
65. Whitlock 2007, p. 12.
66. Ibid., p. 13.
67. Amireh and Majaj 2001, p. 1.
68. Ibid.
69. Whitlock 2000, p. 146.
70. Whitlock 2008, p. 81.
71. Whitlock 2007, p. 161.
72. Vaughan and Clark 1981, p. 2.
73. Ibid.
74. Derounian 1988, p. 239.
75. Castiglia 1996, pp. ix–x.
76. Ibid.
77. Ibid.
78. Edwards 2010, p. 364.
79. Ibid., p. 362.
80. Ibid.
81. Ibid.
82. McAlister 2005, p. 6.
83. Tierney 2010, p. 134.
84. Little 2005, p. 9.

85. Ibid., p.10.
86. McAlister 'Saving Private Lynch' in *The New York Times* <http://www.nytimes.com/2003/04/06/opinion/saving-private-lynch.html>.
87. Edwards 2010, p. 340.
88. McAlister 'Saving Private Lynch' in *The New York Times* <http://www.nytimes.com/2003/04/06/opinion/saving-private-lynch.html>.
89. McAlister 2005, p. 198.
90. Ibid., p. 199.
91. Scott 2000, p. 178.
92. McAlister 2005, p. 199.
93. Darznik 2008, p. 57.
94. Whitlock 2007, p. 12.
95. Ibid.
96. Whitlock 2007, p. 54.
97. Ibid., p. 12.
98. Ibid., p. 13.
99. Ibid., p. 163.
100. Ibid., p. 165.
101. Genette 1997, p. xviii.
102. Whitlock 2007, p. 59.
103. Ibid., p. 58.
104. Whitlock 2008, p. 81.
105. Whitlock 2007, p. 59.
106. Ibid.
107. See for instance Burwell 2007, p. 290; Whitlock 2007, p. 21.
108. See Burwell 2007, p. 290; Whitlock 2007, p. 21.
109. Burwell 2007, p. 291.
110. Ibid.
111. Bahramitash 2005; Rastegar 2006; Dabashi 2006; Burwell 2007; Donadeh and Ahmed-Ghosh 2008.
112. Bahramitash 2006, p. 233.
113. Dabashi 'Native informer and the making of the American empire', *Al-Ahram Weekly Online* <http://weekly.ahram.org.eg/2006/797/special.htm>.
114. Ibid.
115. Bakhash 'Our family hostage crisis', *The New York Times* <http://www.nytimes.com/2007/06/27/opinion/27bakhash.html>.
116. Lamb 'Haleh Esfandiari: I would not let them break me', *TimesOnline* <http://www.allvoices.com/news/4923288-haleh-esfandiari-i-would-not-let-them-break-me>.
117. Wright 'Freed by Iran, scholar reunites with her family', *The Washington Post* <http://www.washingtonpost.com/wp-dyn/content/article/2007/09/06/AR2007090602375.html>.
118. <http://www.halehesfandiari.net>.
119. 'Interview with Reza Kahlili, the author of a time to betray', *JIMON* 4.

120. Rosenberg, http://flashtrafficblog.wordpress.com/2011/07/03/summer-reading-recommendations-top-pick-a-time-tobetray.
121. Oliver 2001, p. 9.
122. Keshavarz 2007, p. 2.
123. Ibid.
124. Ibid., p. 3.
125. Ibid., p. 11.
126. Ebtekar 2000, p. 34.
127. Ibid.
128. Ibid.
129. Ibid.
130. Kaufman 2006, 'Iranian women in exile finding voices through literature', *Payvand News Iran* <http://www.payvand.com/news/06/nov/1079.html>.
131. Amireh and Majaj 2001, p. 2.
132. Whitlock 2007, p. 55.

Chapter 4 Mothers and Daughters – Writing 'Beyond the Homeland'

1. Milani 1992, p. 2.
2. Ibid., p. 1.
3. Ibid.
4. Naficy is alternatively spelled Nafisi. Here, it is spelled and referenced as the article cites.
5. Naficy 1994, p. 117.
6. Ibid.
7. Ibid., p. 120.
8. Najmabadi 1997, p. 442.
9. Ibid., p. 446.
10. Ibid.
11. Ibid., p. 447.
12. Ibid.
13. Ibid., pp. 447–8.
14. Ibid., p. 449.
15. Ibid., p. 444.
16. Ibid., p. 445.
17. For an examination of the concept of brotherhood and Iranian modernity see Joanna de Groot's '"Brothers of the Iranian Race"'.
18. Boehmer 1995, p. 225.
19. Nasta 1991, p. xiv.
20. Sansarian 1985, p. 24.
21. Boehmer 1995, p. 224.
22. Goldin 2009, p. 88.
23. Bhabha 1994, p. 2.

24. Ibid.
25. Ibid.
26. Ibid., p. 1.
27. Ibid.
28. Boehmer 1995, p. 226.
29. Ibid.
30. Ibid., p. 227.
31. Ibid.
32. Ibid.
33. Ibid.
34. Ibid.
35. Oliver 2001, p. 7.
36. Ibid.
37. Ibid.
38. Ibid.
39. Irigaray 1981, p. 61.
40. Ibid., p. 67.
41. Nahai 2000, p. 14.
42. Meaney 1993, p. 21.
43. Nahai 2000, p. 15.
44. Goldin 2009, p. 93.
45. Nahai 2000, p. 123.
46. Ibid., p. 359.
47. Nahai 2000, p. 367.
48. Oliver 2001, p. 9.
49. Ibid.
50. Nahai 2000, p. 238. Emphasis original.
51. Ibid., p. 367.
52. Ibid., p. 365.
53. Ibid., p. 359.
54. Ibid., p. 374.
55. Ibid., p. 6.
56. Ibid., p. 374.
57. Ramanathan 1993, p. 21.
58. Ibid., p. 28.
59. Marotta 2005, p. 15.
60. Ibid., p. 22.
61. Ibid., p. 23.
62. Ibid.
63. Ibid.
64. Ibid., p. 22.
65. Dagninio 1993, p. 65.
66. Ibid.
67. Boehmer 1995, p. 174.

68. Nahai 2000, p. 358.
69. Nice 1992, p. 50.
70. Ibid.
71. Ibid., p. 9.
72. Fido 1991, p. 339.
73. Ibid., p. 331.
74. Nice 1992, p. 12.
75. O'Reilly 2000, p. 145.
76. Hafizi 2004, p. 2.
77. Ibid.
78. Ibid.
79. Ibid.
80. Ibid.
81. Nahai 2000, p. 360.
82. Ibid., p. 380.
83. Nahai 2007, 'Elegy for a dream', *Jewish Journal* <http://www.jewishjournal.com/opinion/article/elegy_for_a_dream_2070909/>.
84. Wegner 1997, p. xvi.
85. Ibid.
86. Fido 1991, p. 331.
87. Ibid.
88. Ibid., p. 331.
89. Rachlin 1979, p. 45.
90. Ibid., p. 27.
91. Ibid., p. 137.
92. Grice 2002, p. 206.
93. Rachlin 1979, p. 32.
94. Ibid., p. 39.
95. Ibid., p. 192.
96. Najmabadi 1997, p. 445.
97. For an interesting discussion about this topic see Cameron Michael Amin's 'Selling and Saving: Mother Iran: Gender and the Iranian Press in the 1940s' in *International Journal of Middle East Studies* 33 (2001): 335–61.
98. Mirsepassi 2000, p. 76.
99. Faris 1995, p. 163.
100. Ibid., p. 165.
101. Ibid., p. 164.
102. Ibid., p. 166.
103. Ibid.
104. Ibid., p. 167.
105. Nahai 2000, p. 143.
106. Ibid., p. 356.
107. Fotouhi 2004, p. 4.
108. Rachlin 1979, pp. 37–8.

109. Hermans-Janson and Hermans 1995, p. 128.
110. Ibid., p. 57.
111. Rachlin 1979, p. 40.
112. Irigaray 1981, p. 63.
113. Slemon 1996, p. x.
114. D'Haen 1995, p. 195.
115. Ibid., p. 196.
116. Wenzel 1981, p. 59.
117. D'Haen 1995, p. 196.
118. Faris 1995, p. 165.

Chapter 5 Iranian Masculinities – 'Hypervisiblity/Invisiblity'

1. Khosravi 2009, p. 599.

   Similarly, in her essay 'Terrorists, Madmen, and Religious Fanatics?: Revisiting Orientalism and Racist Rhetoric', Anissa Janine Wardi traces the importance of *Not Without My Daughter* in establishing and maintaining a kind of homogenous understanding of Middle Eastern people, especially in collapsing the difference between the various cultures of the Middle East at large.
2. The book was eventually published in 2013 by Thistle Publishers.
3. Said 1978, p. 287.
4. Scott 2000, p. 178.
5. Ibid.
6. Khosravi 2009, p. 599.

   Also, in *Islamophobia* Peter Gottschalk and Gabriel Greenberg demonstrate how the image of the Iranian man was portrayed immediately after the Iranian revolution and the hostage crisis through cartoons in popular America newspapers. They depicted Imam Khomeini 'and the Islamic revolutionaries of Iran as crazy, backward, and violent' (2008, p. 124).
7. Ouzgane 2006, p. 1.
8. Bahramitash 2006, p. 223.
9. Fernea 1977, p. xii.
10. Naghibi 2007, p. x.
11. Ibid.
12. Tavakoli-Targhi 2001, p. 4.
13. Ibid.
14. Ibid., p. 54.
15. In *Women with Moustaches and Men Without Beards* (2005), Afsaneh Najmabadi outlines some of the most significant and earliest contributions that Iranian women have made to the feminist discourse in Iran.
16. Rahimieh 2003, p. 148.
17. Ibid.

18. Said 1978, p. 325.
19. Naghibi 2007, p. xvii.
20. Ibid.
21. Nafisi 2004, p. 14.
22. Ibid., p. 17.
23. Ibid., p. 356.
24. Ibid., p. 49.
25. Ibid., p. 28.
26. Ibid., pp. 27–8.
27. Ibid., pp. 103–14.
28. Najmabadi 1997, p. 92.
29. Oliver 2001, p. 149.
30. Ibid.
31. Mobasher 2006, p. 101.
32. Ibid.
33. Stanovsky 2007, p. 495.
34. See her interview with The Alcove <http://www.youtube.com/watch?v=z-ZZ5sLEZGM>.
35. Ibid.
36. Keshavarz 2007, pp. 59–60.
37. Bhattacharyya 2008, p. 19.
38. Nafisi 2004, p. 38.
39. Khosravi 2009, p. 591.
40. Baniameri 2005, p. 3.
41. <http://www.mortbaharloo.blogspot.com>.
42. Mobasher 2006, p. 107.
43. Ibid., p. 112.
44. Ibid., p. 111.
45. Ibid., p. 101.
46. Behdad, qtd. in Sullivan 2001, p. 249.
47. Mulkay 1988, p. 177.
48. Stein and Reichel 2005, p. 9.
49. Pfister qtd. in Stein and Reichel 2005, p. 9.
50. Baniameri 2005, p. 74.
51. Ibid., p. 75.
52. Ibid., p. 76.
53. Stein and Reichel 2005, p. 11.
54. Boskin 1997, p. 48.
55. Sayrafiezadeh 2009, p. 183.
56. Ibid.
57. Ibid., p. 193.
58. Ibid., p. 200.
59. Oliver 2001, p. 4.
60. Ibid., p. 5.

61. Ibid., p. 23.
62. Ibid., p. 24.
63. Ibid.
64. Ibid., p. 149.
65. Ibid., p. 150.
66. Sayrafiezadeh 2009, p. 286.
67. Ibid., p. 286.
68. Seraji n.d., 'Mahbod Seraji: Thank You, My Friend' <http://www.readinggroupguides.com/blog/2009/06/mahbod-seraji-thank-you-my-friend.asp>.
69. Oliver 2001, p. 9.
70. Ibid.
71. <http://www.rooftopsoftehran.com>.
72. Simidchieva 1997, p. 408.
73. Ibid.
74. Ibid.
75. Parvin 1996, p. 113.
76. Najmabadi 2005, p. 3.
77. Whitaker 2006, p. 11.
78. Ahmadinejad's comments soon spread all over the media, to date being quoted in numerous outlets.
79. Whitaker 2005, p. 10.
80. Afary 2005, p. 158.
81. Qtd. in Afary 2005, p. 158.
82. Dr Ali 2011, p. 1.
83. Ibid.

Conclusion – The 'Not-Yet' Future of Iranian Writing

1. For an interesting analysis of the role of blogs in Iran, see Nasrin Alavi's *We are Iran.*
2. Akhavan 2013, p. 9.
3. Ibid., p. 10.
4. Much study has been done already on the significance of social media in forming and shaping the events of 2009. For an insightful analysis of the importance of cyberspace in this period see Cyrus Farivar's 'A Brief History of Iranian Internet', and Mehdi Yahyanejad's 'The internet and the Protests in Iran' in *Iran and the New Media.*
5. In an intriguing article, 'The 7K Report', Hugh Howey traces the history, significance and success of the online and self-publishing industry through an analysis of Amazon and Barnes & Noble. See <http://authorearnings.com/the-report>.
6. Persian writing has a strong presence in Australia. Numerous Iranian poets and writers have established a body of writing, particularly concerned with the process of migration and resettlement. To name a few examples, Azadeh Davachi is a poet and a feminist who is completing her PhD on Iranian women's memoirs

at the University of Wollongong. Saba Vasefi is another well-known poet and feminist who fled Iran with her young daughter after the student protests, and has re-established herself in Sydney. Gronaz Mousavi, an established poet in Iran, also continues to write poetry in Australia. Mousavi is also the director of the controversial and first ever Iranian-Australian co-production, *My Tehran for Sale* (2009). Roshanak Amrein is another poet who continues to write in Persian after migration.

7. Hejazi 2011, p. xvii.

BIBLIOGRAPHY

Abdoh, S. (2000), *The Poet Game*, Picador, New York.

——— (2004), *Opium*, Faber and Faber, London.

Afary, J. and K.B. Anderson (2005), *Foucault and the Iranian Revolution: Gender and the Seductions of Islamism*, University of Chicago Press, Chicago IL.

Akhavan, N. (2013), *Electronic Iran*, Rutgers, New York.

Alavi, N. (2006), *We are Iran*, Portobello Books, London.

Alemi, M. (2008), *Interruptions: a Novel*, Ibex, Bethesda MD.

Dr. Ali (2011), *Modern Gay Persian Poetry about Love*, Lulu Online.

Amin, C.M. (2001), 'Selling and saving "mother Iran": gender and the Iranian press in the 1940s', *International Journal of Middle East Studies* 33/3, pp. 335–61.

Amini, M. (1985), *The Sunset Drifters*, Afsaneh Consulting Company, Canoga Park CA.

——— (1987), *Dreams of a Native Son*, Afsaneh Consulting Company, Canoga Park CA.

——— (1989), *The Howling Leopard*, Afsaneh Consulting Company, Canoga Park CA.

——— (2004), *Escape from Paradise*, Afsaneh Consulting Company, Canoga Park CA.

Amireh, A. and S.L. Majaj (2001), *Going Global: The Transnational Reception of Third World Women Writers*, Garland, New York.

Amirrezvani, A. (2007), *Blood of Flowers*, Little, Brown and Company, New York.

——— (2012), Equal of the sun, Scibner, New York.

Amory, C. (1928), *Persian Days*, Methuen, London.

Asadi, H. (2010), *Letters to my Torturer: Love, Revolution and Imprisonment in Iran*, Oneworld Publications, Oxford.

Asayesh, G. (1999), *Saffron Sky: a Life between Iran and America*, Beacon Press, Boston MA.

Assefi, N. (2006), *Aria*, Harcourt Books, Orlando FL.

Ashcroft, B. (2001a), *On Post-colonial Futures: Transformations of Colonial Culture*, Continuum, New York.

——— (2001b), *Post-colonial Transformation*, Routledge, London.

——— (2007), 'Critical utopias', *Textual Practices* 21/3, pp. 411–31.

——— (2009a), 'Ambiguous necessities of utopia', *Social Alternative* 28/3, pp. 8–14.

——— (2009b), *Caliban's Voice: the Transformation of English in Post-colonial Literatures*, Routledge, New York.

——— (2009c), 'Remembering the future: utopianism in African literature', *Textual Practices* 23/5, pp. 703–22.

Association of Iranian American Writers (n.d.), viewed April 2008 <http://www.Iranianamericanwriters.org>

Azadi, S. (1987), *Out of Iran: One Woman's Escape from the Ayatollahs*, Macdonald, London.

Baharloo, M. (2004), *The Quince Seed Potion*, Bridgeworks, New York.

——— (n.d.), 'Biography', viewed 3 June 2009 <http://www.mortbaharloo.com/?cnt=bio>

Bahramitash, R. (2005), 'The War on Terror, feminist Orientalism and Orientalist feminism: case studies of two North American bestsellers', *Middle East Critique* 14/2, pp. 221–35.

Bahrampour, T. (1999), *To See and See Again: a Life in Iran and America*, Farrar, Straus and Giroux, New York.

Bakhsh, S. (2007), 'Our family hostage crisis', *The New York Times*. 27 June, viewed 5 July 2009 <http://www.nytimes.com/2007/06/27/opinion/27bakhash.html>

Baniameri, S. (2005), *Iranican Dream*, Virtualbookworm.com.

Behdad, A. (2001), 'Ali Behdad' in Z. Sullivan (ed.), *Exiled Memories: Stories of Iranian Diaspora*, Temple University Press, Philadelphia PA, pp. 247–51.

Benjamin, S.G.W. (1887), *Persia and the Persians*, John Murray, London.

Bhabha, H. (1994), *The Location of Culture*, Routledge, New York.

Bhattacharyya, G. (2008), *Dangerous Brown Men: Exploiting Sex, Violence and Feminism in the War on Terror*, Zed Books, London.

Bloch, E. (1986), *The Principles of Hope*, MIT Press, Cambridge.

Boehmer, E. (1995), *Colonial and Postcolonial Literature: Migrant Metaphors*, Oxford University Press, Oxford.

Boskin, J. (1997), *Rebellious Laughter: People's Humour in American Culture*, Syracuse University Press, Syracuse NY.

Brah, A. (1999), *Cartographies of Diaspora: Contesting Identities*, Routledge, New York.

De Bruijn, J.T.P. (1997), *Persian Sufi Poetry: an Introduction to the Mystical Use of Classical Poems*, Curzon Press, Richmond.

Burckhardt, T. (2008), *Introduction to Sufi Doctrine*, World Wisdom, Bloomington IN.

Burwell, C. (2007), 'Reading *Lolita* in times of war: women's book clubs and the politics of reception', *Intercultural Education* 18/4, pp. 281–96.

Butler, K. (2008), 'Thirty days in Iran's worst prison', *Mother Jones*, 4 January, viewed 5 March 2009 <http://motherjones.com/politics/2008/01/thirty-days-irans-worst-prison>

Castiglia, C. (1996), *Bound and Determined: Captivity, Culture-crossing, and White Womanhood from Mary Rowlandson to Patty Hearst*, University of Chicago Press, Chicago IL.

Cottam, R. (1979), *Nationalism in Iran*, University of Pittsburgh Press, Pittsburgh PA.

Dabashi, H. (2006), 'Native informers and the making of the American empire', *Al-Ahram Weekly Online*, 1 June, viewed 2 July 2008 <http://weekly.ahram.org.eg/2006/797/special.htm>

Dagninio, P. (1993), 'Quest of Question', in C. Arkinstall (ed.), *Literature and Quest*, Rodoi, Amsterdam.

Darvishpour, M. (2009), 'The new nest and horizons of exile: sociology of diasporic Iranian literature', *Gozaar: A Forum on Human Rights and Democracy in Iran*,

1 February, viewed 3 January 2010 <http://www.gozaar.org/english/articles-en/The-New-Nest-and-Horizons-of-Exile.html>

Darznik, J. (2008), 'The perils and seductions of home: return narratives of the Iranian diaspora', *MELUS* 33/2, pp. 55–71.

——— (2010), 'Writing outside the veil: literature by women of Iranian diaspora', PhD thesis, Princeton University.

——— (2011), *The Good Daughter*, Grand Central Publishing, New York.

Davidson, A. and K. Kuah-Pearce (eds) (2007), *At Home in the Chinese Diaspora: Memories, Identities and Belongings*, Palgrave Macmillan, New York.

——— and H. Muppidi (eds) (2011), *The World is My Home: a Hamid Dabashi Reader*, Transaction Publishers, New Brunswick.

Derounian, K. (1988), 'The publication, promotion, and distribution of Mary Rowlandson's Indian captivity narrative in the seventeenth century', *Early American Literature* 23, pp. 239–61.

Donadeh, A. and H. Ahmed-Ghosh (2008), 'Why Americans love Azar Nafisi's Reading *Lolita* in Tehran', *Signs: Journal of Women in Culture and Society* 33/3, pp. 623–46.

Dutton, J. (2010), '"Non-Western" utopian traditions', in G. Claeys (ed.), *The Cambridge Companion to Utopian Literature*, Cambridge University Press, Cambridge.

Ebadi, S. (2006), *Iran Awakening: from Prison to Peace Prize: One Woman's Struggle at the Crossroads of History*, Random House, Toronto ON.

Ebtekar, M. (2000), *Takeover in Tehran: the Inside Story of the 1979 U.S Embassy Capture*, Talonbooks, Vancouver BC.

Edwards, B. (2010), 'Disorienting captivity: a response to Gordon Sayre', *American Literary History* 22/2, pp. 360–7.

Elahi, B. (2006), 'Translating the self: language and identity in Iranian–American women's memoirs', *Iranian Studies* 39, pp. 461–80.

——— and P. Karim (2011), 'Introduction: Iranian diaspora', *Comparative Studies of South Asia, Africa and the Middle East* 31/2, pp. 381–7.

Esfandiari, F. (1955), *Identity Card*, New York.

——— (1959), *Day of Sacrifice*, New York.

——— (1965), *The Beggar*, New York.

Esfandiari, H. (1997), *Reconstructed Lives: Women and Iran's Islamic revolution*, Johns Hopkins University Press, Washington DC.

——— (2009), *My Prison, My Home*, Harper Collins, New York.

Falk Jones, L. and S. Webster Goodwin (eds) (1990), *Feminism, Utopia, and Narrative*, University of Tennessee Press, Knoxville.

Faris, W.B. (1995), 'Magical realism and postmodernism', in W.B. Faris and L.P. Zamora (eds), *Magical Realism: Theory, History, Community*, Duke University Press, Durham NC.

——— and L.P. Zamora (eds) (1995), *Magical Realism: Theory, History, Community*, Duke University Press, Durham NC.

Farivar, C. (2011), 'A Brief History of Iranian Internet', in *Iran and the New Media*, Institut fur Auslandsbeziehungen e.V., Stuttgart.

Farman-Farmaian, S. (1996), *Daughter of Persia: a Woman's Journey from her Father's Harem through the Islamic Revolution*, Corgi Press, Auckland.

Fathi, N. (2014), The Lonely War: One Woman's Account for the Struggle of Modern Iran, Basic Books, New York.

Fernea, E. (1977), *Middle Eastern Muslim Women Speak*, University of Texas Press, TX.

Fido, E.S. (1991), 'Mother/lands: self and separation in the work of Buchi Emecheta, Bessie Head and Jean Rhys', in S. Nasta (ed.), *Motherlands*, The Women's Press, London.

Firouz, A. (n.d.), (2003), *In the Walled Garden*, Little, Brown and Company, New York.

——— 'Interviews', viewed 3 March 2007 <http://www.anahitafirouz.com>

Fotouhi, S. (2004), '"That Other World That Was the World": A Study of the Short Fiction of Katherine Mansfield and Nadine Gordimer', MPhil thesis, University of Hong Kong.

Genette, G. (1997), *Paratexts: Thresholds of Interpretation*, Cambridge University Press, New York.

Ghahramani, Z. (2008), *My Life as a Traitor*, Farrar, Straus, and Giroux, New York.

Ghahremani, Z. (2009), 'Writing: on wings of memory', *Zoe Ghahremani*, 6 January, viewed 3 August 2010 <http://www.zoeghahremani.com/blog1/?p=299>

——— (2010), *Sky of Red Poppies*, Turquoise Books, New York.

Goldin, F. (2004), 'Iranian women and contemporary memoirs', *Iranian Chamber Society*, viewed 3 October 2011 <http://www.iranchamber.com/culture/articles/iranian_women_contemporary_memoirs.php>

——— (2009), 'The ghosts of our mothers: from oral tradition to written words', *Nashim: A Journal of Jewish Women's Studies and Gender Issues* 18, pp. 87–124.

Gottschalk, P. and G. Greenberge (2008) (eds), *Islamophobia: Making Muslims the Enemy*, Rowman and Littlefield, Lanham.

Grassian, D. (2013), *Iranian and Diasporic Literature in the 21st Century: a Critical Study*, McFarland and Company, London.

Grice, H. (2002), *Negotiating Identities: an Introduction to Asian American Women's Writing*, Manchester University Press, New York.

De Groot, J. (2004), '"Brotherhood of the Iranian race": manhood, nationhood, and modernity in Iran c. 1870–1914', in Stephan Dadink and John Tosh (eds), *Masculinities in Politics and War*, Manchester University Press, Manchester.

Guppy, S. (1988), *The Blindfold Horse: Memories of a Persian Childhood*, Heinemann, London.

D'Haen, T. (1995), 'Decentering privileged centers', in W.B. Faris and L.P. Zamora (eds), *Magical Realism: Theory, History, Community*, Duke University Press, Durham NC.

Hafizi, M. (2004), 'Toward a general economy of travel: identity, memory, and death', PhD thesis, University of Florida.

Hakakian, R. (2004), *Journey from the Land of No*, Bantam, Auckland.

Hall, S. (1996), 'Who needs identity?' in S. Hall and P. du Gay, *Questions of Cultural Identity*, SAGE, London.

——— (2003), 'Cultural identity and diaspora', in J.E. Braziel and A. Mannur (eds), *Theorizing Diaspora: a Reader*, Blackwell, Oxford.

Hejazi, A. (2011), *The Gaze of the Gazelle*, Seagull Books, London.

Henke, S. (2000), *Shattered Subjects: Trauma and Testimony in Women's Life-writing*, St Martin's Press, New York.

Hermans-Janson, E. and H. Hermans (1995), *Self Narratives: the Construction of Meaning in Psychotherapy*, Guilford Press, New York.

Hiro, D. (1985), *Iran Under the Ayatollahs*, Routledge, London.

Hoffman, D. (1989), 'Self and culture revisited: culture acquisition among Iranians in the United States', in *Ethos* 17/1, pp. 32–49.

Hoveida, F. (1961), *Le quranraines*, Gallimard, Paris.
——— (1965), *L'aerogare*, Gallimard, Paris.
——— (1968), *Dans une terre etrangee*, Gallimard, Paris.
——— (1969), *Le losange*, Gallimard, Paris.
——— (2003), *The Shah and the Ayatollah: Iranian Mythology and Islamic Revolution*, Greenwood Publishing, Westport CT.
Howey, H. (n.d.), 'The 7K Report', viewed January 2014 <http://authorearnings.com/the-report>
Irigaray, L. (1981), 'And the one doesn't stir without the other', *Signs* 7/1, pp. 60–7.
Kahlili, R. (2010), *A Time to Betray: the Astonishing Life of a CIA Double Agent inside Iran's Revolutionary Guard*, Threshold Editions, New York.
——— (2011), 'Interview with Reza Kahlili, the author of a time to betray', *JIMON* 4.
Karim, P. and N. Rahimieh (2008), 'Introduction: writing Iranian Americans into the American literature canon', *MELUS* 32/2, pp. 2–8.
Karimi-Hakkak, A. (1995), *Recasting Persian Poetry: Scenarios of Poetic Modernity in Iran*, University of Utah Press, UT.
——— (2003), 'Exiled to freedom: a memoir of censorship in Iran', *The Drama Review* 47/4, pp.17–50.
Kasem, A. (2002), 'Islam and poetry', viewed 30 March 2009 <http://www.faithfreedom.org/Articles/abulkazem/Islam_and_poverty.htm>
Kashani-Sabet, F. (2010), *Martyrdom Street*, Syracuse University Press, Syracuse NY.
Kaufman, S. (2006), 'Iranian women in exile finding voices through literature', *Payvand News Iran*, 6 July, viewed 9 July 2006 <http://www.payvand.com/news/06/nov/1079.html>
Keshavarz, F. (2007), *Jasmine and Stars: Reading More Than* Lolita *in Tehran*, Caravan Books, NC.
Kho'i, E. (2008), 'To the aged mulberry branch', in N. Talebi (ed.), *Belonging: New Poetry by Iranians around the World,* Scala Press House, Seattle.
Khosravi, S. (2009), 'Displaced masculinity: gender and ethnicity among Iranian men in Sweden', *Iranian Studies* 42/4, pp. 591–609.
King, J.R. (1988), 'Religious and therapeutic elements in Sufi teaching stories', *Journal of Religion and Health* 27/3, pp. 221–35.
Lamb, C. (2010), 'Haleh Esfandiari: I would not let them break me', *TimesOnline*, 2 January, viewed July 2011 <http://www.allvoices.com/news/4923288-haleh-esfandiari-i-would-not-let-them-break-me>
Latifi, A. (2005), *Even After all this Time: a Story of Love, Revolution, and Leaving Iran*, Regan Books, New York.
Lewisohn, L. (1992), *The Legacy of Medieval Persian Sufism*, Khaniqahi-Nimatullahi Publications, New York.
Little, D. (2005), *American Orientalism: the United States and the Middle East since 1945*, University of North Carolina Press, Chapel Hill NC.
Lotfalian, M. (1996), 'Working through psychological understandings of the diasporic condition', *Ethos* 24/1, pp. 36–70.
Lownie, A. (2010), 'Lost without my daughter', viewed 13 July 2010 <http://www.andrewlownie.co.uk/authors/sayed-mahmoody/books/lost-without-my-daughter>
Mabro, J. (1991), *Veiled Half-truths: Western Travelers' Perceptions of Middle Eastern Women*, I.B. Tauris, New York.

Madadi, B. (2004), 'Glorious Loneliness', *Iranian.com*, viewed 22 March 2004 <http://www.iranian.com/Opinion/2004/November/Ben/index.html>

Mahdi, A.A. (1997), 'The Second Generation Iranians: Questions and Concerns', published on Iranian.com, viewed July 2006 <http://www.iranian.com/Feb97/Features/IrAms/IrAmsSum.shtml>

Mahloujian, A. (2003), 'Phoenix from the Ashes: a Tale for the Book in Iran', viewed 15 January 2010 <http://www.iranchamber.com/literature/articles/tale_of_book_iran.php>

Mahmoody, B. (1987), *Not without my Daughter*, Corgi, New York.

Malcolm, J. (1861), *Sketches of Persia*, John Murray, London.

Mandanipour, S. (2009), *Censoring an Iranian Love Story*, Vintage, New York.

Martin, V. (2007), *Creating an Islamic State: Khomeini and the Making of a new Iran*, I.B. Tauris, New York.

Marotta, M. (2005), 'MotherSpace: Disciplining through the Material and Discursive', in S. Hardy and C. Wiedmer (eds), *Motherhood and the Space*, Palgrave, New York.

Masud, F. (1969), *The Airplane Ticket*, New York.

McAlister, M. (2003), 'Saving Private Lynch', *The New York Times*, 6 April, viewed 28 February 2009 <http://www.nytimes.com/2003/04/06/opinion/saving-private-lynch.html>

——— (2005), *Epic Encounters: Culture, Media, and U.S. Interests in the Middle East since 1945*, University of California Press, Berkeley CA.

McCarron, M. (n.d.), 'Baha'i, Sufi and Gnostic Shi'a spiritual cosmology', *Symbol Language and Cosmology*, viewed 2 March 2011 <https://sites.google.com/site/causeofgod/home/papers/cosmos-as-meditation/symbolic-language-cosmology>

Meaney, G. (1993), *(Un)Like Subjects: Women, Theory, Fiction*, Routledge, New York.

Mehran, M. (2005), Pomegranate Soup, Fourth Estate, Harper Collins, Sydney.

Meisami, J.S. (1985), 'Allegorical gardens in the Persian tradition: Nezami, Rumi, Hafez', *International Journal of Middle East Studies* 17/2, pp. 229–60.

Meskoob, S. (1992), *Iranian Nationality and the Persian Language,* Mage Publishers, Washington DC.

Milani, F. (1985), 'Conflict between traditional roles and poetry in the works of Forough Farrokhzad', in Asghar Fathi (ed.), *Women and the Family in Iran*, Brill, Leiden.

——— (1992), *Veils and Words: the Emerging Voices of Iranian Women Writers*, Syracuse University Press, Syracuse NY.

Mirsepassi, A. (2000), *Intellectual Discourse and the Politics of Modernization: Negotiating Modernity in Iran*, Cambridge University Press, Cambridge.

Moaveni, A. (2005), *Lipstick Jihad*, Perseus Books, New York.

Mobasher, M. (2006), 'Cultural trauma and ethnic identity formation among Iranian immigrants in the United States', *American Behavioural Scientist* 50/1, pp. 100–17.

Mogadam, A. (2010), *Death to the Dictator*, Farrar, Straus and Giroux, New York.

Moghissi, H. (1994), *Populism and Feminism in Iran: Women's Struggle in a Male-defined Revolutionary Movement*, St Martin's Press, New York.

Monadjemi, L.I. (1993), *Blood and Carnations*, Eldorado, Kirribilli NSW.

——— (2010), *A Matter of Survival*, Austin and Macauley Publishers, London.

Moshiri F. (2000), *At the Wall of the Almighty*, Interlink Books, New York.

——— (2001), *The Bathhouse*, Black Heron Press, Washington DC.

——— (2005), *Against Gravity*, Penguin Books, London.

Mostashari, A. and A. Khodamhosseini (2000), 'An overview of socioeconomic characteristics of the Iranian–American community based on the 2000 U.S

Census', *Iranian Studies Group at MIT*, viewed 28 July 2006 <http://www.iranian.com/Diaspora/2004/July/Census/Images/US2000census>

Mosteshar, C. (1995), *Unveiled: Love and Death among the Ayatollahs*, Hodder and Stoughton, London.

Mostofi, N. (2003), 'Who we are: the perplexity of Iranian–American identity', *The Sociological Quarterly* 44/4, pp. 681–703.

Motlagh, A. (2008), 'Towards a theory of Iranian–American life writing', *MELUS* 32/2, pp. 17–36.

Mottahedeh, N. (2004), 'Off the grid: reading Iranian memoirs in our time of total War', *Middle East Report Online*, September 2004, viewed 11 June 2014 <http://www.merip.org/mero/interventions/grid>

Mottahedeh, R. (1987), *The Mantle of the Prophet: Religion and Politics in Iran*, Penguin, Middlesex.

Mulkay, M. (1988), *On Humor: Its Nature and its Place in Modern Society*, Blackwell Publication, London.

Naficy, A. (1994), 'Images of women in classical Persian literature and the contemporary Iranian novel', in M. Afkhami and E. Friedl (eds), *In the Eye of the Storm: Women in Post-Revolutionary Iran*, Syracuse University Press, Syracuse NY.

Naficy, H. (2001), *An Accented Cinema: Exilic and Diasporic Filmmaking*, Princeton University Press, Princeton NJ.

Nafisi, A. (2004), *Reading* Lolita *in Tehran*, Fourth Estate, New York.

——— (2008), 'Azar Nafisi: Vladimir Nabokov', *Big Think*, 18 March, viewed 8 May 2009 <http://bigthink.com/ideas/1966>

——— (2010), *Things I've Been Silent About*, Random House, New York.

Naghibi, N. (2007), *Rethinking Global Sisterhood: Western Feminism and Iran*, University of Minnesota Press, Minneapolis MN.

Nahai, G. (2000), *Moonlight on the Avenue of Faith*, Scribner, Berkshire.

——— (2001), *Cry of the Peacock*, Scribner, London.

——— (2007a), 'So what's with all the Iranian memoirs?' *Publishers Weekly*, 26 November, viewed 2 March 2008 <http://www.publishersweekly.com/pw/by-topic/columns-and-blogs/soapbox/article/4048-so-what-s-with-all-the-iranian-memoirs-.html>

——— (2007b), 'Elegy for a dream', *Jewish Journal*, 8 September, viewed 10 March 2012 <http://www.jewishjournal.com/opinion/article/elegy_for_a_dream_2070909/>

Najmabadi, A. (1997), 'The erotic Vatan [homeland] as beloved and mother: to love, to possess, and to protect', *Comparative Studies in Society and History* 39/3, pp. 442–67.

——— (2005), *Women with Moustaches and Men without Beards: Gender and Sexual Anxieties of Iranian Modernity*, University of California Press, Los Angeles CA.

Nanquette, L. (2010), 'The Eye Sees Not Itself? Mutual Images of Iran and France Through Their Literature (1979–2009)', PhD thesis, University of London.

——— (2012), *Orientalism versus Occidentalism: Literary and Cultural Imaging Between France and Iran since the Islamic Revolution*, I.B.Tauris, New York.

Nasr. S.H. (1991), *Islamic Spirituality: Manifestations Vol.2*, The Crossroad Publishing Company, New York.

——— (1999), 'Persian Sufi literature: its spiritual and cultural significance', in L. Lewishon (ed.), *Heritage of Sufism Vol. II*, OneWorld, London.

Nasta, S. (1991), *Motherlands*, The Women's Press, London.

Nemat, M. (2008), *Prisoner of Tehran*, Free Press, New York.

Netton, I.R. and Z.I. Salhi (eds) (2006), *The Arab Diaspora: Voices of an Anguished Scream*, Routledge, London.

Nice, V. (1992), *Mothers and Daughters: the Distortion of a Relationship*, Macmillan, New York.

Oliver, K. (2001), *Witnessing: Beyond Recognition*, University of Minnesota Press, London.

O'Reilly, A. and S. Abbey (eds) (2000), *Mothers and Daughters: Connection, Empowerment, and Transformation*, Rowman and Littlefield, Lanham MD.

Osanloo, A. (2006), 'Imperative: the pressure to be exotic', *Poets and Writers*, viewed 26 January 2010 <http://www.pw.org/content/imperative_pressure_be_exotic?cmnt_all=1>

Ouzgane, L. (2006), *Islamic Masculinities*, Zed Books, London.

Pakravan, A. (1921), *Le prince sans histoire.*

——— (1960), *Destinees persanes.*

Pakravan, S. (1988), *The Arrest of Hoveyda: Stories of the Iranian Revolution*, Mazda Publishers, Costa Mesa, CA.

——— (2011), *Azadi: a Novel of Protest on the Streets of Tehran*, Parallel Books.

Papan-Matin, F. (2003), 'The crisis of identity in Rumi's "Tale of the Reed"', *Comparative Studies of South Asia, Africa and the Middle East* 23/1–2, pp. 246–53.

Pari, S. (1997), *The Fortune Catcher*, Warner Books, New York.

Parsipour, S. (2004), *Women Without Men,* The Feminist Press at the City University of New York, New York.

Parvin, M. (1996), *Avicenna and I: the Journey of Spirits*, Mazda Publishers, Costa Mesa CA.

——— (2003), *Dardedel: Rumi, Hafez, and Love in New York*, The Permanent Press, New York.

Pazouki, R. (2010), *Watch Me*, Lulu.com.

Pordzik, R. (2001), *The Quest for Postcolonial Utopia,* Peter Lang, New York.

Rabinow, P. (1984), *The Foucault Reader*, Pantheon Press, MI.

Rachlin, N. (1979), *Foreigner*, W.W. Norton and Company, New York.

——— (1995), *The Heart's Desire*, City Lights Books, San Francisco CA.

——— (2006), *Persian Girls*, Tarcher, New York.

Raffat, D. (1978), *The Caspian Circle*, Houghton Mifflin, New York.

Rahimieh, N. (1992), 'The quince-orange tree, or Iranian writers in exile', *World Literature Today* 66/1, pp. 39–42.

——— (2002), 'Marking gender and difference in the myth of the nation: a post-revolutionary Iranian film', in R. Tapper (ed.), *The New Iranian Cinema: Politics, Representation and Identity*, I.B. Tauris, New York.

——— (2003), 'Overcoming the Orientalist legacy of Iranian modernity', *Thamyris/Intersecting* 10, pp. 147–63.

Ramanathan, G. (1993), 'Sexual violence/textual violence: Desai's "Fire on the Mountain" and Shirazi's "Javady Alley"', *Modern Fiction Studies* 39/1, pp. 17–28.

Rashidian, J. (2010), 'Our Iranian Identity', viewed 23 November 2010 <http://jahanshahrashidian-rashidian-blog.blogspot.com/2010/10/our-iranian-identity.html>

Rastegar, M. (2006), 'Reading Nafisi in the West: authenticity, Orientalism, and "liberating" Iranian women', *Women's Studies Quarterly* 34/1–2, pp. 108–28.

Rosenberge, J.C. (2011), 'Summer reading recommendation: A Time To Betray', *Joel C. Rosenberge's Blog*, viewed 3 August 2011 <http://flashtrafficblog.wordpress.

com/2011/07/03/summer-reading-recommendations-top-pick-a-time-to-betray>

Saberi, R. (2010), *Between Two Worlds: My Life and Captivity in Iran*, Harper Collins, New York.

Sabri-Tabrizi, G.R. (1989), *Iran: a Child's Story, a Man's Experience*, International Publishers, New York.

Sadegh (2008), 'The trial of Khosrow Golsorkhi', viewed 3 July 2010 <http://iranian.com/main/blog/sadegh/trial-khosro-golsorkhi-victim-shahs-firing-squad.html>

Saeidi, A and T. Unwin (2004), 'Persian wine tradition and symbolism: evidence from the medieval poetry of Hafiz', *Journal of Wine Research* 15/2, pp. 97–114.

Said, E. (1978), *Orientalism*, Penguin, New York.

Sansarian, E. (1985), 'Characteristics of women's movement in Iran', in A. Fathi (ed.), *Women and the Family in Iran*, E.J. Brill, Leiden.

Sayrafiezadeh, S. (2009), *When Skateboards will be Free*, The Dial Press, New York.

Scott, C.V. (2000), 'Bound for glory: the hostage crisis as captivity narrative in Iran', *International Studies Quarterly* 44/1, pp. 177–88.

Sheehan, P. (2007), 'The unattainable feminist dream', *Sydney Morning Herald*, 28 May, viewed 12 March 2011 <http://www.smh.com.au/news/opinion/the-unattainable-feminist-dream/2007/05/27/1180205070029.html>

Seraji, M. (n.d.), (2009), *Rooftops of Tehran*, New American Library, London.

——— '*Mahbod Seraji: Thank You, My Friend*', viewed June 2010 <http://www.readinggroupguides.com/blog/2009/06/mahbod-seraji-thank-you-my-friend.asp>

Serov, B. (2008), *Under a Starless Sky: a Family's Escape from Tehran*, Hacehtte Livre, Sydney.

Shirazi, M. (1984), *Javady Alley*, Women's Press, London.

——— (1992), *Seige of Azadi Square*, Women's Press, London.

Simidchieva, M. (1997), 'Review of Avecina and I: Journey of the Spirits', *Iranian Studies* 30/3, pp. 406–8.

Slemon, S. (1996), 'Post-colonial critical theories', in B. King (ed.), *New National and Post-Colonial Literatures: an Introduction*, Clarendon Press, New York.

Stanovsky, D. (2007), 'Postcolonial masculinities', in M. Flood, J. Kegan and B. Pease (eds), *International Encyclopedia of Men and Masculinities*, Routledge, London.

Stein, M. and S. Reichel (eds) (2005), *Cheeky Fictions: Laughter and the Postcolonial*, Rodopi BV, New York.

Sullivan, Z. (2001), *Exiled Memories*, Temple University Press, Philadelphia PA.

Synovitz, R. (2007), 'Iran: clashes highlight "demonization" of Sufi Muslims', viewed 5 December 2008 <http://www.unhcr.org/cgi-bin/texis/vtx/refworld/rwmain?docid=4742edf92d>

Tavakoli-Targhi, M. (2001), *Refashioning Iran: Orientalism, Occidentalism and Histography*, Palgrave, New York.

Thompson, E. (2003), 'Public and private in Middle Eastern women's history', in *Journal of Women's History* 15/1, pp. 52–69.

Tierney, D. (2010), 'Prisoner dilemmas: the American obsession with POWs and hostages', *Orbis* 54/1, pp. 130–45.

Tirgan, M.H. (2012), Goodbye Iran, Amazon Digital Services.*.

Tiregol, M. (n.d.), 'Thirty years of exilic literature', viewed 21 January 2010 <http://www.mtirehgol.com/>

Trimingham, J.S. (1971), *The Sufi Orders in Islam*, Clarendon Press, Oxford.

Van Den Bos, M. (2002), *Mystic Regime: Sufism in Iran, from the Late Qajar Era to the Islamic Republic*, Leiden, Brill.

Vaughan, A. and W. E. Clark (1981), *Puritans among the Indians*, John Harvard, New York.

Wanner, I. (2004), '"Journey from the Land of No": Memoir paints child's life in shifting 1970s Iran', *The Seattle Times*, 22 August, viewed 21 June 2006 <http://community.seattletimes.nwsource.com/archive/?date=20040822andslug=landofno22>

Wardi, A.J. (1999), 'Terrorists, madmen, and religious fanatics?: revisiting Orientalism and racist rhetoric', in *Race, Rhetoric, and Composition*, Western Washington University Press, Washington DC.

Wegner, P. (2002), *Imaginary Communities: Utopia, the Nation and the Spatial Histories of Modernity*, University of California Press, Los Angeles CA.

Wenzel, V. (1981), 'Introduction to Luce Irigaray's "And the One Doesn't Stir without the Other"', *Signs* 7/1, pp. 56–9.

Whitaker, B. (2006), *Unspeakable Love: Gay and Lesbian Life in the Middle East*, Saqi Books, Beirut.

Whitlock, G. (2000), *The Intimate Empire: Reading Women's Autobiography*, Cassell, New York.

——— (2007), *Soft Weapons: Autobiography in Transit*, University of Chicago Press, Chicago IL.

——— (2008), 'From Tehran to Tehrangeles: the generic fix of diasporic Iranian memoirs', *ARIEL* 39/1–2, pp. 7–27.

Willford, C. (1990), 'The Mantle of the Prophet', *Washington Report on Middle East Affairs*, viewed 30 March 2006 <http://www.wrmea.com/component/content/article/126/1304-the-mantle-of-the-prophet.html>

Wood, J. (2009), 'Love, Iranian Style', *The New Yorker*, 29 June, viewed January 2010 <http://www.newyorker.com/arts/critics/books/2009/06/29/090629crbo_books_wood>

Wright, R. (2007), 'Freed by Iran, scholar reunites with her family', *The Washington Post*, 7 September, viewed 14 July 2009 <http://www.washingtonpost.com/wp-dyn/content/article/2007/09/06/AR2007090602375.html>

Yahyanejad, M. (2011), 'The internet and the protests in Iran', in *Iran and the New Media*, Institut fur Auslandsbeziehungen, Stuttgart.

Yavari, H. (1995), 'Modern Iranian literature', *Encyclopedia Iranica* 8/6, pp. 599–602.

Zanganeh, L.A. (2006), *My Sister, Guard your Veil; My Brother, Guard your Eyes: Uncensored Iranian Voices*, Beacon Press, Boston MA.

Zarrinkoub, A. (1970), 'Persian Sufism and its historical perspective', *Iranian Studies* 3/3–4, pp.139–220.

Zibart, E. (2004), 'The power of the word: an Iranian writer recalls her youth in "the Land of No"', *Book Page*, viewed March 2006 <http://bookpage.com/review/journey-from-the-land-of-no/the-power-of-the-word>

INDEX

www.ingramcontent.com/pod-product-compliance
Lightning Source LLC
Chambersburg PA
CBHW060250100726
47907CB00003B/834

* 9 7 8 0 7 5 5 6 4 9 2 4 2 *